Relational Mindfulness

RELATIONAL MINDFULNESS

A Handbook for Deepening
Our Connection with Ourselves,
Each Other, and the Planet

DEBORAH EDEN TULL

Wisdom Publications
199 Elm Street
Somerville, MA 02144 USA
wisdomexperience.org

Library of Congress Cataloging-in-Publication Data
Names: Tull, Deborah Eden, author.
Title: Relational mindfulness: a handbook for deepening our connection
   with ourselves, each other, and the planet / Deborah Eden Tull.
Description: Somerville: Wisdom Publications, 2018. | Includes index. |
   Identifiers: LCCN 2017037683 (print) | LCCN 2018003385 (ebook) |
   ISBN 9781614294214 (ebook) | ISBN 9781614294139 (pbk.: alk. paper)
Subjects: LCSH: Meditation. | Mindfulness (Psychology) | Awareness.
Classification: LCC BL627 (ebook) | LCC BL627 .T85 2018 (print) |
   DDC 204/.4—dc23
LC record available at https://lccn.loc.gov/2017037683

ISBN 978-1-61429-413-9   ebook ISBN 978-1-61429-421-4

22 21
5 4 3 2

Cover design by Jim Zaccaria. Interior design by Kristin Goble. Set in
Sabon LT Std 11/16. Author photo by Doug Ellis Photography.

Printed in the United States of America.

Please visit fscus.org.

I hold this to be the highest task for a bond between two people: that each protects the solitude of the other.—Rainer Maria Rilke, *Letters to a Young Poet*

I dedicate this book to my beloved Mark D'Aquila:
You have brought boundless joy to my life;
I bow to the mystery that brought us together.

I offer this book
for all beings of the past, present, and future.
May we find the courage to meet life as students of love.
May we remember the love that is who we already are.

Contents

PART THREE. Cultivating Mindful Relationship with the Planet

PART FOUR. Healing Our Relationship with Global Uncertainty

Preface

Integrating Seven Years
at a Zen Monastery

This day and age carry more uncertainty and threat
to the human species and planet than humanity has
ever experienced in human time. What we need
now is a pathway for global healing. If Buddhism
addresses this, great; if it does not, then the teachings are not relevant enough for this time.

—David R. Loy

I heard these words at the International Dharma Teachers
Gathering at the Omega Institute in Rhinebeck, New York, in
2015. The elder Buddhist teacher was addressing global climate
change. I took this statement to heart with the full awareness
that my personal practice has always, from the beginning, been
merged with my commitment to activism.

Buddhism is about putting an end to *dukkha*, to suffering.
The translation of the Pali word *dukkha* is "subtle, incessant dissatisfaction." Years ago, I sought to address this state in myself
and others by becoming a monk at a Zen Buddhist monastery.

I arrived at the monastery at the age of twenty-six, eager to
address my own suffering and holding big questions about how
to contribute to a more sane and peaceful world. I had grown

up in the city of Los Angeles and by the age of seventeen was in despair about the state of the world I was inheriting. I had witnessed extreme poverty and social injustice alongside mass overconsumption and excess wealth, lack of reverence for our planet in the name of greed, and a level of unconsciousness, denial, and corruption in the city I lived in that seemed like madness to me.

I was hungry for answers, and so I set out on a journey that took me to city and farm and back many times; to spiritual and sustainable communities around the world; and eventually to a Zen Buddhist monastery for seven and a half years. As a student of ecological design and sustainable agriculture, my mind was blown open as I learned about the healing capacity of nature—fungi to clean up oil spills, for instance, design mimicking nature to exponentially cut down on energy use and help people create more sustainable human habitats, and projects re-seeding rainforests that we thought were obliterated. It seemed obvious that if only we could get our egos out of the way, we had a chance at contributing to restoration and balance. If people could actually see, as I had, what is possible when we work with rather than against nature, I was certain they would all get on board.

As a student of meditation, giving myself permission to look within and bring awareness to my own ego, I came to understand that much of the modern world persists in an adversarial relationship—both with human nature and with the natural world. My despair shifted into compassionate action when I understood the possibility of working with rather than against life and making every moment and every relationship an opportunity for awakening.

Within the simple and compassionate architecture of the Zen monastery, following a daily schedule of sitting and working meditation, I began to find my way back home to a more authentic way of being. I describe this as living from nonseparation or interconnection. As I began to shed my own life's conditioning through engaged meditation practice, I realized everything I wanted and had to offer came naturally from becoming more present. The more I saw about how deeply conditioning operated in myself and in our world, perpetuating the myth of separation, the more I was determined to see through it.

My journey as a monk was not always pretty and rarely easy—often far from it. I struggled with layers of fear and the perception of inadequacy and, over the years, was forced to address personal challenges and the releasing of trauma before returning to my own sustained presence. Although I had not identified as someone who suffered from trauma, the more I observed my thoughts and emotions, the more I realized that growing up in a conditionally loving world had left the marks of severe trauma on my psyche. I had internalized the belief that only some parts of myself, and thus humanity, were acceptable, valuable, and worthy of love; and other parts of myself were not—and in fact deserved criticism and punishment. Though I was not conscious of this belief system operating within me, the choice to become a monk was my heart's call to dismantle this distortion. As a result of my own personal journey, I now believe strongly that if I can take steps to wake up from delusion, anyone can. With willingness, courage, kindness, and patience, anyone can wake up from the mind of separation. To do so is our birthright.

I came from a family of artists and activists, steeped in social justice and poverty issues. By the time I became a monastic, I had been a student of and educator in sustainability for years. Until I found the Dharma, I had always felt the need to help people understand interconnection but did not have the true language for it nor did I know how to take it beyond a concept into moment-by-moment embodiment. Most people had an intellectual understanding of interdependence but were nonetheless living their lives in the paradigm of separation, not at peace with their minds, struggling daily for survival, caught in relational challenges, disconnected from the natural world and their subtle body, and seeing through the lens of "other." Even in the well-intentioned world of change agents in which I was immersed, I often noticed a quality of egoic separation. Egoic separation, the tendency to perceive life through our own separate bubble, too often leads to drama, competitiveness, finger-pointing and blame, self-righteousness, burnout, and inefficiency.

During my years as a monk the more I meditated, the more I began to understand that meditation and mindfulness offer a direct means for healing the myth of separation. This is the key to both personal healing and global sustainability. Our native state is nonseparation.

Seven and a half years later, when I left the simplicity of the monastery to live and teach out in the world, my practice took on even greater dimensions. As I devoted myself to practicing in the context of the complex megatropolis of Los Angeles, I gained an even further understanding: the steadfast support of a monastic structure is something we can create inside ourselves wherever we are. This was freeing for me and holds true for all of us. We can create the necessary support for our own awakening by making a commitment to Relational Mindfulness.

In other words, meditation is not just something we do while sitting on a cushion. It is an attitude of mind and way of life. It begins on the cushion, and we then bring it into movement, into our interactions and communication, into our work life, into how we relate with the earth, with politics, and all aspects of our life. We can use every moment of our lives, every interaction, and every relationship as an opportunity to wake up to and affirm the consciousness of interconnection.

This book offers a heartfelt teaching about how to participate wholeheartedly in the inner and outer healing that our time is calling for.

While many people look around at the state of the world through the lens of anger, despair, finger-pointing, fear, or numbness and denial, Relational Mindfulness offers access to exactly the inner resources we need to see clearly and navigate the issues we face—with courage, compassion, and humility. Relational Mindfulness offers a way to connect more intimately with one another and set down the illusion of separation that keeps us estranged and isolated. And it offers tools for how to transform our despair about the state of the world into empowerment and compassionate action. Compassionate action always begins within ourselves and extends outward organically. In other words, true compassion does not take root in our beings until we begin to have compassion for every aspect of our self we have rejected.

This book draws equally upon the lessons of the natural world. The natural world was my first teacher of Relational Mindfulness. Everything in nature demonstrates interconnection. Yet when it comes to the natural world, the separate self sees everything as something to conquer, colonize, claim, fear, understand/explain, control, or improve upon. Signs of the mind of separation are infused everywhere: in our institutions, our social and land use policies, our approach to basic human needs, and even our general attitude toward the elements, animals, insects, and plants. The mind of separation operates in a paradigm of power over rather than power with. It perceives domination/subordination, hierarchy, scarcity, competition, and survival. The mind of separation has carried us far from nature's principles of balance, reciprocity, and interdependence, and these principles need to become a priority if we are going to survive as a species.

Relational Mindfulness invites you to consider the ways that the mind of separation operates in your life and in your world and to deepen your embodiment of whole mind. What is possible when we pay attention more subtly and bring curiosity to our moment by moment experience of life, questioning the actual lens through which we have been perceiving our experiences? What is possible when we remember the still spaciousness within, and allow all of our life experiences—pleasant and unpleasant—to be met by compassionate awareness? What is possible when we align our outer actions with inner stillness?

The good news is that all that is required for our healing is the willingness to remember who we are authentically. Although the mind of separation has carried us far away from the love that is who we are, this love never leaves us—it is only ever we who leave it.

To heal in this way we have to be willing to reconnect with awareness as our guide. We have to be willing to meet one another in the field of compassionate presence rather than through habit, projection, or judgment. We have to be willing to return confidence to nature and to savor our place in it.

Acknowledgments

If your life's work can be accomplished in your lifetime, you're not thinking big enough.

—Wendell Berry

For Mark, my beloved and partner on the path. Thank you for meeting me in the spaciousness that allows love to thrive. Thank you for your steadfast support, affection, honesty, patience, perspective, and humor as I wrote this book. Thank you—every day—for the flowers.

Thank you to Josh Bartok, Ashley Benning, and all of Wisdom Publications. I first met Josh after giving a talk at the International Dharma Teacher's Gathering as we acknowledged a shared passion for integrating Dharma practice with social change, and the necessity of making space to grieve the pain of the world in order to be whole. I am grateful for the opportunity to work with you on behalf of the greater good.

Thank you to my mom, Tanya Tull, for being such an inspiring agent of change in the world, and for encouraging me to honor the power of my true voice. Thank you for affirming fortitude and commitment in my life. Thank you to my stepdad BJ Markel, for your editorial support and good spiritedness, and to my family—Rebecca, Paul, Julian, Dani, Yvonne, Olivia, and

Jim—for cheering me on. The irony of being less available for connection while writing a book about connection has not been lost to me, and I love you.

Thank you to my dear friend Susanna Corcoran, who stepped in with tremendous generosity to help me move beyond doubt and organize and affirm my vision. Your skill, knowledge of the book, and creative support goes above and beyond.

Thank you to Forest Fein who is always there to offer deep listening and Michelle Durand for devoted friendship. Thank you also to the Mindful Living Revolution Board of Directors for offering support in so many ways, including Amanda Bramble, Wendy Meyer, Premlata Poonia, and Samuel Hires. And thank you to all of my students for your willingness to be vulnerable and step into the mystery.

I offer gratitude to Marvin Belzer, who first introduced me to the phrase "relational mindfulness." It was his impassioned and playful devotion to teaching Relational Mindfulness practices that encouraged me in deepening and expanding my own practice of it.

Thank you to all of my teachers over the years. I offer my deepest gratitude to Joanna Macy for inspiring me in times of doubt about the world we live in; Diana Winston for guidance and sisterhood; Cheri Huber for her fierce compassion; Nina Simons for your continual embodiment of the deep feminine; and to the UCLA mindfulness community; the Against the Stream community; and the 5Rhythms Dance community.

I wrote this book while immersed in the process of healing from Lyme disease, and I am grateful to all of the people, plants, animals, and allies who supported me.

Thank you for the spiritual support, Claire Wings and Wolla. Your guidance is immeasurable.

Thank you to all of my friends for modeling authenticity, transparency, vulnerability, joy, and deep listening.

And lastly, thank you to the land of Ojai, California, for holding me in stillness as I wrote this book.

Special thanks also to the following people for supporting the writing of this book:

Athena Carrillo	Christina Martinez
Misha Collins	David Perrin
Melissa Dart	Andrew Rasmussen
Margaret Dunham	Paula Ravets
Cristal Franco	Rich Ray
Luis Frausto	Jileen Russell
Lisa Friedman	Eric Sagaspe
Yanel Gonzalez	Henry Schipper
Aubri Hathaway	Jamie Shea
Kevin Kidd	Sam Stegeman
Jill Knapp	Karen Taylor
Tamar Krames	Justin Tilson
Hilary Kimblin Licht	Maxene Vener
Patty Lin	Jodie Venturelli
BJ Markel	Debra Warmington

Introduction

At a time of global uncertainty, there is an emerging revolution. This revolution has the ability to wake us up to a profoundly kinder and more intelligent relationship with ourselves, with one another, and with our planet. While a revolution usually means to evolve and change, this shift is actually a return to a simple and sacred understanding we seem to have forgotten—one we can only remember when we are present.

Humanity has become highly technologically advanced and developed incredible systems for commerce, transportation, and defense, but when it comes to presence, kindness, and sustainability, we are still living in the dark ages. We have been conditioned to know ourselves as separate rather than as part of the vibrantly alive and interconnected fabric of life on this planet.

If you, the reader, are feeling drained by the state of the world; if you are becoming tired of feeling powerless in the scheme of things; and if you are becoming bored with or fatigued by your own personal struggles or dissatisfaction, you are in the right place. If you are ready to experience deeper connection and intimacy in all of your relationships, read on. If you have had a glimpse of your own essence and want to nurture it in an increasingly stressful world, this book is for you. And if you are curious about the wider application of mindfulness to help seed personal, interpersonal, transpersonal, social, cultural, and societal transformation, these pages can lead the way. If you know that the natural world is our greatest teacher, but sense that nature's teachings can only be realized when we let go of certainty and learn to perceive from curiosity, then you are well-positioned to receive the teachings as you read on.

In this book I invite you to explore the following questions: What if our greatest strength is our shared sensitivity and vulnerability? What if personal awareness practice is the most important skill for impacting social change? What if meditation is simply a pathway for erasing the illusion of separation and returning us to our natural state of interconnection? What if a subtle shift in our attention informs our ability to live in partnership with one another, the natural world, and all forms of life? The teachings and practices of this book point to the belonging that we yearn for at our deepest level. The limiting beliefs weighing upon humanity, beliefs that prevent us from loving one another well and from taking devoted care of our planet, come from one simple misunderstanding—the illusion of separation.

What is the illusion of separation? The separate self, which stands outside of life looking in, sees everything through a veil of judgment and assessment. It disconnects us from our actual experience of life as it is and creates distortion. The mind of separation perceives through the lens of disconnection, dissatisfaction, and competition. It believes in having power over, rather than power with. It compels us to live in survival mode sustaining feelings of fear, threat, and judgment in an effort to have control over life.

The illusion of separation fuels a way of life that is unsustainable both personally and globally. Every seed of violence in our world—war, social injustice, planetary abuse, and any ism—stems from the seed of this illusion. On a global field, we see the ramifications of the mind of separation in every instance of bullying, racism, and bigotry.

Interconnection is our natural state of being. No matter who we are, we feel at home when we experience our common bond. As infants or young children, we knew this state of unity; we were present and in touch with our natural intelligence. As we became conditioned, we learned to stand outside of life looking in. We learned to assess, label, compare, and react to life from a disconnected place, rather than perceive from our oneness with life. Over time, for many of us, these behaviors became more familiar than trusting our own inner guidance. Today we are up against so many conditioned beliefs that make both our internal and external landscapes increasingly unsafe places in which to live.

I work with people from around the world, and everyone who comes to workshops and retreats struggles with the illusion of separate self. We have become so accustomed to living under the illusion of separation that we are not even aware anymore that we are doing it. It just feels like our own skin. Why would we question it? We might, however, sense a dissatisfaction with our life, or, at times, isolation, depression, anxiety, loneliness, or being overwhelmed. We might also be aware of the fact that we spend a lot of time trying to do, acquire, fix, or change things in our life rather than slowing down and savoring life. We may have even decided that the intimacy we long for is not available to us.

Many people have given up on experiencing the quality of connection and belonging they deeply crave. Likewise, many of us have given up our hope of healing our world because the degree of insanity and ignorance we are up against feels overwhelming. When we look around us with a clear heart and open eyes, however, we can begin to see that perhaps this moment in history is the best and most persuasive invitation humanity has ever received to wake up and end suffering. If we are willing to address the myth of separation and become curious about what else is possible, our personal and global healing can occur organically—and much more easily than we might think.

The illusion of separation causes a loss so deep in our hearts that it robs us of the vitality, the power, and the relaxed trust in life that is our birthright. How can we restore peace within ourselves or on our planet until we heal this illusion of separation?

Pause . . . right now, as you are reading. Take a moment to connect to your breath, simply feeling the air as it enters your body, fills your body, and leaves your body. Feel the weight of your body sitting or resting on whatever surface you are on and surrender a bit more to the force of gravity. Allow your curiosity to be alive without any agenda. Notice, subtly, what is going on in your mind . . . your body . . . and your feelings. Notice the touch of air on your skin . . . the sounds surrounding you . . . and allow yourself to "sense into" being where you are, as you are. Be aware of your experience with curiosity and kind neutrality. Allow yourself to stand within the landscape of your experience as a full participant and enjoy just sensing. Whether what you sense feels pleasant or unpleasant, see if you can welcome your experience as it is, allowing yourself to be exactly as you are. As you continue to read this book, set the intention to stay connected with awareness of your breath and your body so that you can experience this teaching as a meditation. Whatever experience you have, moment by moment, can be met with gentle curiosity. Allowing ourselves to meet life with this quality of spacious awareness is the first step in affirming our capacity for love.

It is possible to cultivate long-term sustainable change in our lives through the practice of Relational Mindfulness: using all of our interactions—with self, one another, and the planet—to remember the love that is who we really are. This book offers a joyful process of discovery. Relational Mindfulness gives us tools to navigate the complexity of both the human mind and the modern world at the same time. Our confusion clears up easily when we realize that we have been participating in a case of mistaken identity: perceiving ourselves as alone and separate from one another.

Another translation of the Pali term *sati* that is often translated as "mindfulness" is "remembering"—and the practice of Relational Mindfulness allows us to use our daily life and all of our relationships to remember who we really are.

Relational Mindfulness invites us to stop standing outside of life looking in, and to instead engage wholeheartedly within the web of life in present moment awareness. This opens up an entirely different quality of relating to ourselves and to one another.

You will be challenged to let go of your limiting beliefs and assumptions, and to risk freeing yourself of the illusion of separation. Even if you have been practicing meditation for years, you will be asked to look at things with fresh eyes and go deeper.

Throughout this book, I use a number of terms to point to the same things, drawing from various traditions such as Buddhism, secular mindfulness, and my own experience:

- The mind of separation: This is used synonymously with conditioning, conditioned mind, separate self, ego.
- The authentic self: This is used synonymously with whole mind, center, the consciousness of interconnection, no-self, true nature, essence, nonduality.

Many of these teachings came to me through Zen; however, mindfulness is woven into many other religions and spiritual/secular traditions across the globe and over the vast span of human history, from many indigenous and Native American cultures to shamanism to Christianity. If we are going to address the global challenges we face, it is vital to move beyond the labels and categories that have separated us and embrace our shared teachings that point us to interconnection and freedom.

Cultivating change requires taking a stand . . . so if you are ready to take yours for interconnection, read on.

Beginner's Mind

As you read this book, I invite you to cultivate beginner's mind. Beginner's mind is the quality of meeting each moment with openness and receptivity, rather than through the filter of thought and assessment. Beginner's mind is the most helpful attitude to bring to meditation and to life.

This book is not meant to bring revelation to the intellect. It is meant to guide you through a personal inquiry process into presence and interconnection.

Rather than turn the teachings here into a belief system, I encourage you to reflect and inquire for yourself: How do these ideas match my experience of being human? What is my actual experience when I try on the practices offered?

Guidance for Using the Exercises in This Book

O rdinary life is the best laboratory for Relational Mindfulness. At the end of every chapter I offer Mindful Inquiry exercises and a Daily Practice to help you integrate these teachings into your daily life. You are invited to pick one question, or more if you like, in each chapter to work with, or work with all of them. You can go as deeply or as gently as you choose.

There are also formal Relational Mindfulness practices to do with a partner or in a group. These practices, offered in appendix 2 invite you to step beyond habitual ways of relating and experience relating as a meditation. Some of us learn better on our own and some of us learn better in groups. If you are the latter, you may want to read this book with a group—a mindfulness practice group, meditation sangha, book club, church group, circle of friends, or a collective of activists committed to a cause. You might also want to read it with your spouse, colleague, or a close friend whom you can do the exercises with. The practices are simple and based in compassion.

This book is applicable to people of any and all backgrounds, religious traditions, or secular pathways. It holds insights for Buddhists and non-Buddhists. While my core practice is Zen, my aspiration as a teacher is to make the essence of Zen and its teachings on intimacy accessible to people everywhere. My intention is to honor mindfulness as the universal language that it is. Please note that there is a glossary in the back of the book that defines any language and terminology that may be new to you.

This book invites and encourages a change in the way you see yourself and the world—a paradigm shift, if you will. As you begin to identify and release limiting beliefs and habits, I cannot emphasize enough that judging yourself (or our culture) for previous beliefs and/or habits is not necessary or helpful. We all have a golden opportunity to release old cobwebby ways of being and embrace change.

Appreciate yourself for your willingness to seek deeper intimacy, courage, truth, and authenticity in all of your relationships—beginning with your relationship with yourself.

Here are some suggestions for general practice:

- Cultivating compassionate relationships begins within yourself. Give yourself extra time for meditation, journaling, and reflection and self-care while you are reading this book.

- The spirit of nonjudgment is the most useful, wise, and honest approach to mindfulness and to learning anything new. Please do not hold Relational Mindfulness as a standard to use against yourself, but as an invitation for growth.

- Likewise, please do not use the principles of Relational Mindfulness as a standard for anyone else. It is never helpful to use the language of consciousness against someone, for instance, to say, "You should be more mindful."

- Just like building muscle in our bodies, presence is developed through repetition. Each time you show up to practice, your capacity for presence is strengthened.

- At times you may run into resistance. Ego might kick and scream a bit as you meet new edges. This is natural. These teachings invite you to let go of old conditioning and move into a much larger sense of yourself. Do not be alarmed, nor take resistance personally. Just notice it, breathe deeply, and keep going. Ego's discomfort is generally a sign that you are heading in the right direction.

- If you are working with a partner or group, please see appendix 2 for Helpful Guidelines for Working with a Partner or Group.

PART ONE

Relationship with Our Self

The quality of every relationship we will ever have begins with the quality of our relationship with our self. Having a committed and compassionate relationship with our self means staying present to our experience of life without turning away when it gets difficult. It means learning to trust our authentic self over our conditioning. It means aligning our outer actions with inner listening. And it means having tools for seeing through the myth of separation to the love that is always there.

1

Our Sensitivity Is Our Strength

The tragedy is that through fear of vulnerability, we choose numbness and complacency over aliveness and action. We choose isolation rather than connection with one another.*

I grew up witnessing two competing paradigms of the human experience. Throughout my childhood, I saw my parents serving people who had been truly marginalized and could barely survive day to day without support. My mother worked with homeless children and families, first in Los Angeles's Skid Row and eventually throughout LA County and nationally. My father was a social worker who worked with mentally ill people released into the city from state mental hospitals and he studied law at night.

Regardless of our limited resources and struggle at times to afford basic groceries, our house was the place where anyone could come for help. My parents took a lot of people under their wings in times of need and even opened up our modest living

*Epigraphs without attributions are the author's own words.

room to house homeless youth. This reflected my parents' human-itarian values and their compassion for the human experience. It also positioned me to grow up aware of the world around me and to experience life through a lens of "We are all in this together."

At the same time, I experienced a competitive Los Angeles mentality within which the primary values were success, image, fame, and wealth. In school, I learned that one's value depended upon performance, and those who were not able to keep up with these particular academic standards were judged, rejected, or bullied. I learned to appear strong and independent in order to succeed. I tried to hide my weakness and sensitivity when I felt I had to and to appear to have it all together even when I did not.

As a female, I was not conditioned to exhibit masculine traits. However, the exaggerated masculine conditioning of the culture around me impacted me deeply. I took on the message that the masculine aspects of my personality (active, extroverted, com-petitive, and intellect-based) were more worthy than my femi-nine traits (receptive, intuitive, gentle, and nonlinear). Ironically, I attended an all-girls middle and high school, but it was primar-ily a training ground for success in a man's world.

I was often more sensitive than my peers, sensitive to how I saw people being treated, sensitive to how I saw the earth being treated, and empathetic to animals and other forms of life. I felt disempowered and burdened by the masculine paradigm of strength, competition, and power over. Later in my life, the realization of the ultimate strength of sensitivity became a core teaching on my spiritual path.

I had a close community of friends throughout my child-hood, and this support system helped me to survive the trials of growing up. But my primary survival mechanism was to escape every summer to a sleep-away camp in the nearby mountains, one that was immersed in nature and based on humanitarian values. My time in the woods there each year gave me a glimpse into a different lifestyle and ignited in me a hope that I might find an alternative way to live as an adult. Nonetheless, witnessing the human suffering I saw through my parents' work, while experiencing the upper-middle-class and money-oriented lifestyles around me that seemed to be based on completely different values, was continually challenging and eventually led to an existential crisis.

I began to question the order of things, the randomness of it all, and the gravity of the marginalization I witnessed. I was painfully aware of the vulnerability and fragility of the diverse groups of people living their lives out around me. As my own experiences became more global, I realized the even deeper fragility of today's world and did not know what to do with the powerlessenss I felt.

The Inevitable Vulnerability of Being Human

> Life is like stepping onto a boat which is about to sail out to sea and sink.
>
> —Shunryu Suzuki

Being human is an inevitably vulnerable experience. Once the umbilical cord is cut, we are completely dependent upon our parents' care moment by moment to meet our needs for love, nutrients, affection, attention, acceptance, touch, and forming healthy attachments. As human beings, we rely on access to clean soil, water, sunlight, and air, and we are susceptible to environmental, climatic, microbial, and atmospheric changes. We are each alive only temporarily—and learning what we need to learn in our lives is not always easy and sometimes grueling. We are susceptible to the rules, customs, and biases of our culture and government.

Though we might think we can control life, there is little we can actually control. If we are honest, we can say that the human experience involves some form of disappointment every single day. Death is the only thing we actually know with certainty will happen to us in this life.

We suffer when we resist our innate vulnerability and view it as a weakness, rather than embrace it with acceptance. As human beings, there is no way around being vulnerable. We try to build scaffolding and protection in the form of met goals, gated communities, and future planning to cope with the innate uncertainty with which we live. We have myriad ways to guard, defend, fill, escape, and turn away from the vulnerability that is actually the key to our authentic power and our shared compassion for one another.

Each time we turn away from vulnerability, we give our power away, reinforcing a story that we do not have what it takes to meet our life experience. The surrounding environment we create for ourselves—with its walls, barricades, and defenses—reflects our fears and therefore reinforces states of fear. We live in a vulnerable state, yet avoid this reality so we are never put in touch with the resilience of our deeper being.

Imagine if, as young people, our parents had sat us down and said to us some version of this: "Welcome to this incredible and sobering journey called life. In this lifetime, you are going to experience more love and beauty than you could possibly imagine. And you will also experience more pain and suffering than you think you can bear. Given this reality, let us prepare you with as much awareness, wisdom, courage, resilience, and self-compassion as you are going to need for this journey. You will experience all of it, and so let us prepare you with the ability to see clearly and listen deeply as you navigate the journey called life. You have what it takes to meet whatever life brings you. Your unique contribution matters here. And you are not alone."

Imagine the world that generation of young people would create!

Why Our Sensitivity Is Our Strength as a Species

Authentic power is the ability to give and receive love.

Often, when someone returns from a retreat, they say to me, "My heart feels wide open now. I'm crying tears for everything, tears for the beauty of a rose I pass on my morning walk, tears for the homeless person in a tent under the underpass. I'm afraid I'm too open to live in this world. And at the same time I don't want my open heart to return to the numb state of the past." I encourage these students to use the opportunity to explore their personal mechanisms for habitually turning away from their sensitive nature, so that they can ultimately release these habits and find the courage to soften.

Consider some of the messages you may have received in life encouraging you to hide your sensitivity:

- Stay strong.
- Be cool.
- Toughen up.
- Don't cry.
- You're too sensitive.
- Be independent.
- Don't ask for help.
- Don't speak up if it will rock the boat.

Consider how some of these identities have become a means of hiding your sensitivity and vulnerability:

- tough guy
- independent woman
- boss
- expert
- pessimist/cynic/"I don't really care"
- caretaker who focuses on everyone else's needs

- "I'm too busy," living in survival mode
- constant comedian
- spiritual bliss/the yoga gal who "keeps things pretty"
- the peacemaker/diplomat

Consider if you have ever employed any of these means to cover up vulnerability or perceived weakness:

- trying to look good/acceptable/positive when you don't feel good/acceptable/positive
- putting other people down to pump yourself up
- withdrawing or isolating when you feel vulnerable
- not asking for help when you are in a challenging place
- editing your words to appear strong or cool
- overcompensating for yourself in one area due to feeling weak in another area
- downplaying your true feelings because it's too painful
- choosing defeat or checking out rather than risking appearing vulnerable in a situation

All of these mechanisms for hiding our sensitive nature support an "I"-versus-"you" rather than a "We" world. These are expressions of false bravado that we use as a substitute for authentic power, which I define as the ability to give and receive love. Authentic power is our ability to stay present through whatever we are experiencing and to meet it with compassion. When we are perceiving through the lens of ego, we identify with a separate self who often feels weak and under threat. We find an artificial substitute for power in the form of "power over," rather than seeking the "power with" that comes from embracing our weakness and being willing to give and receive love.

If turning toward that which we instinctively want to turn away from seems frightening, consider how much more frightening it is to live burdened by the belief that there is always something to fear. It is much more frightening to live in a world in which we feel isolated and alone. It is also much more frightening to live with the belief that there is something wrong with us because our sensitive self is feeling.

Before we understand that we have the capacity to meet everything that arises with love, we are stuck in the duality of positive/negative. If we wake up with vitality and sunshine, we label that as "positive." If we wake up with sadness and stormy weather, we label it "negative." This kind of dualistic approach to life is inherently unhelpful.

Discomfort is a part of life. It is our greatest teacher and does not need to be labeled "negative." When we allow ourselves to meet every feeling state with compassionate awareness, we remember that who we are is love. We find very little use for the duality of positive/negative. Awareness does not live in a field of judgment. Awareness is accepting. Every time we turn away from something that we label "negative" or "difficult," we feed the part of us that feels inadequate to meet life. Every time we pop a pill or turn away instead of learning how to meet and "be with" discomfort, we turn away from who we really are.

Psychic Numbing and Turning Toward Rather Than Away

That which we turn toward strengthens our aliveness, our compassion, and ultimately our resilience as living organisms. That which we reject further affirms the myth of separation and isolation.

A seventy-five-year-old male retreatant once told me that he believed it was absolutely necessary for him to stay numb to all of the pain he felt from his lifetime and for our world. He said he found it needful to cut off his ability to feel, and he was certain that if he began to feel again, he would be swallowed whole by a dark pit of despair. I asked the man to do a simple assignment: to write a love letter to himself. At first he resisted, but when he did finally compose the letter, the floodgates opened. And when they opened, he cried and cried and allowed his heart to open. He cried tears especially for all of the time he had wasted being afraid of feeling and just "going through the motions of his life. And then the emotions passed." In his own words, he got in touch with the little boy who was buried and forgotten, and this little boy brought light, vitality, and renewed purpose back to his life. His willingness to turn toward his pain for our world healed a part of him that had been left behind.

It is natural for every single human being alive today to feel some degree of sadness, confusion, rage, powerlessness, and grief about the state of the world. We would have to be utterly numb to not be impacted by the destruction of the living systems on this planet that has already taken place. When we witness life with an unguarded heart, we feel our deep cellular sensitivity and pain for the 500-year-old tree being cut down, for the whale being blasted out of its habitat by sound pollution, and for the young man incarcerated due to a bias related to his skin color.

When we ignore our feelings and allow ourselves to "numb out," we diminish our power. We also diminish our sensitivity to life, which is the signature of interconnection. We dig ourselves deeper into an illusion of isolation and communicate the message to others that we and they are alone. We dull our natural feedback system and thus our ability to respond appropriately to all that is happening in our world. Instead of allowing the painful things we see and experience to strengthen our commitment to wakefulness, we often choose fear. By numbing our capacity to feel pain, we equally numb our capacity for joy. In the words of Buddhist writer Joanna Macy,

> This is a dark time, filled with suffering and uncertainty. Like living cells in a larger body, it is natural that we feel the trauma of our world. So don't be afraid of the anguish you feel, or the anger or fear, because these responses arise from the depth of your caring and the truth of your interconnectedness with all beings.

Consider the myriad ways we have invented to turn away from feelings through over-thinking, over-consuming, internet-binging, sex, eating, drinking, shopping, and endless other forms of escapism. We can pop a pill to evade temporarily almost any unwanted emotion we experience. Luckily, there is no pill through which we can truly escape ourselves or relieve our pain for the world. Though "lucky" may sound counterintuitive, it is a gift that there is no pill that can claim to do that which only the human heart can accomplish for us.

Relational Mindfulness calls forth our willingness to remain aware and to fully feel. The act of turning away temporarily closes our hearts, but that which we turn away from does not go anywhere. In turning away, we are left feeling isolated on the inside and cold or hardened on the outside, while the emotion we turned away from only goes deeper into our psyches. To turn toward our pain opens our hearts and offers the part of us that is in pain the embrace that is needed.

How Meditation Expands Our Capacity for Love

> Every part of us that feels pain needs to know that it is not alone. Each aspect of us that suffers needs to know that there is someone to listen.

I have always loved morning meditation practice. It is a space for turning toward and honoring myself however I am feeling that day. I know that how I meet myself in the morning sets the tone for the quality of presence I bring to the day. When I ring the bell and begin my morning sit, I ring it as a sign of my commitment to be with what is. I allow myself to be open and permeable, feeling each layer of experience that moves through me. For a moment there might be a feeling of "oh no, not this emotion" or "not this physical experience," but the very act of turning toward whatever is difficult returns me to love. This is how we learn wholeness, and the entire point of practice is not to attain rose-colored happiness, but an unconditional sense of completeness.

Picture a clay vessel—round, smooth, and organic—with empty, hollow space inside. When we first come to practice, we are like a very small vessel for life energy. Accordingly, we accept certain emotions but reject many others; we welcome certain parts of the human experience, but resist much more. Sitting meditation invites us to gently, kindly, and gradually allow our vessel for life to expand. As we learn to sit with comfort and discomfort, light and shadow, the vessel expands. As we learn to be with our emotional body more intimately, the vessel expands. As we welcome parts of us we have denied and pushed away, the vessel expands. As we turn towards those feelings we have ignored and numbed out to and instead meet ourselves with love, the vessel expands. We come back to life.

Literally, moment by moment in meditation, we expand our capacity for love through the spirit of repetition. The true invitation is to become a crucible for life energy that is big enough and generous enough to contain all of life, welcoming everything in and leaving no one out. Remembering that our true size is vast enough to contain it all can be a lifelong practice.

Each time we show up to sit, we are given a golden opportunity to deepen our understanding of human kindness. We are given multiple invitations throughout the day to choose to meet ourselves with kindness. Every time we experience physical discomfort, a strong emotion, mental stress, or resistance, we have the capacity to meet it with kindness.

To be the soft strength of love is the ultimate strength. This is the strength that allows us to be resilient, flexible, and to use everything that arises to remind us of our vibrant aliveness and capacity for love. This love is not Hallmark-card love; nor is it the romantic walking-into-the-sunset type of love glorified by Hollywood. This love does not require our doing anything, nor does it necessarily erase pain. It is simply the gentle motion of turning toward, rather than away, and being with our naked experience. In our world of distraction and escapism, this in itself is a revolutionary act. The willingness to sit with no other agenda but being with seeds a dramatic shift in our lives.

Addressing Spiritual Bypassing in the Modern World: Letting Go of Keeping Things Pretty

> The best people I know are inadequate and
>   unashamed.
> We have to learn to live with our own frailties.
> —Stanley Kunitz

I once had a student in an introductory meditation class tell me that she did not have any discomfort to be with, because she had recently learned to "follow her bliss" through ecstatic dancing.

Two weeks later she returned in great despair: she had torn a ligament and because she could not dance, her bliss had disappeared. One of the ways we resist spiritual growth is through spiritual bypassing. Self-improvement, bliss, inner peace, and ecstasy get held up as some ideal or destination. Equanimity gets misinterpreted as a static impermeable state, and we continue to push away real life and our wounds in the name of spiritual pursuit. When we feed the notion that freedom equates to positivity, popularity, and glamour, we misinterpret an ancient practice through the passive consumer filter. In other words, we "buy in" to the notion that we can "escape real life" by acquiring something—whatever it may be—that we do not have.

Ego is incessant about seeking ways to justify escaping from consciousness. Doing this, however, comes at great cost, from over-investing in how we appear to others to over-engaging in projecting an image of who we think we should be. Drugs, pharmaceuticals, the internet, and sex addiction are traditional forms of escape in the modern world, but in today's new age world we also misuse other seemingly healthy activities, such as cleansing, bliss retreats, consuming energy bars and green drinks, and even yoga, as substitutes for the real work. Spiritual capitalism takes advantage of many of us daily who are trying to improve ourselves through healthy alternatives. From conditional love and the illusion of self-improvement, we strive for spiritual elevation rather than spiritual awakening.

These healthy alternatives to drugs and other addictions can certainly support our bodies and bring some more enjoyment and understanding. However, without clarity about the end goal, these pursuits can instead become a means of avoiding the real work that leads to wholeness and embodiment. We can confuse meditation for a means of affirming and protecting our own bubble of separation. We can further close ourselves off from the personal responsibility that is the essence of practice. What is harmful about these pursuits is not the pursuit itself but the mindset behind them. The more we feed the notion that freedom looks like positivity, elevation, and popularity, the more we feed duality. We must let go of promoting uninformed ideas about spiritual bliss and ecstasy if we really want to be free.

It is true that meditation can take us to pretty blissful states of mind sometimes. But this is neither the purpose nor the promise of meditation. To find some static disconnected island of bliss would offer only a crumb of the satisfaction our souls are looking for. Bliss is not going to help us make peace with the reality of the human experience. Bliss is not going to point us to the boundless nature of unconditional love.

Love is the unconditional embrace that is willing to be here with us, in a grounded and unwavering way, however we are, in any state. We feel it as tenderness, grace, acceptance, reassurance. We hear it as the still small voice within. Love allows us to relax and feel safe, to feel at ease in our skin, to trust our capacity to meet life, and to trust life to support us. Love allows us to bring care and skillfulness to our engagement with life.

· · · · · · · · **Mindful Inquiry** · · · · · · · ·

What messages did you receive about sensitivity growing up?

How have you been impacted by the conventional definition of strength as "power over" rather than "power with"?

In what ways do you cover up your sensitivity and vulnerability?

In what ways do you turn away from, rather than turn toward, difficult feelings? What is the impact of this?

How have you allowed yourself to be courageously vulnerable so that others can see you and support you? What has vulnerability taught you?

How has another's vulnerability inspired or strengthened you?

Do you ever bypass the real work of bringing compassion to discomfort in the name of "keeping things pretty" or "positive"?

• • • • • • • • Daily Practice • • • • • • • •

Today, bring more awareness to your relationship with vulnerability. Be gently aware of the particular ways that you cover up vulnerability. What thoughts and actions express fear of vulnerability? Ask yourself: Who, internally, turns away from vulnerability? What is the impact of turning away from your vulnerability? What happens in your body? Your mind? And your emotional experience?

What helps you to turn toward your vulnerability and softly embrace it? What helps you to risk being vulnerable with others? Become more aware of the gift that the willingness to be vulnerable offers your self and others.

2

The Choice in Every Moment

Healing the Myth of Separation

What is imposed on you from the outside is of no value whatsoever. It doesn't count.

—Bertrand Russell

When I first visited the Zen monastery where I eventually trained as a monk, I witnessed a new paradigm for life based on interconnection. During orientation in the meditation hall, the monk presenting paused for a good five minutes to carefully and gently remove a tiny insect from the hall and deliver it outside to safe grounds. I watched another monk using the whole vegetable with great care and intention in dinner preparation rather than create any waste. Outside, I observed two monks working together in silence, building a rock wall in the courtyard with caring gentle attention to detail. After dinner, when everyone went into the kitchen to wash dishes and clean up, I realized that even the head Zen teacher was right there with us scrubbing pots. And in evening group discussion, people listened to one another speak with a quality of deep listening and respect that I was unaccustomed to. There was an honesty and lack of pretense in people's speech that I found relieving.

The monastery expressed a profound commitment to simplicity, kindness, and attunement in a world tangled up in complexity and distraction. The monks had twinkles in their eyes, a steadiness in their focus, and calmness in their hearts. They worked together in a way that embodied care and intention and stewarded the land with respect. Monastic life was not easy in any sense. The monks were dedicated to taking responsibility for their unconscious patterns of thought and action, and this is the work of a lifetime. Without fetishizing monastic living, which is as full of light and shadow as every other manifestation of life, the monastery taught me that when we align with our willingness to let go of suffering and move beyond the bubble of "I" or separate self, life supports us to reclaim the wholeness and unity that are our natural state.

What I witnessed at this first contact with the monastery made an inscrutable kind of sense to me. There was nothing ritualistic or exotic going on there. The monks were ordinary people from all walks of life committed to living from the extraordinariness of the human heart. Everyone followed a disciplined schedule of sitting and working meditation, offering their service to the land and the community. The monks lived simply, free of the trappings of the modern world and without distraction. This monastic environment invited people to question their basic orientation to life and to make a fundamental shift from an "I" or ego-based to a "We" consciousness, which provides a much larger field of awareness.

A monk is just like everyone else. However, a monk is willing to make spiritual growth the full priority. This means turning toward, rather than away from, our shadows and "triggers." This means questioning whether fear is a necessary installation in human life. This means being willing to stop looking outside the self for answers and to instead access the authority of the heart. This means understanding that deep joy doesn't actually come from getting what we want and avoiding what we don't. It means releasing the habits of both self-deprecation and self-aggrandizement and knowing the beauty of ordinary self. It means learning how to pay attention, with curiosity, to every moment of life. And it means understanding that authentic power comes from acting in service to the whole. In monastic training we were asked to use everything in our life experience—whether pleasant or unpleasant—to see how we caused ourselves to suffer, so that we could return to presence and end our suffering.

Helping people to meet this commitment in modern life in order to cultivate a kinder, more sustainable world is the foundation for this book.

Given that most human beings on the planet will never experience monastic living nor the privilege of silent retreat, I believe that ordinary life can provide the perfect opportunity to dissolve the trance of separation and remember our oneness with the whole. Relational Mindfulness offers a means for dismantling the ways that we as individuals and as a species have failed to remember this. Relational Mindfulness and its lessons can bring a mindful way of being to every aspect of our lives.

The quality of our life experience is governed by the focus of our attention. If our attention is focused on the conditioned mind, we suffer. When our attention rests in present moment awareness, we are free. All of our experiences, whether enjoyable or difficult, can be met with compassionate awareness. The simple instruction and motivation for Relational Mindfulness is this: In every moment, we have a choice in how we direct our attention. We can return to interconnection in every moment—and we can allow our relationships to help us to do so.

Relational Mindfulness is based on the understanding that the subtlest form of love is attention. It is about paying attention

to ourselves, to one another, and to our planet, with more intention . . . and, in so doing, to affirm who we really are.

Listening: The Essence of Relational Mindfulness

To perceive meaning is a distortion on perception.
Meaning annihilates curiosity.

On my first retreat, deep in the mountains of Yosemite National
Park, the weather was cold and rainy. I stayed in an uninsulated
wooden cabin with no electricity for the ten full days. After a day
of sitting and walking meditation, I huddled up in my blankets
on the first night and thought to myself, "I am freezing. I hate
this. This is miserable. I am not going to make it through this
retreat. I've made the wrong choice. What am I doing here?"

When I noticed how caught up I was in this internal story, I
paused, took in a deep breath, and became truly curious about
my actual experience. I noticed how loud the story was, but at
the same time I realized that my body was actually having a completely different experience than my mind. My body felt relaxed
and awake. The air felt exhilarating and sensual on my skin.
There was something inherently peaceful and nurturing about
the cool winter air.

My mind had talked me into deep dissatisfaction in a moment
of absolute perfection and serenity. In that moment, a doorway
opened that never closed again, and I began to understand the
wisdom of living in curiosity by questioning the conditioned
mind.

In today's fast-paced world, it is all too easy to experience our
lives through distortion, unconscious habit, and autopilot. We
allow our minds to control how we experience the world around

us. We are unaware that we have a choice in every moment to be free of the conditioned stories that control us, personally and in community.

The word *listen* comes from the root "to obey." Most of us have not been taught how to listen to our authentic self, but instead to obey the mind of separation. Life is new and full of possibility in every moment, yet we allow the filter of conditioning to weigh heavily upon us and keep us from being fully aware and operating from a deeper truth. This deeper truth is who we are when we are free from conditioning.

Learning from the Coral Reef

A coral reef is an incredibly complex organism that can extend for hundreds of thousands of miles. Its many parts function, communicate, and sustain its life through subtle vibration. In my early twenties, I had the opportunity to study the health of coral reefs and was shocked to learn that the sound of a motorboat speeding through the water disrupts the organism's capacity to hear this vibration. This is a primary cause of the decline of coral reefs. Similarly, as human organisms, our survival and well-being also depend on attunement to our natural feedback system. When we are distracted by the loud voices of conditioning, we are not able to hear the subtler messages of our bodies, our emotions, our needs, our intuition, or one another. We are not available to take care of ourselves or to pay genuine attention to one another.

The mind of separation takes the form of many voices: judgment, dissatisfaction, fear, doubt, projection, evaluating and reviewing, and a continual internal commentary about life. It tends to be loud, repetitious, demanding, all-knowing, adversarial, self-focused, fear-based, and often urgent. It lives in an "I"-versus-"you"/"us"-versus-"them" world.

When our attention is on the mind of separation, we are a step removed from our authentic experience of life. This can best be described as shallow/habitual listening. When our attention rests in present moment awareness, we can begin to access deep listening. When we listen shallowly, distracted by the volume of conditioning, just like the coral reef we are unable to receive the subtle information we need to thrive.

Returning Authority to the Heart

> While the mind of separation is loud and lives in shallow waters, whole mind is quiet and lives in deep waters. It hears the heart beating . . . the waves on the shore . . . the rhythmic experience of embodiment.

During my first springtime at the monastery, on a day when I was experiencing a particularly strong pull toward resistance and dissatisfaction, I entered the meditation hall and sat down with no agenda other than meeting my difficult experience with presence. I felt relieved to have space to be with my naked experience with no one intervening. I slowly began to focus all of my attention on my breath, and I allowed its rhythm to anchor me in presence. I sat there for a couple of hours, meeting my uncomfortable experience with attention and curiosity and allowing my awareness to expand organically. When I did rise, I noticed almost immediately that everything in my perception had dramatically shifted. I palpably felt my unquestionable oneness with everything around me: the spider on the wall, the lavender and rosemary growing outside the meditation hall, the sun's rays touching my skin, the body I was so used to judging, my cup of tea. I had given myself the gift of my own attention, and through paying attention, everything that I was experiencing could be perceived through a lens of love.

This feeling of love was simply a visceral experience of non-separation. I experienced everything around me as connected *to* me and felt a mutual regard for all beings. There was no one to resist and no one to assess. I was free. While I had experienced similar feelings of unity many times before, I had never understood so clearly that all that was required to get there was a gentle but profound shift in my attention.

Whole mind exists in balance, in being rather than in doing, and in experiential perception rather than duality. It is characterized by an active and receptive field of mutual support and well-being that operates in subtlety and timelessness. It is felt as spaciousness. It can be thought of as consciousness or the seat of consciousness. It is difficult to point to whole mind, because it is an experience rather than a concept to mentally grasp. Consider that rather than perceiving through judgment and hierarchy, whole mind perceives the simple truth: I am no more or less perfect than the tree in the forest.

Whole mind equally perceives the tree in the forest and the forest as a whole. It is awareness vast enough to notice both the bigger picture and the details in the picture. Whole mind meets life with acceptance. By welcoming *what is* with kind neutrality, our experiences are allowed to come and go, to arise and pass, to move through us without resistance.

In the modern terms of brain science, there is a lot of talk about the two-brain hemispheres: the right and the left, the linear and the nonlinear. Whole mind can be understood quite differently. Whole mind does not, of course, refer to a part of the brain. It does not refer to body versus mind. It is the seat of conscious, compassionate awareness which contains it all. This interconnected perception cannot be accessed through the conditioned mind because whole mind is an experience, not an assessment, because we are fully in it when we are having it, and because it does not affirm the notion that the human sphere is the only sphere that matters. This is a radical view.

Whole mind is our natural state, and it is where we feel at home . . . However, many of us tell ourselves that we cannot access that same state in the dynamic realm of daily life.

The Principles for Relational Mindfulness

> Intimate relating begins with the self. It is a toxic fantasy to believe that we can be intimate with others when we have not learned (or are afraid) to be intimate with ourselves.
>
> — Gerry Greenswald

When I entered college, I became immersed in an impassioned exploration of community. Studying conscious communities around the world of the present and in the past, I found myself asking: What makes communities work? What gets in the way? What allows relationships to thrive? And what systems support humans to live in greater harmony with the natural world?

During this same time period, I also committed to daily meditation. As my meditation practice deepened, I became inquisitive about all of the ways that meditation shifted my orientation to life and to community. Sitting changed me and shifted my perception of everything—and this included how I related with others. It allowed me to respond consciously rather than react to my experiences and to not take life so personally. I became aware that meditation was cultivating certain foundational qualities in me, such as deep listening, transparency, personal responsibility, and clear seeing. These qualities deepened the more my perception deepened of the reality of interconnection. These qualities began to serve me in my human relationships but also and equally in my relationship with the natural world.

Through workshops and retreats at various centers of learning through the ensuing years, I have had numerous immeasurable experiences of intimacy and community. I experienced the quality of connectedness and kinship that is possible when we meet one another fully present. I also became more painfully aware of the compromised quality of connection when we are not present with one another.

As I began to share these practices I had learned with more and more people, the dire need for them in the world became clearer to me. It also became clear to me that there were simple practices that people could integrate informally into their lives on a daily basis.

While studying and teaching at UCLA's Mindful Awareness Research Center, I was introduced to Professor Marvin Belzer and the term *relational mindfulness*, which he had coined while sharing mindfulness with adults and teens. Marv had a similar obsession with relational practice and intimacy, and he was also exploring formal practices to share with people to deepen their understanding of what is possible when we give one another our full attention. We now had a term to use for these practices we were exploring: Relational Mindfulness.

Relational Mindfulness encompasses diverse practices that help us to cut through the habit of disconnect. Some practices focus on *receptivity* and some focus on *expressiveness*. Through my practice, I have identified nine fundamental principles in Relational Mindfulness, which we will explore in depth for the rest of this book. They are: *Intention, The Mindful Pause, Deep Listening, Mindful Inquiry, Turning Toward Rather Than Away, Not Taking Personally, Taking Responsibility, Transparency,* and *Compassionate Action*. We learn to embody these principles through formal and informal practice, and they help us to remember whole mind through the relational field.

Intention. Relational Mindfulness begins with the intention to pay attention moment by moment and to use our life experience to wake up to our true nature. In this practice we learn to pay attention more fully to ourselves and to one another as we engage.

The Mindful Pause. Each time we take a mindful pause and turn our attention within, we invite ourselves to relax and return—from the mind of separation—to whole mind. We pause in order to access the spaciousness within and notice what lens we are perceiving through. Only from spaciousness can we connect and attune fully with our self and with one another.

Deep Listening. To listen deeply is to listen from full presence. It is the essence of Relational Mindfulness: To listen to one another in a more attentive way, and to listen to life, moment by moment, as it unfolds. We listen beyond surface thoughts or words to what is actually going on underneath. Relational Mindfulness invites us to cultivate deep listening or awake receptivity with every opportunity. We do this through formal and informal practice.

Mindful Inquiry. Mindful Inquiry means to inquire into our present moment experience, to investigate our personal and collective conditioning. We ask questions that help to point us back to whole mind, such as, "Is this thought really true?" "Am I listening to truth or delusion?" "What if this emotion too, could be met with welcome and curiosity?" We don't fill in the answer. We wait for it to present itself and remain in the receptivity of deep listening. We become aware of the amounts of energy that we've been giving to stories, and we begin to return to undistorted reality.

Turning Toward Rather Than Away. When discomfort, pain, or fear of intimacy arises, we turn toward, rather than away from it. Most of have been conditioned to turn away from or try to escape the challenges we face or to escape vulnerability. But challenge is a natural and inevitable part of being human. Relational Mindfulness invites us to turn toward discomfort and to be with it instead, with the same quality of kindness and welcome with which we would meet comfort.

Not Taking Personally. One of the ways that we maintain the bubble of a separate self is by taking things personally. We take our thoughts and emotions personally. We take things other people say personally, whether or not they have anything to do with us. We even take the weather personally. We strengthen our self-referencing bubble every time we take things personally. By practicing *not* taking life personally, we are better positioned to see clearly. This means both seeing the bigger picture and seeing ourselves within the bigger picture. Not taking personally helps us to stay connected to the consciousness of "We."

Taking Responsibility. As we deepen awareness, we become more accepting of the fact that each of us contains authenticity and goodness and each of us contains conditioning. We learn to take responsibility for our own conditioning—our thoughts and actions—so that we can impact the world around us more consciously. It brings joy to affirm who we really are and to bring our authentic self to how we relate to the world.

Transparency. As we deepen in Relational Mindfulness, we learn to be transparent about our experience within ourselves and with others. This means allowing ourselves to be vulnerable and honest, even when it is difficult. Transparency helps us to see ourselves and others with acceptance and clear perspective, acknowledging the complexity and contradiction that we can embody in any given moment as human beings. Transparency affirms the interconnected self, while judgment and masking affirm the separate self or ego.

Compassionate Action. When we practice these principles, compassionate action can arise organically. Compassionate action generally does not come to us through analysis or trying to figure out the right next move. Kindness exists in our hearts, and by settling into compassionate awareness, the action that feels most kind and skillful will be apparent. Sometimes compassionate action means to just be with ourselves or another in the field of spaciousness. Sometimes it requires an expressive gesture or courageous action.

Relational Mindfulness is based on the understanding that we are inherently whole, connected, and lovable—even with our imperfections. It asks us to affirm this understanding through how we relate.

While the mind of separation speaks to us loudly and busily, the guidance that comes from present moment awareness speaks to us kindly. This guidance may come to us in words or be experienced as a sense of grace, insight, or relaxation in our nervous system. It speaks lovingly, through insight, intuition, reassurance, and gentle knowing, guiding us step by step and breath by breath.

From presence we can perceive life as it actually is and receive information undiluted by our conditioned thoughts. We can access openness and wonder when we are having an enjoyable human experience and equally when we are having a difficult human experience. Shamans, many indigenous peoples who have a strong connection to the land, healers, Zen masters, and artists know this place of nonseparate awareness. As adults, we tend to know nonseparation on occasion, isolated from our usual experience. In fact, we may only allow ourselves to experience nonseparation when we are in nature, immersed in a sport or other physically strenuous activity, playing music or making art, spending time with children, or falling in love. We've come to know this feeling of nonseparation as a temporary state that we attain rather than as our natural state.

The first symptom of separation is the illusion of lack. From separation, we can be chopping carrots for dinner while berating ourselves for something we said the day before. We can be appearing to listen to someone speak while actually listening to our own mind planning our response. We can be carefully executing a yoga pose while judging our body and constricting our breath. We can be meeting with our new boss while projecting upon this new associate the character of an unkind person from the past. We can be making love while distracted by thoughts about our performance and not tuning in to our actual sensory experience. We can be at work while wishing we were on vacation. We can be on vacation while worrying continually about challenges at work.

Signs and Clues That the Mind of Separation Is Operating

It is not necessary or helpful to take the mind of separation personally or judge ourselves when we catch ourselves in it, but it is useful to understand how it operates. The more we pay attention and bring a sense of fascination to its workings, the more we are able to see it for what it is: a distraction clothed in conditioning that we do not need to follow. We can become increasingly aware of how it distracts us and pulls us away from presence. We can bring compassionate neutrality rather than judgment to the experience.

Here are some clues that the mind of separation is operating within us. This list can serve as a set of "red flags" inviting us to notice where our attention is, to bring our attention back to the present, and to help us deepen our embodiment of whole mind:

- The mind of separation assesses rather than lives life. It labels, measures, categorizes, and draws conclusions about everything.
- The mind of separation tends to focus on the message that "There is something wrong."
- The mind of separation notices what is missing. "There is not enough."
- The mind of separation focuses on "There's something I've got to do," even when there is not.
- The mind of separation walks into a room and spots difference rather than connectivity.
- The mind of separation turns difference into "other than" rather than just different. It often then perceives "other than" as a threat.
- The mind of separation zeros in on one small thing, like a dot in the big picture, while awareness holds the big picture.
- The mind of separation seeks to impose control. Rather than being in the flow of life, the separate self feels the need to try to control and micromanage life, often working against natural flow.
- The mind of separation also seeks to impose control by projecting meaning on everything. When we have a physical health symptom, for example, it concludes that "I'm going to be sick all week and my vacation plans are ruined!" or "I must have a major illness!" The mind of separation would rather come up with meaning or take a

position without facts, rather than dwell in the field of not knowing.

- The mind of separation makes a big deal out of anything and everything. It feeds off the sensation of drama rather than the deeper nourishment of well-being. Just listen to CNN or pick up a magazine for a few minutes and you will hear or read in the way the stories are told the drama of the mind of separation.
- The mind of separation takes life personally.

The mind of separation perceives itself as an island and gives little weight to the bigger picture. The mind of separation lacks a sense of responsibility and operates from ignorance. "I want to smoke and so I will. It doesn't really impact anyone else around me." "I feel like speeding, and since I'm a good driver, I'm not concerned about how this might impact other people on the road." It also carries a sense of powerlessness, implicitly believing "I don't really matter, so whatever I do can't really make a difference." We can see this in the driver who ignores other drivers and in the person who inserts him/herself into a conversation inappropriately. We see this in the gardener who puts chemicals into the soil rather than observing and working with the soil to rebalance it. We also see this in ourselves when we ignore signs that our bodies are exhausted or depleted and need to rest.

Consider that the mind of separation is not embodied; it is a mental construction with a physiological impact. In Buddhism it is sometimes referred to as a parasite feeding off humanity's energy. Similarly, in the Hopi language, there is reference made to it as Powaniqqatsi, an entity, a way of life that consumes the life forces of beings in order to further its life. The mind of separation does not operate in service to life. If we do not have the tools to step back from the myth of separation, it can drain our life force. Within the mind of separation we cannot see clearly or experience life as it is. When we turn our attention within, we hear beyond separation and return to the present moment awareness that is grounded, accepting, awake, relaxed, and alive. It is possible to live our lives free from the myth of separation in this place of empowered and embodied aliveness.

Releasing Passive Consumerism and Reinstating the Authority Within

It is up to each of us to restore the authority of our authentic self. There is no pill to take or shortcut to getting there. It requires tenacity and commitment. It is not actually hard work, because who we are is interconnection, but it requires devoted practice to remember this truth. It requires formal and informal practice. Most important, it requires the willingness to look within and acknowledge that this is perhaps our best moment in time to wake up. Given that our life will not last forever, why wait?

Relational Mindfulness invites us to acknowledge our innate capacity for intimacy. It invites us to release or let go of who we've been and the perceived limitations we've been operating under and instead to be willing to risk. As we do so, we find that we do indeed have the capacity to meet each moment with loving presence. We find out that we become more loving and receptive to love. We find that when we are powerfully present we are equipped for intimacy with others. We find that by reclaiming our inner authority, we give others permission to do the same. We find that we have increased capacity to navigate challenges and conflict from the heart and are more empowered to contribute positively to any situation.

A golden rule for this work is to trust the process. These practices work. Trust your intention and the opportunities life gives you to make the choice of nonseparation in every moment. We are all accustomed to feeling a bit powerless to confront our thoughts and emotions, just as we have become accustomed to feeling disempowered by participating in a society that is not aligned with compassion.

• • • • • • • Mindful Inquiry • • • • • • •

When do you feel most at peace? At home in your body? What pulls you away from peace?

How does the mind of separation operate in your life? How does it impact your relationship with your self?

How do you experience subtle incessant dissatisfaction?

What are your versions of "When I have X, then I will be fully happy"?

What are your favorite memories of interconnection as a child? At other particular times in your life? When do you experience interconnection most fully in your daily life?

What conscious habits or practices do you engage in to affirm interconnection in your daily life and align your lifestyle with interconnection?

Think of one place, perhaps in nature or somewhere you visited as a child, where you fell the most safe, connected, relaxed, and cared for. Close your eyes and imagine yourself resting in this place. What qualities do you experience in this place?

Think of one person in whose presence you experience safety and intimacy. Close your eyes and imagine being in the presence of this person. What qualities do you experience with this person?

• • • • • • • • **Daily Practice** • • • • • • • •

Today, begin to bring curiosity to how the mind of separation operates within you.

Notice how it gets your attention and unnecessarily adds meaning and story.

Every time you notice the mind of separation in action, pause and bring your full attention to your breath and body. Breathe deeply into the center of your heart, feeling the air as it enters your body, fills your body, and leaves your body, and ask the questions, "Is this true? Is this really so? How do I know this is actually true?"

Rest your full attention with your breath and body. See if you can be aware of the deeper stillness within you, even while the mind of separation is operating at the surface. Just this subtle shift is all that is required to remember nonseparation.

3

The Wisdom of Turning Our Attention Within

As we remember our authenticity, we cease to have an appetite or artificial need for distraction and outer focus. We learn to relax into the steadfast nourishment of awareness, with nothing to do and nowhere to get to that is more worth it than being here, where we already are.

I f I had one wish for the world, it would be that every person be given the opportunity to spend ten days on silent retreat. On retreat, we pause from daily life, look within, and get in touch with the deep listening and clear seeing that is possible through present moment awareness. When we observe our minds while on retreat, we see clearly the habit of turning to the mind of separation for information instead of to our own actual experience. We have the space to experience the peace and ease of non-doing awareness. All that is required is a subtle shift in our attention.

To my first retreat I brought with me a host of anxieties: relationship difficulties, self-doubt, and angst about the state of the world. During the first Dharma talk at the retreat, the teacher introduced the definition of suffering or *dukkha* as a "wheel off center." If the wheel of a vehicle is off center, then the vehicle does not run properly. Everything that the body of the vehicle carries is impacted. When we are off center, the vehicle of our life wobbles, veers off course, and often crashes. When not equipped to meet life's challenges with presence, we react to everything we encounter through habitual patterns. When we return to center, our experience of everything we are carrying realigns. It is not that our problems necessarily disappear. It is that we see our mind's role in creating them. We can respond consciously to all we encounter, and our challenges take their place in a larger perspective.

So many concerns in my life at the time were addressed by the simple medicine of turning within and learning how to center. This was my initiation into seeing that my stories and fears were an inside, not an outside, job. They could only be fully be addressed by attending to the inner landscape.

Turning Toward Our Self

> The best way is to understand yourself, and then you will understand everything.
>
> —Shunryu Suzuki

By the time I made the choice to become a Zen monk at age twenty-six, I had come to believe in the messages that so many of us receive . . . that we are somehow not good enough, that we don't measure up, and that there is always a higher standard to reach. I carried around a heavy inner critic. I had learned to see myself as someone to be measured and judged. I was accustomed to looking outside of myself for validation, while true validation can only be accessed from within.

In the cultural context in which I grew up—Los Angeles in the 1980s—I often felt different. I was much smaller than my peers, more introverted, and came from an unconventional family of freethinkers and activists. As I never grew past 4'11", I felt judged for my size throughout my childhood, and took on the message that there was something wrong with me, I learned to compensate for my perceived inadequacies by being rigorous about excelling in other areas of my life.

For me, an external focus was a way to assure that I got approval and acceptance—by making others happy and being hypervigilant about how I was perceived. Although I was both talented and intelligent, I did not realize my own inherent value. I traded in my personal peace for a devoted relationship with an internal standard keeper.

I recall a significant conversation with my dad when I was five years old. He sat me down one day after kindergarten, under a shady oak tree at Griffith Park in the Hollywood Hills, which was one of his favorite places for us to go walking and exploring. In a voice of gentle concern, he said that I seemed less free than I had been prior to that point. He said that I had been joyful the whole time he had known me, but that recently I seemed to be less happy and more worried. He asked how he could support me.

I imagine the pain in all parents when they notice their children becoming conditioned and self-conscious for the first time. It is the recognition of the loss of innocence in our own self. My dad was a deeply perceptive and attentive parent, with a contemplative practice of his own, and I am blessed to have had such a good listener and clear seer in my life. I imagine him witnessing the beginning of a conditioned pattern back then, his joyful carefree little girl going to kindergarten and for the first time perceiving herself as lacking somehow. I do not recall my response on

that autumn day, but it was my dad's honest and compassionate inquiry in that and many other conversations throughout my
childhood that enabled me to learn how to ask compassionate
questions and to inquire into my own capacity for joy throughout my life—and to do so with nonjudgment and gentle concern.
When I was eleven years old, my dad, who was a health devotee,
yogi, and marathon runner, received the harsh news one day that
he had one month left to live. He had spotted a dark, uneven
mole a couple of years earlier and had it removed, but due to a
misdiagnosis, the melanoma had spread and thus was not treated
until it was too late. My best friend's parents drove my sister and
me to the hospital where my dad sat us down to tell us this news.
I remember the palpable silence of tragedy in the car and tears
building as I intuited bad news. In his hospital room, my dad told
us honestly what he had heard.

It was as if the whole world cracked apart in that moment,
and my sister and I broke down for what felt like hours. We
covered his face with kisses, while we all wept, in shock at this
inconceivable news that we would be losing each other. This
was my first time of many of being hit by the avalanche of
impermanence.

During that time, we helped my father bring closure to his
life and our family's life as it had been and never would be again.
It was a heart-wrenching and intimate time. On a rainy night in
February, we were all snuggled in bed together as he took his last
breath. My father had a role in our community as friend, mentor,
and coach to many kids, and he was beloved by all. After he died,
a period of great instability ensued. With an emotion as strong
and tumultuous as grief, maintaining the mask of normalcy came
at great cost. I quickly learned that grief is not welcome in this
world. I learned how to disassociate, leave my body, and check
out from reality at will—although I continued to perform well

enough to meet the standards of the high-expectation world I lived in. I learned to smile regardless of how I felt inside.

The outer landscape in which I was living, however, became increasingly unsafe and unsettling. I took on an outward identity while perpetuating a deepening well of aloneness within. I learned how to attend to other people's emotional needs despite being out of touch with my own. Ironically, many people knew me as "Eden who was always smiling."

It was this mask that got revealed and unearthed the first time I went on retreat. I had learned to survive well, but at great cost. At the end of his life, my dad had expressed clearly that what mattered in life was not what he had accomplished or not, but the quality of his relationships—with himself and with God, with people, and with the earth. A part of me never forgot this, and practice has taught me that the quality of each of our relationships stems from the quality of our relationship with ourselves. I needed to bring my focus back within to address my relationship with myself before continuing to relate and serve in the world in all of the ways I wanted to.

When I did turn within, I quickly realized the healing power of grief and that it was okay to not feel okay. I also realized the degree to which my personal pain was tied into my pain for our broken world.

The Collective Agreement

The message of conditional love is pervasive in our society. It is as if over the past 100 years we have turned up the volume on conditional love, broadcasting it to the masses through television, advertising, and the internet. Hollywood, where I grew up, is the epicenter of this machine of conditional love. Society perpetuates the message that parts of our humanity are acceptable and parts are not. Some get rewarded, and some get rejected and ignored.

The message is streamed globally through the media and advertising that a particular lifestyle lived by people who look a certain way and buy specific products is the model to follow.

Young women are taught that their attractiveness to men is the most important thing in life, robbing many at an early age of the wholeness that allows a woman to find her authentic power. We teach little boys that being successful is a contest they can pass or fail, whether it is in the arena of sports, money, fame, or profession.

The image of the American dream leaves most of the globe out (and most of the United States out, too), yet it pervades the global community, from indigenous farmers to the developing middle class in many countries who strive to purchase homes in facsimiles of American suburbs. Traditional societies in many parts of the world have accepted the "modern way" as superior and, as a result, have abandoned their cultural customs and values—and, along with them, their sanity. The American dream has eroded our global quality of life and the self-esteem of countless billions. Rather than valuing diversity, resilience, and cooperation, we have become resigned to living in a world of judgment, competition, and fear.

It is tragic to consider the amount of money and time humanity devotes to the energy-draining pursuit of attaining conditional love. Trying to perfect the way we are perceived is a waste of time. This kind of external focus can never lead to happiness, but it is often mistaken for happiness, and then followed by painful loss. Receiving attention or approval from without is an inadequate substitute for a much deeper experience of wholeness available within each of us as individuals.

Instead, our energy should be directed to cultivating and sustaining a centered relationship with ourselves. Our energy should be going to generating well-being and health, integrity, intimacy, and partnership with nature. Our energy and creativity should be going to the unique expression of the authentic self and to the larger question of how to create a socially just and equitable world for generations to come. Our energy could be expended on developing our widely untapped capacity for relational intelligence and sustainable design. And when it is, we can expect to lead lives that generate and sustain the fulfillment that is our birthright.

People are encouraged to look good rather than feel good. The media even promulgates the message that to feel good, you must look good in a particular way. Society teaches people to follow a script for behavior rather than to be in touch with their unique essence and to express that essence fully.

In teaching mindful eating workshops, I have learned that people refer more to magazines and books for information on how to eat than to the intelligence of their own bodies. In teaching workshops about mindful sexuality, I have learned that many young people turn to the media in the form of movies and TV for information about how to engage in sex rather than to their bodies and their own erotic intelligence.

Children are conditioned to look outward to an external authority rather than supported in developing their relationship with the authority within, which is where we access the inner guidance to navigate life's ups and downs.

In my own life, I spent years comparing myself to what I saw celebrated externally and missing the unique gifts and rare beauty that I carry and embody today with pleasure and gratitude. Instead of savoring my introverted nature, I compared myself to all the extroverts I knew. Instead of enjoying my petite body, I compared my body to the tall blonde models of Hollywood culture. I even compared my current self to the "future me" when my spiritual work would finally pay off. I did not understand that the difference I carried was my unique contribution.

Practice invites us to examine ourselves and to inquire honestly into the questions: What really matters deep within, beyond survival in a world of conditional love? What do we gain by taking on the made-up standards of society? What would it be like if we could see ourselves clearly, without the overlay of judgment? Beyond the ego, from where do we access true confidence, joy, trust? What is possible when we relieve ourselves of the habit of conditional love and risk taking a stand for the unconditional?

Finding the Refuge Within

Turning our attention within, we learn to perceive through loving presence rather than judgment. Awareness gives us a compassionate and neutral refuge to relax into. When we realize that we have a refuge to come home to, a still, clear, spacious place within, how we act in the world changes. We are no longer poised for survival and approval, fear, or competition. We can meet our emotional experience with kind neutrality. We can take responsibility for our "stuff" to a degree that it does not leak out into the world and muddy our perceptions even more. We make fewer judgments and feel less frustration with others. Our energy is not drained by identity maintenance or efforts at self-improvement.

Becoming centered does not make us perfect, but it reminds us of the perfection of our imperfect selves. Once we start practicing awareness, we find great joy in cleaning up our act and releasing the misconceptions we believed in so thoroughly. We begin to see that each and every one of the parts of our self we have mistakenly judged or pushed away is a gift for us. The first gift our shadows carry is that they can to teach us how to accept that there is nothing inherently wrong with us, once we stop looking through the eyes of judgment. The second gift our shadows carry is that they can teach us how to access real compassion—for ourselves and for others.

Stillness Is the Doorway to Awareness

It is common in this day and age for people to allow themselves glimpses and moments of inner awareness and to then spend the majority of their time focusing outwardly, plugged into the conditioning of their mind, the internet, external conversations, and the demands of life in the modern world. The glimpses become a moment to refuel, a pause to exhale, but then people return to the conditioned busyness they believe is required to navigate the day.

I believe that the world would be a different place if more people were able to turn within and find center. Finding our center and cultivating a sustained relationship with that center are, I believe, the biggest contributions we can make as human beings. When we turn our attention within, we find out both how pure and powerful our authentic nature is and how easily we, susceptible to the forces of conditioning, can lose sight of our authentic self if we are not present. Our greatest untapped resource is the stillness within. This does not necessarily mean physical stillness, but energetic stillness that comes from being centered. From stillness we can accept life as it is and respond appropriately and with care.

Stillness can be found through a daily meditation practice, but we also nourish stillness through the following:

- spending time in silence
- taking devoted care of our minds and bodies every day
- spending time immersed in nature
- experiencing intimacy and vulnerability with others
- getting in touch with our bodies as fully as we can
- giving our full attention to ordinary daily activities
- being aware of the crowding of time and leaving blocks of time unscheduled
- releasing toxic relationships and activities
- fasting from media from time to time

- letting go of gossipy relationships or habits of interaction that feed drama
- making choices that simplify rather than complicate our lives
- spending time with the landscapes and people that help us to remember stillness
- eating mindfully . . . paying attention more subtly to our sensory experience of food and to the web of interconnection that the food on our plates represents

Is It Selfish to Focus Within?

It might seem ironic that it is through an inward focus that our outer connections are nourished, but without being centered we cannot participate consciously in the world around us. As long as we see ourselves through a tainted lens, we view others through a tainted lens. To clarify, an inner focus is not equivalent to being self-absorbed or self-centered. In fact, it's the very opposite. It does not mean that all of our attention is directed within; it's that our attention is rooted in awareness of mind, feelings, and body and extends out to engage mindfully with the world. We are settled into the sacredness of each ordinary moment, aware rather than indulging in the dogma of conditioning that makes us only partially available. When our attention is not focused within, we make meaning out of everything. We take life personally. Awareness is by nature nonjudgmental. When we meet life from the spaciousness of awareness, we experience life as whole, rather than as good versus bad or positive versus negative. We are able to meet our experiences with the kind neutrality that gives rise to genuine service or compassionate action, rather than with the reaction of fear trying to "fix" what we think might be wrong.

We often say that we want to contribute and be of more service to others, to our community, to the world. Being of service starts with finding center. If we find our center, then we will know how to be of service in each moment. Instead of over-filling our calendars in order to "help," we ensure that we make time to cultivate stillness and become centered. We are then empowered to engage from the effortless intelligence of our own essence. I cannot think of anything less selfish than the willingness to give ourselves the gift of our own attention. Not only does this show us how to meet ourselves with love and to love others, but it is also how we access genuine compassion.

Encouragement for Finding Your Authentic Self

> Your task is not to seek for love, but merely to seek and find all the barriers within yourself that you have built against it.
>
> —Rumi

The more clearly we understand that we are not our conditioning, the more we become in touch with our authentic self or essence. Our essence is the unique beauty and wholeness that is who we are seen through the eyes of compassion. It is the unique way that consciousness illuminates us. As long as we maintain an outward focus, our attention is turned away from our essence.

Our essence carries innate qualities that have nothing to do with effort, performance, and judgment. The qualities it carries are timeless, ordinary, and immeasurable. It means being inherently special just as we are—where we are smooth and where we are cracked. The ordinary self has no self-consciousness, no pretense, and no need to be seen as "special" for it perceives no lack and does not live in the realm of comparison. It can also be called "no self" because it points to the quality of presence we emanate when we allow ourselves to be free of identity and surrender to the spaciousness of awareness.

I compare finding one's essence to discovering a unique and exceptionally beautiful flower in the wilderness. We cannot seek it out intentionally because we would not know where to look. But in turning within and allowing awareness to guide us, we might unintentionally find it. We begin to soften, let go of conditioned ways, and surrender more fully to innocence. We open our eyes to seeing more clearly and eventually behold ourselves more clearly. We see ourselves, finally, as we actually are—our inherent goodness and the perfection of the unique signature that we carry.

Our essence does not call out loudly to be seen, but instead gently reveals itself to us. Shadows can become a welcome part of that revelation. When we find our essence, we find a humility at the same time that we shine more brightly. There is a sense of shining fully and freely for the benefit of the whole.

This is not egoic love. There is no need for self-aggrandizement or self-deprecation when we discover our authentic self. We can relax and enjoy our own presence, with nothing to prove or make happen. We can accept all that has occurred in our life up to this point, and all that will happen in the future. We can acknowledge the wholeness of our lives and of the path that we are taking.

As we remember our inherent wholeness, we cease to have an appetite or artificial need to participate in the conditioning that is telling us that what we have and who we are simply are not enough. It is an extraordinary relief to encounter the perfection of ordinary self in a world that is screaming loudly, "There is something better out there! There is someplace else that you need to be. There is something more you need to prove! There is something you might not find!" Embracing our essence ends the charade of conditioning, and all that is left is acknowledgement of the preciousness of our unique expression of life and all forms of life. We finally relax, aware that there is nothing worth more than being who we already are.

Choosing to Belong . . . to Ourselves, to Our World, to One Another

> The simplest path to happiness is to remember non-separation. Nothing can replace the joy of knowing our own inherent and shared goodness.

When we return to the consciousness of interconnection, our needs are fulfilled and our resistance is addressed because we understand at a bone-deep level that we are not alone. If we are not alone, then there is nothing to prove, nowhere to get to, and no need to exert control over another human being.

We are often surprised when we experience genuine connection, as well as the synchronicity that often accompanies it. A stranger is profoundly kind. Our best friend calls just as we are thinking of them. We choose to walk down a particular street at the moment that someone we've been thinking about appears on that same street. We look up from our work at the exact moment a deer is walking by the window. The more present we become, the more this synchronicity occurs, because we are more in tune with the whole. We begin to understand that it is natural to live in the alignment of synchronicity. Synchronicity is not magic. It is natural.

The more we understand this, the more we learn that even our own healing is not isolated. We are healing not just for ourselves, but for all beings we share this planet with—all people who have suffered from delusion as we have, all beings who have suffered from human greed and hatred, the generation before us and the generations before them, and for future generations yet to come.

Nonseparation erases the idea that we are only connected to those who are human and alive right now. It expands our understanding that the heart holds the capacity for connection beyond time and beyond form. Anyone who has lost someone they love but felt the connection remain intact knows this to be true deep within.

The future of life on earth requires that we move beyond the myth of separation. As we return to whole mind, we accept and treasure all aspects of who we are and therefore accept and treasure humanity. We learn to treasure all states of being.

· · · · · · · · · **Mindful Inquiry** · · · · · · · ·

Consider, on this day, what the external factors are that have had your attention.

Other people's needs? Text messages? Emails or the internet? Things on your to-do list? Standards you are trying to meet, consciously or subconsciously?

What thought formations or emotions have had your focus?

- Distractions?
- Mind obsessions?
- Fantasies?
- Fear or worry?
- Other strong emotions?
- Pressures?
- Relational dramas?
- Self-improvement schemes?

What made-up standards do you hold yourself to?

Who do you compare yourself to?

In what activities do you allow yourself to set aside distraction and give your focused, relaxed, and sustained attention?

What are the qualities of your essence or true self, when you are simply present and in spacious awareness?

How do you nurture your essence?

What activities help you get in touch with your essence?

• • • • • • • • Daily Practice • • • • • • • •

STOP

This practice will help you to turn your attention within regularly, as often as you would like, throughout the day. Over time this practice cultivates a conscious habit of pausing and remembering that spaciousness is always available to us.

S—Stop—simply pause.

T—Take a couple of conscious breaths and turn your attention within.

O—Observe what is arising in your body, feelings, and mind with curiosity and nonjudgment.

P—Proceed.

Today, set a timer to go off as a reminder to STOP throughout your day, or pick a reminder, such as each time you get a text alert, to invite yourself to STOP each time you hear it. Each time you pause, allow yourself to meet whatever is moving through your awareness with welcome.

4

Cultivating a Daily Practice of Presence and Power

Perhaps all the dragons in our lives are princesses
who are only waiting to see us act, just once, with
beauty and courage. Perhaps everything that frightens us is, in its deepest essence, something helpless
that wants our love.

—Rainer Maria Rilke

first learned to meditate as a little girl on a camping trip with
my grandparents in the High Sierra mountains of California.
We had pitched a tent amid a forest of pine trees near one
of the Mammoth Lakes, and we spent our days swimming in
the lake, hiking, fishing, and cooking our meals over a camp-
fire, with no one around for miles. My grandparents were lovers of the wilderness and made sure to instill that experience in
their children and grandchildren. I have memories as a child of
my grandmother, an artist and bohemian who ran an alternative
school for children, sitting me down on a shaded log by a creek
and inviting me to be still and listen. In the middle of a busy

day, she used to say "let's think of something quiet" as a way to invite us into presence. We would pause and pay attention to the quiet undercurrent of life, such as clouds floating in the sky, a slow-moving insect, a still tree, a sturdy rock, or trickling water. I remember a palpable and visceral feeling of peace and aliveness while being in the forest with her in this way. These experiences left an imprint on me of the value of pausing and listening within.

In the imaginative way that children can, I turned that experience into a game I would play throughout my childhood. I would pretend that my entire body from head to toes was an ear and listen carefully to everything around me. Like a tuning fork, in this game I was an instrument of deep listening. Little did I know that this was the beginning of a lifelong meditation practice and love affair with the receptivity of awareness. I did not take on daily practice until I was nineteen years old, but the experience of meditating by the creek with my grandmother paved the way.

The Darkness of the New Moon

Practicing meditation is easier than we think. When we stop considering meditation a means for changing something within ourselves and realize that it is instead a remembering, something shifts. We let go more easily of striving and more willingly surrender to the spaciousness within.

Before this realization, we resist awareness by filling our lives with distraction. The groundlessness of empty space frightens us. At first, meditation can seem like sitting outside at night in the darkness of the new moon, wondering why it is so dark and hoping to get away. Gradually we become curious about the darkness, and so we continue to sit. As we continue to sit in the dark, we slowly begin to perceive in a new way. At some point, it begins to dawn on us that the gift of the new moon is the pure darkness it offers. Something within us changes, and the world around us changes too. We relax and begin to notice stars in the night sky that we could not see before. We surrender to the darkness, and rather than being fearful, we turn to greet it with open curiosity. The discipline itself transforms us, and we lose the fear of being in the dark. We let ourselves forget every story we have created in our minds and projected onto darkness, stories we have become captive to, and we welcome instead the mystery that envelops us with love.

The more we learn to savor awareness for the sake of awareness, the more we can savor the ordinary moments of our life. We can enjoy our morning chores with the same quality of presence and serenity as our morning tea. We can anchor ourselves in the rhythm of our breath moving through our body even as we meet work deadlines. We can relax in our interactions with others, and thus experience greater intimacy.

Remembering the Already-Awakened State

Real practice does not begin until we altogether drop our reasons for practicing. Mindfulness is not about self-improvement. It is only ego that cares about "fixing ourselves," "getting somewhere," and "attaining something." When we sit in meditation, there is nowhere to get to and nothing to change or improve upon. We sit to remember the compassionate awareness that exists when we stop doing everything else. We sit to learn to meet life's ups and downs from true compassion.

There is great emphasis in modern spiritual conversations on reaching an awakened state. What meditation actually teaches us is to learn to live in a continual remembrance of the awakened state that is already here. Awareness is already awake. We leave awareness regularly for the mind of separation, but the awakened state never leaves us. It is the very consciousness that illuminates us. Even in our most stressful moments there remains a thread of awareness within. Rather than remain obsessed with attaining a peak awakened state, we can live in a continual state of affirming awareness or whole mind.

Some people think of meditation as a special event. They compare awakening to the dawn that occurs for one instant early every morning and then not again for twenty-four hours. People justify spending twenty-three hours in a less than wakeful mode while waiting for one enlightened moment. We can instead find the willingness to remember, moment by moment, throughout the day. We can pause as many times as we choose to, to turn toward the already-awakened state of whole mind.

Compassionate Self-Discipline

When I attended my first daylong meditation retreat (called *sesshin* in the Zen tradition), at Green Gulch Farm Zen Center on the coast of Marin, California, I fell in love with Zen practice and decided I would meditate for two hours a day, every day— one hour in the morning and one hour at night. I was certain that if I could just maintain the state of well-being that I experienced on this retreat, which included one full day of sitting and walking meditation, everything in my life would improve.

This intention lasted for about three weeks and then petered out completely.

I did not want to let go of the expanded states I had reached during retreat and thought that scheduling time for meditation would ensure this. When I failed to maintain the schedule, I beat myself up for failing at my intention and having to start all over again. Ego had taken meditation into its hands and had once again used something that was initially for my well-being against me.

I had become accustomed to engaging in self-improvement programs. I would embark on a long, ambitious juice cleanse, and then reward myself for being so disciplined. I would set goals such as, "I will follow a 100% pure macrobiotic diet. I will do sit-ups every day. I will write poetry every day. I will be disciplined." My motivation in the past usually had to do with reaching a romanticized state of perfection, without being present to the process or honoring the messages from my body. Predictably, I would regress, stop whatever regimen I was on, and feel badly through the process. I did not see clearly the underlying mistake of allowing ego to set the standard and demanding that the rest of me meet that standard.

It was akin to living with a military sergeant as my companion instead of a wise mentor or friend. I did not see the lack of wisdom in assigning my "potential" to ego. I did not realize that our potential is already realized when we get ego out of the way. A mentor would have taught me compassionate self-discipline and how to enjoy exercising for my body's pleasure and sustained well-being. A friend would have helped me to bring a light heart and playfulness to macrobiotics, without turning it into a pass/fail test.

There is a tremendous amount of distortion in the promotion of modern meditation and mindfulness. The primary distortion is that mindfulness is another passive consumer product we can buy to improve ourselves and our lives. Meditation is marketed as a means of relieving our suffering rather than ending our suffering. This subtle (or not-so-subtle) promise pervades our society. But because we're so conditioned by the consumer mentality, it's sometimes difficult to see. When we cease affiliating meditation with self-improvement, we can find our way to the greater work, which is to find freedom from the cycle of suffering.

My early days as a meditator taught me the importance of clarity of intention. Even if we approach meditation with an egotistic motivation initially, if we persist, we naturally find our way to clarity of intention. Ego might lead us to practice, but eventually the ego falls away and we can access something much deeper. If we try to approach meditation as a self-improvement program, it will never work. By perceiving meditation as a "should," our human instinct is to rebel against it. Any parent who has demanded that their child do something, knows this all too well.

By letting go of the idea that we meditate to attain a particular state within or to "heal our broken self," and instead just showing up to sit with willingness and curiosity, we are positioned to sustain a practice. By releasing ego's agenda, our deeper heart's desire is free to emerge. We are then able to feel fully alive, free of the delusions and distortions that cause suffering. It is only from our heart's desire that we can sustain practice.

It is likely that, initially, conditioning will bring all of our extraneous stories to practice, and there is nothing wrong with that. Some such stories I've seen in myself and my students are:

I'm finding an island of peace and I need to hold on to it.

I'm meditating to fix my broken self.

I'm meditating to prove my worthiness.

I'm meditating ever so seriously, to be allowed into the gates of enlightenment.

Meditation is a special/precious/exotic experience.

I'm meditating because I should meditate.

I'm special or wiser than others because I meditate.

Once we have removed ego from the driver's seat, then our practice can go much deeper. We then sit in the spirit of willingness, fascination, humility, and surrender. It can take time to develop a distilled and committed relationship to meditation, so patience and self-forgiveness are essential.

The Balance of Receptivity and Expressiveness in Practice

Establishing a meditation practice is the discipline and art of establishing a kind and loving landscape within ourselves. Sustaining a meditation practice requires that we access the qualities of *receptivity* and *expressiveness*. Both are requirements for Relational Mindfulness. Balancing these qualities within us invites us to adopt an attitude of fierce wholeness.

We can think of receptivity as the willingness to relax into stillness and non-doing, paying attention and accepting whatever the moment brings. As we notice a thought arise, we call on our willingness to observe the thought, let it go, and bring our full attention back to our breath. Receptivity is the soft, nurturing, neutral quality of presence that we access in meditation. Our receptive nature gives us the ability to "just be" without agenda.

Expressiveness is the tenacious, persevering, and fierce quality that helps us to show up to meditate every day. It allows us to cut through delusion. It is the source of structure and discipline needed to sustain a practice. It is also the quality needed at times to speak or act courageously from our authentic self. This can seem somewhat frightening at first, especially if we are used to discounting our authentic self.

Often, as a teacher, I will meet people who have become comfortable with "just being"—embodying the receptive aspect of meditation; however, they have not yet learned to access their expressive nature, the perseverance and tenacity required to step back from their thoughts. I also encounter people who bring a hyper-discipline to their practice, holding themselves in a very rigid approach to "cutting through delusion." This does not allow them to relax into full receptivity. It does not allow them to enjoy the effortlessness of awareness.

When we balance the receptive and expressive, in our sitting practice and in our way of being in daily life, we have the safety, structure, and discipline we need to thrive, as well as the compassion, flexibility, and ease of equanimity. We create a singular expression in ourselves that carries the grace and strength of a spiritual warrior. This balance is not modeled for us often in today's world. We are more used to seeing force and rigidity positioned against relaxation and self-care. Restoring this balance within ourselves is imperative to cultivating a wakeful life. At the same time, we contribute to the possibility of rebalancing these two elements in our society.

Considerations for Sustaining a Practice

A committed meditation practice is like a committed relationship with a beloved. Our willingness to show up may at first be fueled by elated states of mind and body and positive reward. We might perceive the relationship through the lens of "specialness" and "expectation." As time passes, we experience both joy and challenge in the relationship. Our meditation practice illuminates every unconscious mechanism within us. We begin to find the willingness to show up both when ego wants to and when that is the last thing ego wants to do. We sense the immeasurable treasure of sustained love, and may start to perceive love as our teacher of personal growth. We are no longer in the relationship for what we get, but equally for what we bring and how we show up. As this shift begins to happen, compassionate self-discipline becomes less of an issue. Instead, acceptance and fortitude emerge and we are more able to show up with love, no matter what.

Helpful questions to inquire into in order to sustain a practice are:

- Do I have a structure to support and sustain my practice (perhaps a set schedule and/or people to meditate with, a teacher to work with)?

- How can I support myself to STOP regularly throughout the day and remember the already-awakened state?
- Am I in this to achieve a specific goal or to surrender to the process?
- What forms of resistance arise in me? Can I allow my resistance to be here without adding a layer of judgment? What would help me to show up to meditate even when I don't want to?
- Am I meeting my practice with lovingkindness?
- Do I have accountability for staying on course when I hit rough patches?

Affirming Wholeness

The love we access through meditation teaches us not to feel *good* but to feel *whole*. Wholeness means knowing that who you are—your ordinary self and ordinary experience—is enough. It means understanding that there is no part of you unworthy of compassion. Affirming wholeness requires that we move toward all those places where we are caught in the mind of separation, whether from a mild irritation or a life trauma.

To have a practice means to continually turn toward whatever is there and greet it with the welcome of an open heart. Here, with space around it, whatever arises can move through us. We can accept what arises rather than resist it or give it more power than it needs by taking it personally. Accepting our feelings with loving presence means not wasting precious time in an effort to escape, judge, resist, manage, or analyze. It means making room for "this human experience too." When we understand that the inner landscape contains it all—every texture, season, mood, color, and expression of humanity—we stop resisting and show up for the task at hand. The task at hand is always to meet what *is* with love.

In daily life, we often abandon ourselves in the name of "feeling good" and "avoiding discomfort." We are provided constant opportunities, however, to come back to ourselves and affirm wholeness over "feeling good." There are seemingly small choices all day long that either support ego or authenticity. Some examples of this are:

- showing up to sit even when we are experiencing resistance
- choosing to remain open in an uncomfortable interaction
- keeping commitments one has made even when resistance arises
- not reaching out for that drink, cigarette, or _____ (*fill in the blank*) when we know it would distract us from discomfort
- prioritizing self-care even when it is inconvenient
- asking for help in a moment when it is difficult and we feel weak
- making choices that feed our growth and integrity rather than ego
- making choices that serve long-term well-being rather than the shortsighted view of separate self
- making the choices that express our common bond with all beings
- practicing restraint when we feel reactive, so we can investigate the nature of our reactivity and respond consciously

Does This Mean I Have to Be Mindful All the Time?

On the last day of a beginners' retreat, someone always asks, "Does this mean I have to be mindful all the time? This sounds like a lot of work." If we are not careful, we can find ourselves using mindfulness to justify constantly judging ourselves or trying to shape ourselves into an inauthentic but seemingly superior way of being. In other words, we can turn mindfulness practice into a form of personal hypervigilance.

"Having a practice" of mindfulness does not mean turning mindfulness into a standard. Mindfulness means to pay attention. Yes, it serves us to be mindful at all times. It serves our hearts to pay attention to our life experience, whatever we may be doing at the time. It is useful to always be aware of the choice we have in every moment. If we find ourselves becoming hypervigilant, it is a sign that, once again, ego has taken hold of our practice. Separate self is trying to "manage" our practice. This is not a problem, and we will eventually see through it. It helps to take our practice sincerely but not seriously, maintaining a light heart and sense of humor at the same time, especially about all the ways that the mind of separation pulls us off course along the way.

Meeting Trauma: Turning toward Our Demons

Sometimes we are provided with opportunities to heal past trauma through our personal mindfulness practice—trauma that we are conscious of or perhaps not aware of at all. As human beings, we all experience trauma to varying degrees in our lives. Trauma can take the form of loss, illness or injury, abuse, heartbreak, shame, addiction, or any emotional, physical, mental, or spiritual stressor that is too much for our system to integrate at the time it occurs. A temporal experience becomes frozen in place, and our ability to respond to life in the moment from a place of clarity, trust, and freedom narrows.

Meditation practice illuminates the traumas held in our bodies as we become more present to life. As a meditator I have been surprised and humbled by the power that past trauma can have over the present. I have also been continually grateful for the reliable and sturdy tools that mindfulness offers. From the perspective of practice, we can know that our past traumas are surfacing not to ruin our day, but to be healed. Some of the questions that working with trauma elicits are:

How can I find safety and ease, even as my most stimulated states of past trauma are arising?

How can I remember that I am whole when I am the most triggered?

How can meditation help me to gradually release past trauma?

I have found meditation and mindful inquiry to be dependable guides for meeting any trauma from the past. It helps to remember that if something difficult is coming up, it is coming up to be healed. Here are five simple steps for meeting trauma when it arises:

1. Turn toward, rather than away from, ourselves when we get triggered.
2. Pause, and through mindful investigation, ask: What does it feel like in my body right now? Notice sensations, temperature, and movement. What thoughts am I aware of? What is my self-talk? What emotions am I experiencing? Where in my body do I feel these emotions? What do I do to cope when this trauma gets triggered?
3. Continue to investigate by asking: Who is this part of me? How old is this part of me? Do I have a sense of where this trauma comes from in my life history?
4. Without getting analytical, spend time turning toward, being with, and feeling with this part of you.
5. Then ask: What does this part of me really need? What would compassion offer this part of me?

Generally when we turn toward an aspect of ourselves that has been pushed away, and listen with patience, we will sense what is needed. The need is often just to experience feeling seen, safe, reassured, and loved. We might ask ourselves: If a friend or child came to me with this emotion, what would I offer them from compassion? If someone who truly loved me were here now, what form of compassion would they offer me? Those questions may point the way to the kind of reassurances we need to hear.

Sometimes the reassurance can be as simple as:

It's okay.

You're not alone, I'm right here.

You are safe. You can relax.

I love you just the way you are.

When we are alone or isolated with our traumas, and when we resist them, they appear to us as "demons." When we take a step backward and can see the wounded aspects of our psyche locked in memory, we become more willing to listen to that part of us and more understanding of the wound. We are then empowered to meet this "demon" with love.

Listening and looking deeper, we often find a lingering memory of a vital need or genuine hurt that was not attended to. It is possible to have a loving relationship with every part of ourselves when we inquire in this way. While this may not fix or resolve the trauma, turning toward the trauma and being with it offer an expression of compassion that can, over time, help to heal damaged memories or feelings carried deep within. With repetition and patience, eventually past trauma may be released. In some situations we need the support of a counselor or somatic therapist to work in conjunction with our mindfulness practice; but it always serves to have tools for meeting our trauma when we are triggered.

Embodiment and Getting Down to Earth

We can read all the books in the world about meditation and come to a deep intellectual understanding of it without having embodied meditation's teachings in any way. A good teacher can point to the experience of awareness, but it is up to each individual to cultivate an actualized practice. Practice does not just mean sitting on the cushion and finding stillness, but also learning to pay attention in every aspect of our lives.

Practice takes time.

Practice takes kindness.

Practice takes commitment.

Practice requires us to look deeper than most of those around us might be looking and to make choices from this depth of perspective. Practice invites us to see ourselves and our world more clearly. And when we open our eyes, what we see is not always pretty. Practice also invites us to continually *let go* in order to be wholeheartedly alive, unburdened by the distractions of a deluded mind.

· · · · · · · · **Mindful Inquiry** · · · · · · · ·

What is your motivation when it comes to meditation?

What ways can you identify that self-improvement, achievement, or "getting somewhere" distort your relationship with practice?

What nonessential agendas have you brought to pursuits that were initially intended for your heart?

How does conditioning compromise your relationship with discipline? Do you ever fall into the duality of all or nothing? Of effort versus laziness?

How do you embody the qualities of the receptive and the expressive in your practice? In your life? Would it serve you to strengthen either the expressive or receptive at this time?

In what situations is it easiest for you to dwell in spacious awareness?

In what situations is it most difficult? Where is your attention in this difficult situation? How might you meet yourself with more kindness in this situation?

· · · · · · · · **Daily Practice** · · · · · · · ·

Today, set the intention to, at least once during the day, do the following things:

Enjoy the spaciousness of pure awareness or doing nothing but being.

Slow down and savor an ordinary life experience, such as drinking tea or cleaning the kitchen.

Welcome yourself exactly as you are during an uncomfortable moment, meeting discomfort with curiosity rather than judgment.

Make yourself available to experience genuine connection with another being.

At the end of the day:

Reflect on a moment today when you experienced the spaciousness of pure awareness or doing nothing but being.

Reflect on a moment when you savored an ordinary life experience, such as drinking tea or cleaning the kitchen.

Reflect on a moment when you welcomed an uncomfortable experience, meeting discomfort with curiosity rather than judgment.

Reflect on a moment when you experienced genuine connection.

What were the qualities that you experienced in each of these moments?

Be kind and forgiving with yourself if you didn't fully actualize each of your intentions. And revisit this exercise again tomorrow!

5

Deep Time

Slowing Down as a Revolutionary Act

Energy is our most precious resource, for it is the means through which we transform our creative potential into meaningful action.

—Tarthang Tulku

Nature does not hurry and yet everything is completed.

—Lao Tzu

When I was twenty-four, living as a farm apprentice at a Zen center on the fertile green peninsula of Muir Beach in Northern California, I received the teaching of Uji or "being-time." This practice stems from the writings of Eihei Dogen, the thirteenth-century founder of Japanese Soto Zen. Attending a Dharma talk in a Japanese-style zendo, the teacher introduced Uji as the practice of being one with the unfolding of time, moment by moment, in a nonseparate way that allows time to be experienced as spacious and boundless.

When we are fully present, we are "being time." The more conditioned we become, the more we develop an artificial and adversarial relationship with time. We treat spaciousness and leisure as a rewarding treat, like dessert. Time out, vacations, a yoga or meditation class—and those moments of grace that sometimes appear in our lives—are experienced as disruptions in state of productivity that we dedicate so much of our time to.

Uji invites us to question the notion that the only way to experience time is linear. Anyone who has sat in deep meditation, trekked up a mountain peak, spent time immersed in play with an infant, fallen in love, or experienced the stillness of deep prayer has had an experience of time that felt limitless. Meditation is a direct means for softening our obsession with productivity and returning us instead to a more vast presence of being.

When I was a monk, the phrase "deep time" came to me as a way to describe the state of spaciousness that meditation made available. This state could only be entered through a doorway that took me beyond my conditioned beliefs. As my practice deepened, it became helpful to gauge how present I was by noticing when and how often I left the well-being of deep time.

The myth of there being "not enough time" is perhaps the most pervasive story of modern society—a story that feeds the collective conditioning that causes anxiety and stress. When we believe the story of "not enough time," we justify making compromised choices in how we treat ourselves, one another, and our world. The story of "not enough time" creates an entire society of people resigned to living under pressure, multitasking, speeding up to meet both real and imagined deadlines, forgetting how to tune in to their authentic pace, disobeying their bodies, and giving energy to time management all day long. This story line allows us to justify high levels of stress, to glorify "busyness," and, in so doing, to compromise vital aspects of well-being—including rest, enjoyment, relationships, and sometimes simply doing nothing. We compromise quality for quantity.

Many people today give more attention to planning, preparing, and managing their lives than to actually living their lives. They tell themselves, "Once I meet this deadline, I'll take a break," or "Once the holidays are over, I'll make time to care for my body." Way too much time is spent in an internal conversation about time management, and harmful choices are made as a result.

The motivation of "convenience" takes over, rather than concerns regarding sustainability, kindness, and "what is best for all." Every habit of suffering results from a limiting belief. If we explore within, we begin to see that the "not enough time" story is an extension of the "I'm not good enough" story that so many people carry at a subconscious level. This story is fed at its core by the illusions of a separate self.

Letting Go of Limiting Beliefs and Realigning with Kindness

Growing up in Los Angeles in the 1980s in a middle-class family, multitasking, rushing to get somewhere on time, and the stresses that accompany life in a big city became a familiar backdrop to our lives. This was a lifestyle in which there truly seemed to be "not enough time." When I moved to a Zen monastery, the residue of the "not enough time" story replayed in my psyche. Whether it was while serving as the cook in charge of preparing gourmet meals for retreatants following a rigorous Zen protocol, serving as the work director managing hundreds of details every day, or being assigned tasks that I felt inadequate to perform successfully, I became increasingly aware of the seduction of this story.

Whenever the "not enough time" story arose in my mind, I began to realize that this was a sign that separate self had arisen. I could either meet the task I was given with a relaxed, trusting, focused, and attentive state, which allowed me to pay attention to detail and also to enjoy the process of fully engaging in whatever I was doing, or, if the "not enough time" story got my attention, I would notice my body tensing up and a habit of worry and hurry taking over. Gradually, with the monastery's support, I learned to disidentify from this story and meet my work from presence and trust in natural timing. This process required me to allow the underlying beliefs supporting the myth of insufficient time to be revealed.

When I first contracted Lyme disease at the age of thirty, it was not properly diagnosed—and so my symptoms became a valuable practice opportunity for me. This illness at times has compromised my ability to even pretend to keep up with the pace of the modern world and has taught me invaluable lessons about self-care.

Eventually I took a medical leave from the monastery where I had trained, in order to receive health care support in the city. I was given medication and ordered to rest on my back for as long as it took for the medicine to work. I was warned that, as the medicine set in, it would cause more pain than was originally there. I willingly surrendered to all of this. But as days turned into weeks, I began to experience feelings of panic and despair arise when I considered the impact of being horizontal on my back for who knew how long. In addition to the severe physical pain I was experiencing, I struggled with stories of fear: What if I am always this way? What if I am this incapacitated long-term? Who will love me? What does this mean for the goals I hoped to accomplish in my life?

As I grieved my circumstances, I slowly began to realize that even after my monastic training, a part of me still believed that being lovable depended upon me reaching threshholds of performance. I had taken on this limiting story—that we are loved based on what we do or achieve—from the culture around me. I grieved the time spent in my life trying to keep up with others and meet the so-called performance standards around me. Then, as I slowly settled into acceptance of the situation as it was, not knowing if I would ever actually heal, a moment of clear insight arose. Wise words from the messenger of kindness arose in my mind:

Your Presence Is Your Greatest Contribution

This whisper of truth soon relaxed my whole being. It touched me like the steady embrace of a good friend . . . someone who could see me clearly and knew that my essence itself is the gift I have to offer. I finally integrated at a bone-deep level something I had not fully understood before and have not forgotten since, that my presence alone is my gift. This is true for all of us. This gift can only be accessed when we leave story behind and are willing to be present, awake, and aware, exactly as we are.

I also began to understand on a deeper level that I can only contribute attentively in any context when I am fully present. Nothing else actually mattered. So, if nothing was more important than being present, or honoring my natural state, then I could take a big exhale around the notion of accomplishment, around being ill—and even the fear of being in a horizontal incapacitated body forever—and just be me.

This was an important marker on my path to understanding unconditional love. If nothing is more important than cultivating loving presence in each moment, then even if that required letting go completely of the achieving productive self, it was worth it. If presence is our most valuable resource, then why would we ever give it up? If presence is what matters most, how could there not be "enough time" to be present?

Permission to Slow Down

I was taught at a young age by the culture around me to discount my body and mind's natural feedback system in order to be productive. As an adolescent, having lost my father to cancer just prior to entering a competitive college prep school, I quickly learned to hide my feelings, and even disregard the somatic experience and messages from my body; I felt that if I did not keep up, I would be judged. It took me years to let go of this habit, and to learn the wisdom of honoring my natural feedback system no matter what.

Many of us have had similar experiences during childhood and adolescence, where we allowed the fear of being judged to negatively impact our mental, emotional, and physical well-being. As adults, even with awareness, we learn to get through each day at a hurried and often frenetic pace that is not actually natural for us.

Sometimes, if we are lucky, life intervenes when we are operating at an inauthentic pace. We are forced to question the pace at which we are living our lives when:

- we become too busy to find time to feed the quality of relationship with ourself;
- we are ill and cannot move as fast and efficiently as we have been used to;
- the quality of relationships with loved ones we value diminishes and we are aware enough to respond;
- a disability—mental or physical—requires us to slow down;
- we feel that our lives are being wasted on menial rather than meaningful activities and take this feeling to heart;
- a trauma or crisis occurs and we are forced to make space in our fast-paced life to integrate it.

When we realign with kindness as our guide, we begin to understand the real value of self-care. We see that our contribution to the larger world extends out from our willingness to bring care to every moment. The wisdom of self-care is the foundation of sustainability, and self-care is modeled in how the natural world works. To disobey the natural feedback system of an ecosystem is to abuse life and results in imbalance or disease.

It takes an immersion in self-care to understand that it is a quality of authentic strength when we let go of that which abuses our natural state. Consider time a precious currency that is yours to spend. If you give the spending power to the conditioned mind, which believes the story of "not enough time," the impact can be dramatic. Reclaiming a conscous relationship with time is key to well-being—personally and collectively.

With awareness, every time the "not enough time" story arises can be viewed as a mindfulness bell pointing out that we have left the present moment. Without judging ourselves for becoming confused, we can make a gentle correction. There are always situations where we are not in charge of the timeline—a crisis at the office, a computer glitch that needs to be addressed, an unexpected deadline to be met—but there is tremendous choice in how we address these moments. There is also choice in how we arrange the structure and schedule of our lives. The overall question is, which is in charge—kindness or conditioning?

Practices for Cultivating a Kind Relationship with Time

I brought as much intention as I could to the transition from living in a silent sanctuary in the wilderness to the hustle and bustle of Los Angeles. Committed to the greater task of living from authenticity in a world that does not always reinforce this, I supported myself in all the ways I knew how. I tried to remain in contact with my inner stillness and not get caught up in the fast paced momentum of the world around me. I gave myself the gift of silence one day each week, when I would arise and spend the day without any contact or intrusion from external voices— human or media. Most days I would wake up at 4 or 5 a.m. to spend time alone with the stillness of the city in the early hours. I would meditate, make tea, and set my intentions for the day, being kind to my body by letting it take in more gentle sounds and silence before the world awoke. These daily practices helped me to remember that the mega-city in which I lived was rooted in the soil of stillness beneath the buzz of the modern world. It reminded me that I was rooted in the soil of stillness. I also created a schedule for myself, as I had at the monastery, to support simplicity.

Despite my efforts, there came a time when I noticed myself feeling more susceptible to some of the collective conditioning and thought patterns of the society around me. I found myself making less wise choices about my schedule, and saying yes to time commitments more often. What I learned in this period was how to take a stand for deep time in a world that does not.

Deep time is the time we spend in expanded awareness, without opening the window even a crack for multitasking or distraction. It is time that we spend committed to spaciousness, away from the internet and with cell phones off.

I find it vital to schedule the nourishment of deep time on my calendar, in order to cultivate this as a way of being and help the body to remember what it is like to live without busyness, distraction, or stress. In relationships or family, it can be important to claim deep time together as a regular intention, no matter how full life becomes.

A celebrity client once said to me, "I wish I could have back what I had before I made a lot of money." Part of what he had lost was more deep time. With his success had come more bills to pay, a bigger house to maintain, more work to manage, and more image to uphold. These all brought more complexity and "doing" rather than simplicity and ease to his life, primarily because of the way he was approaching it.

What is the real cost of this conditioned relationship with time? We have become increasingly disconnected from our natural rhythm and pace. We are increasingly willing to treat ourselves and one another like tools and machines. Our somatic and emotional experiences do not have time to be integrated fully within.

A Kinder Schedule

In the Zen tradition, the schedule holds a vitally important role. By following a disciplined schedule, a student is able to release the conditioned habit of time management and learn to simply show up wholeheartedly to whatever he/she is scheduled to do. The schedule also supports the student to take a sacred pause regularly throughout the day to maintain the mind of meditation.

When I left the monastery where I trained, I found that there was little support for this type of simplicity in urban life. Surrounded by the messages that "doing more is better," I found my schedule being gradually overtaken by my ego and my life becoming more complicated as a result. Happy to share my teachings, for example, I found invitations to speak and teach very compelling and generally agreed to do so. I scheduled sessions with students who were often very much in need, even when I myself was deeply depleted. I worked hard into the evening even on days when I had already given of myself fully.

My life changed dramatically the day I remembered that I could trust my body to create a far saner schedule than my mind. In other words, it is possible to let our bodies do our scheduling. My mind will always, in a seemingly innocent way, try to pack more in, forget to schedule periods of rest after events that require great output, and take on more than is reasonable. What if every time you sat down to make your weekly schedule, including scheduling meetings, trips, and creating timelines for projects, you asked your body for feedback on the choices made?

The body will always give clear somatic feedback about what is the right amount and what is too much, if we are willing to listen. The conditioned mind can easily talk us into distortion and wishful thinking when it comes to scheduling. And we pay for its ambition later.

What Is This the Season For?

It is helpful, when looking at the overall picture of our lives, to view our life as a garden, and to ask the simple question that always points to clear and graceful organization: What is this the season for? If we try to address everything growing in the garden of our life and attend to it all at once, or believe we should address all of it at once, we are being dishonest with ourselves. Nature models natural progression and right timing for each step required.

The question "What is this the season for?" invites us to see the natural step-by-step progression of a project or goal. It also requires us to let go of that which is not necessary for personal sustainability. Whether we are setting intentions for the next year of our life or prioritizing goals for the coming week, this simple question can keep us honest and aligned with our deeper purpose. This in turn allows us to focus on "one thing at a time" and "one step at a time" and experience more of a sense of being in the flow of life, rather than racing to catch up with life.

Letting the Soil Rest

The separate self, with its propensity to focus on accomplishment and productivity, cannot acknowledge the wisdom of restoration. The conditioned mind makes a strong argument to "keep working" or to stay out late even when the body projects symptoms of fatigue. An organic gardener knows that if we do not let the soil rest, we deplete it, and the consequences of this are not casual. With this reminder applied internally, we can acknowledge the many effects of depletion—from health imbalance to lack of joy to speeding up the aging process. We can learn to see rest as equally important to productivity as activity. It is also a vital nutrient for longevity.

As a monk, I fell into the habit of working past the schedule and was then called out by my teacher for being spiritually lazy. Ironically, I thought I was being a good practitioner by devoting extra time to work. When I investigated my behavior more deeply, however, I realized that I was actually motivated by my ego and a desire to prove my worthiness. The more I learned to obey the schedule and let go of my mind's measurements of achievement, the more relaxed life became. I felt supported by the wisdom of simplicity. This empowered me to choose to not listen to ego's habit of measuring myself or "overdoing" in other aspects of my life. I began to learn the wisdom of sufficiency.

One Thing at a Time

Mindfulness reminds us to live life one breath at a time, one step at a time, and one task at a time. One thing at a time is the attitude that allows us to dwell in the spaciousness of interconnection, fully receiving life in this moment, and then the next moment, and then the next.

When we focus on product over process, we have one foot out the door of this moment. In a world where so many people identify as busy and busy is perceived as the right way to be, it is important to question the impact of this way of being. It is possible for us to remain in touch with the compassionate awareness that does not feel busy, even when we have a lot on our plates.

When I teach personal sustainability workshops, I am astounded by the number of people who meet busyness and stress with a "buckle up and push through" attitude. They regularly tell themselves that there is no alternative but to keep going and tough it out when feeling overwhelmed. Is this really the quality of life we want for ourselves, given how short our time here on this earth really is?

The Sacred Pause

All that is really needed for us to stay present is that we pause, and that we do so often enough to notice if we are immersed in the momentous stream of conditioning or if we are settled instead into spacious awareness. Each time we take a momentary pause, we step back as a compassionate observer and notice what is happening in our mind, our body, and our feelings. Sitting in front of a computer checking email, we pause and notice perhaps that our hands are tiring from the keyboard and could use a rest or that we are feeling less grounded than when we started and need to take a break to replenish our body and our mind. Upon observing this, we can make a gentle self-correction. We can take a few deep breaths, stretch, or get up and close our computers to meditate until we are ready to return to being fully present to our work.

In my early days as a meditator, I became aware of how often I was trying to reach a threshold in meditation, trying to make something happen. I noticed that I was somatically leaning forward—and energetically leaning forward in my life a lot of the time. Other times while meditating, I would notice that I was leaning back, withholding, procrastinating, tentative, and not fully showing up to life. I learned to ask myself, at the start of a meditation session, "Am I physically positioned at center, neither leaning forward nor leaning back, but showing up to meet life with a balance, both engaged and relaxed at the same time?" This simple inquiry can help us to find presence through our intention and physical posture, just as in sitting meditation.

Befriending Fatigue

The dominant paradigm has minimal understanding and respect for low energy and fatigue. For years in my practice, I experienced an internal voice judging or diminishing me when I had particularly low energy. I was conditioned to view productivity as *positive* and low energy/fatigue as *negative*, because it forced me to slow down. When I experienced fatigue at an inconvenient time, my mind would ask, "What's wrong with me? Was it something I ate or something I did wrong?" My mind would scan for solutions to fix this "problem" of low energy.

The more time I spent observing the ever-changing landscape within me, while at the same time also observing the natural world, the more my perspective on low energy changed completely. I began to respect nature's energy cycle with much more reverence. I came to see myself clearly, rather than through the filter that measured my productivity or energy. As I began to understand how useless and egocentric it is to try to give nature's energy a linear measurement, the more I learned to welcome the energy variances in my own body. I realized that trying to resist or control energy cycles fed a conditional relationship to well-being. Even the severe low energy states that illness sometimes asked me to endure could be rich in lessons and purpose.

By learning to accept all energy levels that I might experience, I was able to release a vicious cycle of self-monitoring and self-assessment that had been operating in my psyche. Ironically, this freed up even more vitality and clarity of mind, even on tired days.

My capacity to soften into compassion and attunement with other beings was in no way disrupted by low energy. In fact, I became even more available for subtle awareness in certain low energy states; however, my ability to speed up, produce, or focus on the superficial diminished. I became suspicious of our collective distaste for the natural low energy states that visit us as we integrate our life experiences, self-heal our bodies, restore ourselves, communicate with others, and feel as one with the larger world around us.

Today I see fatigue as a friend, and I am grateful for my healthy body's ability to tell me when it is time to stop in order to digest the nutrient of restoration. The gift or purpose of low energy is to diminish our capacity to participate in superficial habit patterns and the trance of productivity. If kindness and balance are our priorities, we meet low energy and fatigue as messengers to be honored without question.

Mindful Juggling

There are different phases to a mindfulness practice, and while the earliest phase focuses on one task at a time, there is a time when practice asks us to learn what we might call *mindful juggling*. The juggler, as an archetype, has many balls in their awareness and the balls are moving quickly; however, the juggler is focused, centered, and in a sense, attending to both one ball at a time and the coordination of many balls simultaneously.

Sometimes, despite our best efforts, we become genuinely overwhelmed by how much is on our plates and by the story of "not enough time." We begin to notice how much energy, vitality, and time (!) the "not enough time" story actually requires of us. It is at this point that we can consciously choose to show up wholeheartedly and stay present. We can accept the practice of mindful juggling and trust our capacity to stay relaxed, focused, and awake as we juggle, rather than resist our feelings and thus suffer from the experience. One of the qualities of a juggler is the ability to focus, another is balance, and I would hope that two others are a lightheartedness and nonjudgment should one of the balls falter and fall.

Wakeful Transitions

Students tell me time and time again that they do not have time for daily practice. I have witnessed those same students complete their morning meditation and immediately become caught up in rushing through the day, not taking a breath and pausing again until their evening meditation.

In practice, we say that when sitting meditation ends, practice begins. Because we acknowledge that transitions are the times in which we are most likely to "go to sleep," we make conscious transitions central to our practice. In other words, we understand that it is necessary to show up for important activities, but consider the transitions in between as mere bridges from one important activity to the next. When we forget this vital part of practice, we find ourselves present for work meetings but completely unaware during the break in between. We show up for the gym but are not present on the drive over.

These examples can be applied to all of our human activities and interactions. When we take on the practice of staying awake in transition, our practice deepens immeasurably. We realize that there is no moment that cannot be met as meditation, moment to moment, and we become more alive, relaxed, and grounded as we move through each day. Life is transition and life is change. Learning to becoming subtly aware in each passing moment prepares us to meet transition and change with grace.

· · · · · · · · **Mindful Inquiry** · · · · · · · ·

Do you give yourself permission to move, work, and live at your authentic pace?

To what degree and how often do you believe the "not enough time" story?

What are the signs (physical, mental, emotional) that you are becoming stressed by a sense of time constriction?

How often are mistakes made or is more work created for yourself or others because you rushed through a task in order to save time?

How often do you push yourself? Multitask? Make choices in the name of "convenience" that you might not otherwise choose from your heart? Do you feel the subtle residue of these choices after you make them?

How often do you allow yourself to relax into timelessness?

In what activities do you allow yourself to relish the task just for the task and release any pressure of time (cooking, parenting, a craft or hobby)?

The story of "not enough time" can be easily identified in our language. Pay attention to how often you hear yourself using language such as the following:

- "pack in as much as I can"
- "hurry up"
- "when there's time"
- "got too much to do"
- "I'm behind"
- "grab a bite"

What other phrases do you use that reflect a conditioned perception of "not enough time"?

· · · · · · · · · **Daily Practice** · · · · · · · ·

Today, notice how the mind of separation talks you into the story of "not enough time."

Be aware of how much time can go to the story of "not enough time." Be aware, without judgment, of the impact of this story on your body, feelings, mind, and actions.

Pause, take a deep breath, and take one full minute to soften your body and be where you are. What do you notice?

PART TWO

Relationship with One Another

The first section of this book offers teachings in how to heal the myth of separation and embody wholeness within ourselves. In making this shift from an adversarial relationship to a conscious compassionate relationship, how we engage with all other beings changes.

Part Two is dedicated to bringing Relational Mindfulness to the interpersonal field: our interactions, conversations, relationships, sex life, conflicts, and participation in social change. There is no separation between sitting meditation practice and our engagement with the world. The point is to meet ordinary life and the dynamic, messy, and beautiful world in which we live with compassionate presence.

In Part Two, we ask these questions:

How do we stay connected with our authentic self through social interaction?

How can we use the relational field to affirm intimacy and release the lens of "other"?

How can we work together with more efficacy and less drama?

How can we affirm a "we" world instead of an "I versus you" world?

Please note that formal Relational Mindfulness exercises for pairs and groups are offered at the end of this book. These practices are invitations to learn what is possible when we give one another the gift of our full attention.

6

Making the Shift from "I" Consciousness to "We" Consciousness

Before speaking, consider whether it is an improvement upon the silence.

—Chief Seattle

When I entered the monastery, it was a surprising relief to let go of the unspoken expectations and busyness of socializing. There was a profound intimacy that came from going to that place beyond words as a way of life. The other monks and I worked on the land together in contemplative silence and communicated essential information through notes to coordinate work projects such as preparing garden beds for planting, building new hermitages for retreats, or sewing and stuffing meditation cushions. We shared our meals in silence and used spoken language only in facilitated groups three times per week for mindful inquiry to support one another's inner work.

There was a quality of sincerity without being overly serious, and laughter was a natural part of life. We received training in conscious communication, but we carried out the rituals of each day in silence to support an inward focus and more subtle attunement to our surroundings. As someone who had been social for my entire life in an effort to attain close connection with others, I relished the permission to reconnect with myself without interference from others and to discover the depth of intimacy that is possible between human beings through Relational Mindfulness.

I had known myself as a "successful" social being for my entire life up to that point. I found it easy to make friends and find community. As a result, I had not brought much investigation to my underlying assumptions and habits around connection. Because my relationship with myself was not intact before I came to practice, I was unaware of the many ways I used the relational field unconsciously to get needs met outside of myself instead of from within, to distract myself, and to perpetuate the limiting beliefs and delusions of my ego. It was as if the contract I had signed with myself—one of conditional love—extended into all of my relationships and social contracts.

I often unconsciously used the relational field to affirm self-consciousness. I believed I was separate without being aware of this distortion. I did not open my eyes to this until I moved to the monastery and learned what was possible with others from the foundation of a compassionate relationship with myself first.

Who Socializes? Who Communicates? Who Listens?

One of the first areas of inquiry I approached was "Who socializes? Who communicates? And who listens?" Through this inquiry I began to see all of the ways I was interacting from the trance of separation rather than authenticity. I discovered an assumption I had been blind to: that somehow we are separate from one another and therefore connection and intimacy

required effort. This effort took the form of social etiquette, trying hard to be liked and make interactions successful, hiding the
parts of me I did not want to be seen, and doing relating rather
than simply embodying presence. In reality, all that is required
to be relatable is to let go of effort and to become more present.
Paying attention more fully opens us up to the inherent interconnection that already exists between each and every human
being. Interconnection is the nature of reality, and thus it can be
found easily through noneffort, being with, releasing judgment,
and silent witnessing. It can be found by letting go of trying to
be "special" or of seeking approval from outside ourselves. It can
also be found by asking "What is best for all?" in this interaction
rather than "What is best for me?"

The social etiquette and self-consciousness I had been taught
to bring to interactions actually created separation, lack of understanding, and positionality. To position means to hold on tightly
to a perspective, with the intention of "being right," instead of
being willing to look at an issue with another person. I began to
let go of egoic agendas attached to my communications, such as
getting what I wanted or seeking approval. I began to see ways
my ego complicated communication to serve its own needs and
learned how to communicate essential rather than nonessential
information. Communication became more intentional, clear,
and honest. I relaxed more. And more of my energy was then
available to experience genuine connection and healing in the
field of relationship. My approach to interactions shifted from
someone who was hoping to get something from outside of myself
to someone who was already whole and interested in expanding
consciousness with other human beings.

My motivation for this inquiry was not just personal. I
understood that my contribution to changing the world I lived
in began with how I acted in my corner of the world. I began to
understand how kind and relieving it was to others to show up

without egoic agenda. I suspected there were ways I was participating in the collective madness in my own day-to-day relationships, and I was right.

The Investigation Begins

Picture yourself in any of these scenarios:

- going to a Saturday evening social gathering
- bringing up a sensitive topic with your spouse or partner
- having a conversation with your boss or employee
- meeting an acquaintance you haven't caught up with for a
  while for lunch on a busy day
- making a call to an insurance company
- being interviewed for a job
- going to a meeting at your kid's school on a day that's been
  stressful
- answering the phone on a call from a triggering relative
- going on a date with someone for the first time
- being part of a group conversation where you have a strong
  differing opinion from the rest of the group

It is possible to meet each of these types of interactions from
a relaxed, spacious, and compassionate presence. It is possible to
use each of these examples as a means to deepen the embodiment
of authenticity. It is possible to experience satisfying and meaningful connection in each of these realms.

This begins by setting the intention to use every interaction
for Relational Mindfulness practice, rather than to play out habits and unexamined assumptions. It means to bring an inward
focus to our outer relationships. Once we have set the intention to
being present, we inquire into the first question, "Who is here?"

Personally, I might bring either the people-lover or the her-
mit to a party, depending on the day. I might bring the conflict

avoider to a sensitive conversation with my partner. I might wear a mask of "everything is good" to a meeting with an acquaintance on a day I'm feeling particularly fragile. I would definitely bring either the assumption of "boring interaction" or "they're out to get me" to a call with an insurance company. I might also answer the phone with "I already know how this is going to go" for a phone call with a triggering relative. Although every moment is fresh with possibility, we settle for bringing a closed mind, habit, and assumptions from the past into otherwise uncluttered experiences.

To ask the questions "Who is here?" and "What is going on beneath the surface?" is being honest and taking responsibility for our engagement with the world. It means using the relational field as a mirror and bringing self-awareness to whatever interaction we are engaged in. It means stepping back from our identification with the separate self and being willing to meet someone from our heart rather than habit. From identification with the separate self, we have no choice but to interact in familiar ways and thus affirm expectations and limitations we have already experienced in the relational field. When we inquire within, we make ourselves available for personal discovery and insight, as well as for fresh and in-the-moment interaction. Here are some examples:

> *I am at a gathering, but feeling a bit disconnected. I'm fatigued because I did not sleep well the night before, and I would rather not be around other people, but I am required to be here. I become aware that I am feeling disconnected and, as I step back, I see my identity clearly: I am identifying as "the tired one" and believing a story that this is a problem. In acknowledging "tired" I see that this description of myself is attached to "not feeling my best," judging low energy,, and fearing that others might*

judge me for having low energy. By inquiring, naming, and investigating, I relax and remember that "the tired one" is part of me but not all of me. I step back into a more accepting place. I let go of the idea of a "best" or "worst" self. This gives me more energy and relaxes any self-consciousness. I am available to enjoy myself exactly as I am, connect genuinely with people, even in a tired state, and then go home early to get the sleep I need.

I am in a group workshop and I'm telling myself "I'm different. This workshop might work for the others, but it is not going to work for me." I notice that the "I'm different" label carries with it a sense of isolation and self-righteousness. As I look beneath the self-righteousness, I notice a layer of sadness. This sadness feels familiar and lonely. Tuning in and becoming aware of these feelings enable me to find more willingness to soften and open up about my feelings to the group. My willingness to be vulnerable invites others to be more vulnerable and the entire group is impacted in a positive way.

I'm making an appointment with someone to be interviewed for an article, and I notice intimidation about the interview. I sense that "the one who is intimidated" is speaking instead of my authentic self. My voice sounds careful, tense, and somewhat stressed. I check in with my body and notice that I am not breathing fully into my belly. Just by pausing to bring awareness to these various feelings, I am able to drop that identification, relax and accept the situation, and return to grounded center. The conversation immediately shifts to a more genuine and relaxed exchange, which is gratifying for us both.

I am slightly agitated at my partner for being online during our shared time together. I notice how I'm feeling and discount it, thinking "I'll just brush this off and wait. It's no big deal." But as I investigate within, I notice that I'm slightly withdrawing and separating myself from him. Upon remembering the "We" of our relationship and that we are a team, I find the willingness to step forward and tell him how I feel, without being accusatory. This communication allows him to respond consciously, bring his online time to a close, and return us to a place of connection.

I am at a meeting of activists, and I disagree strongly with what seems to be the agreed-upon perspective. I find it superficial and lacking depth, and I notice a self-righteous part of my ego wanting to speak up and "set them straight." I'm aware of the anger and self-righteousness behind this desire, and as I attend to my own experience of anger (in body, mind, and feelings), I am able to speak up with a voice that is both heartfelt and strong. I am able to share in such a way that honors my unique perspective and offers understanding and transformation to the group as a whole. It is deeply satisfying to speak from center, the place that honors We, rather than just my self-righteous ego, and, in so doing, I am grateful to serve connection rather than disconnection.

I am at a gathering, and I notice a self-aggrandizing internal response to someone impressed by my accomplishments. I realize that my ego is becoming energized by "looking good externally" and that I am feeling a sense of "power over." The interaction no longer feels authentic to me. Without shunning the attention, I refrain from responding to the praise by further elaborating on my accomplishments. The interaction now feels more pure to me. I relax in the awareness that I would rather people know me by my presence rather than by something "special" about my accomplishments.

Noticing Attachment to Outcome/Agenda

As we bring awareness to our identification with separate self, one of the things that gets revealed is attachment to outcome. One of the signposts of ego is that it always has an agenda. The agendas of ego always get in the way of real connection. For instance, if I enter a conversation with a relative with the goal of changing them or helping them to see things my way, I will probably not be very open to actually listening to them. I will not see past my assumption that they are "limited" in their thinking and will be disappointed. If I attend a work-related gathering with an agenda/attachment to "being liked by everyone," it is very likely I will feel stiff and self-conscious rather than being myself, relaxed, courageous, and genuinely open.

Examples of agendas we bring to the relational field are:

- getting approval
- getting positive attention (or being the center of attention)
- being right
- being in control
- being different
- being isolated

Consider how often you approach an interaction or say something attached to one of these agendas. Consider what the impact tends to be—on yourself, and on the people in your life.

When we are motivated by one of these agendas, we easily justify abandoning both authenticity and interconnection. If we allow our attachments and agendas to point us back to self-awareness, there is opportunity for healing and growth.

For instance, if I notice an attachment to receiving approval for how I look, I can trace this back to an insecurity and feeling of inadequacy and then respond in a compassionate, conscious way within myself. Or I can honestly share this feeling with another, enabling us to connect authentically over how easy it is as a human being to fear being inadequate. This allows me to honor an authentic need over ego's interest in approval.

With our needs already being met on a fundamental level, we do not project our neediness on others. We are available for real and satisfying connection.

Stepping Back and Acting on Behalf of "We"

Just by taking responsibility for what we bring to an interaction and choosing to step back from the agendas of separate self, we are in a position to experience a healing interaction that serves all involved, rather than serving just "I." We are in a position to relate from the consciousness of interconnection or the "We" mentality rather than the "I" mentality. We are bringing less ego to the situation, which in itself is of great service.

Here are some examples of stepping back from "I" to "We" in social situations.

In a conflict, for instance, if our first commitment is to self-investigation and clarity and that carries more value than "being right," then we really are not apt to argue for making our point to win. Instead, we can inquire with genuine sincere curiosity and seek a solution to the conflict that meets everyone's needs.

At a party, rather than focusing on our performance or hoping that people will judge us attractive or special, we might avail ourselves instead of the opportunity for spontaneity and playfulness with others on the dance floor. We may find out that it is way more satisfying to connect and create joyfulness together rather than perceiving the occasion as a venue in which to address a personal agenda.

In traffic, instead of being so attached to "getting there quickly" that we curse endlessly at the slow driver in front of us on a one-lane road, we are able to step back, release our agenda, and see that person in the another light, similar to how we might view a friend or sibling: being an annoying slowpoke but doing the best they can, maybe having a hard day themselves, certainly deserving of our understanding, not our judgment.

At a group meeting, rather than speaking up to make ourselves heard or because we want attention, we can bring awareness to the group field. We can honor everyone's voice and wait until what we have to offer is of most benefit.

When we are coming from We, we are more able to empathize. Our focus changes from trying to meet our ego's needs to being free of ego and becoming connected to others. We become more grounded and able to be of service to the sense of We, as a result.

The Principle of Energy

Anytime we do not stay present in an interaction we experience it as an energy drain. Anytime we stay fully present we experience it as energizing. When we check out, we give our attention to the mind of separation and that is innately draining. The person speaking on the phone to the insurance company with impatience and the belief that all bureaucratic interactions are a waste of time becomes drained by the energy expended on the interplay. Staying present, investigating oneself from within, breathing slowly, and choosing to meet the person on the other side of the phone with openness and kindness feed our energy. We are often completely unaware of the fact that we are involved in a situation or interaction to which we have brought a personal agenda. Being fully present allows us insight. This brings about both connection and personal discovery at the same time.

When we fully express ourselves and feel generously received, we are satisfied. When we hold back and don't say what we need to, we feel depleted. When we are in conflict with someone and resist or battle our feelings the whole time, we become depleted. When we stay present, we can listen to what the other person is saying while attending to our own feelings. We can work together to understand the conditioning each person is bringing to the conflict in order to gain clarity about it, and we also gain energy within ourselves.

When we complain or get vented at by someone else, we feel drained. When we ask for support or support another person to disidentify when they are caught in something, we feel energized. When we hold onto a projection (that person is silently judging me and I feel annoyed), we feel drained. When we own our projections (I am aware of my mind projecting onto so-and-so), we feel energized. When we try to be liked (I'm giving a talk and want to appear impressive), that is an energy-draining task. When we let go and speak from our true selves, perhaps naming our desire to be accepted and liked, it feeds our vitality.

The Shared Field of Connection

> Love consists of this: two solitudes that meet, protect and greet each other.
>
> —Rainer Maria Rilke

I have come to know compassionate awareness as a distinctly palpable and welcoming field in which to reside. When I am present, I can invite a hurt part of myself into that field for healing. I can also invite another person to that field of being. As a teacher, I can invite a group of people to connect within that field of intimacy.

Knowing what gets in the way of that field, which we might call shared solitude or shared peace, inspires us to bring great discernment to how we engage. Relating becomes an art of finding presence with people, and some of the ways we know we are there is that it feels safe, alive, and in the moment. It might carry excitement or edge to it, in the sense of stepping into new territory together. There is also a healing and heart-connected component to the experience and generally a sense of shared vulnerability.

I believe that there is an essential soul nourishment that comes from this kind of communal togetherness. It is like finding a hidden treasure that we all long for. In this place, we belong to ourselves, to one another, and to our world. There is no separation. There have been no studies that I am aware of measuring this state and so it is easy to discount, but anyone who has experienced being in the consciousness of interconnection and non-separation with another being or a group knows that it is both our deepest longing and our birthright.

Further Habits That Support a "We" Consciousness

> The eyes are the windows of the soul.
> —Traditional saying

Some of the healthy habits in "We" consciousness are:

- The willingness to look people in the eyes and maintain eye contact throughout an interaction. Even when we put up artificial walls with one another, the eyes are gateways to connectivity and vulnerability.

- The willingness to give one another our full attention and not allow distractions such as thoughts, stories, or cell phones to pull us away.
- The ability to receive feedback. When we lose interest in living in a world of judgment and are committed to growth, we perceive feedback as helpful. We can also offer others feedback in a compassionate way and only when appropriate because we are not actually identified with the judge persona. We have stepped back from being the judge who serves disconnection.
- The willingness to meet conflict resolution with a real intention for mutual understanding and mutual growth. We often say that this is our intent in conflict, when we really only want to win or remain a victim. When we open up to We consciousness, we can equally honor what the other party is feeling and what we feel and allow presence to hold both. There is nothing to be afraid of in conflict from the place of We.
- An interest in communicating essential information well, and refraining from nonessential information. For instance, at work we can distill our communication to simplify rather than complicate circumstances. At a social gathering, we can participate generously and move away from a personal agenda when we become aware of it.
- The willingness to stop trying to be "special." Letting go entirely of the duality of special versus not special frees us to enjoy the perfection of ordinary self.
- Another healthy habit is the ability to just be in silence with another and not fill space when that is what most serves the whole.
- Lastly, it is important to take good care of ourselves so that we are able to meet the relational field from center when we get triggered (and we will get triggered).

All of these habits feed one's personal power, integrity, and compassion. They also support humility. Humility is our ability to let go of both self-aggrandizement and self-deprecation and just be as we are. In other words, it is an invitation to "get over ourselves" and show up available for the field of "We."

• • • • • • • • Mindful Inquiry • • • • • • • •

In what relationships is it easiest for you to stay present?

In what relationships is it most difficult?

Are there unspoken rules and expectations you still abide by in the relational field? What conditioning did you receive about socializing while growing up that no longer serves you?

What are some of the agendas and attachments you might bring to interactions with family? With friends? With your partner/spouse? With work colleagues?

What do these agendas get in the way of? What is the quality of connection you most want to have with people?

Are there any social contracts you have made in the past that you wish to let go of?

Are there any particularly triggering relational dynamics at this time in your life? How might you support yourself to find your center in this dynamic?

When you are present and connected with your essence, what does that enable you to experience in the relational field? What are the gifts that your essence has to offer others?

Where and when do you experience the treasure of shared solitude or shared peace?

• • • • • • • • Daily Practice • • • • • • • •

Today, bring compassionate awareness to investigating how you meet the relational field.

Who shows up to social interactions?

Who communicates?

Who listens?

What helps you to be available for deeper intimacy and ease with people? And what pulls you away?

7

Deep Listening

Finding Freedom and Authenticity in How We Relate

The act of deep listening is an act of love. Listening to life as it unfolds moment by moment, with our full presence, is the essence of meditation.

The Old Paradigm of Relating

My first week back in Los Angeles after leaving the monastery, I was invited to guide a meditation class in a busy urban neighborhood in West Hollywood. When our silent meditation ended, I rang a bell and invited people to break into pairs to engage in a Relational Mindfulness exercise. The instructions were very basic: Each person was to take turns responding to a simple question about presence that I asked, while their partner gave their full sustained attention to listening and witnessing their response. Just as the breath is used as an anchor to presence in sitting meditation, in this practice listening to the other person is used as the anchor. The speaker was asked to be mindfully aware of their internal experience while they spoke.

I instructed the pairs to listen with their whole body and to pause between each response to breathe deeply and connect with their experiences. After the exercise, one by one, each person expressed that this simple exercise was one of the most profound experiences they'd had in a meditation class.

Though some initially felt fear or discomfort at engaging in this nonhabitual way of being present with a stranger or casual acquaintance, they all experienced relaxation and joy in the depth of connection. People expressed their appreciation for being listened to so fully and a desire to go deeper. A student named Alicia, a forty-year-old attorney, had become so accustomed to maintaining emotional distance when talking with a stranger that to look someone in the eyes felt quite intimate. A student named Ryan, a twenty-five-year-old actor, habitually dismissed what older people said. In general people were so accustomed to conversations in the city being casual and superficial and to meditation being solo, that the invitation to connect in a meditative way with a stranger had a meaningful impact.

I too had a profound experience witnessing this simple exercise. I realized that being in LA was an invitation to deepen my own practice, not despite the relational field but directly through the relational field. I realized that this simple exercise and experience were a form of mindfulness practice that perhaps people in our world needed the most.

With no expectation of a specific set of protocols or practices that I was to meet as a teacher, I set the intention to expand my awareness of Relational Mindfulness and help others do the same. I was reconnecting with friends and family, I was socializing and dating, and I sensed there were profound lessons to be learned in the interpersonal field at this time of reentry into urban life. I surrendered to expanding my edges and entering unknown territory. I welcomed dynamics that triggered reactivity or fear and trusted that if I were not experiencing precarious or uncomfortable situations, then I was probably playing it safe. It was those edgy places that presented the greatest opportunity for growth.

I welcomed opportunity to become a beginner again—and to embrace mindful messiness.

While I did not trust the level of unconsciousness I witnessed in the city, I did trust the language of interconnection.

Intimacy from Within

> If you want to know God,
> Then turn your face to your friend,
> and don't look away.
>
> —Rumi

We all desire intimacy—an honest, open-hearted, genuine connection—but most of us are fearful of it or do not have the skills to break the habit of superficial relationships. It can feel easier and more comfortable to communicate from the surface rather than from a deeper place of authenticity, yet to do so perpetuates separation. Many of us have become accustomed to interactions that feel superficial or are generally unsatisfying. For some people, texting, social media, and email have taken the place of face-to-face and heart-to-heart interactions.

We might not even be aware of this until an unusually heart-opening interaction highlights how rare it is. We have an experience of feeling truly seen by someone and we are surprised. From a place of separation, we have become accustomed to believing that we need to be "on" when we are with people and then relax when we are alone. We don't realize that in so doing, our approach to socializing is like performing. We have become accustomed to checking out when relating becomes uncomfortable. We do not allow for the subtle attunement and sense of belonging that is possible when we are fully present with another.

Lack of presence in the relational field can have grave ramifications. Consider how often we overlook an opportunity for real connection with another human being. There is a missed opportunity each time we engage with someone without actually seeing and hearing them, because we are distracted by the conditioned mind. The consequences can range from not understanding what someone is trying to communicate, to competing with someone rather than working as a team. It can include feeling dismissed by someone or projecting that we are being judged or attacked. We might not notice mild irritation in a conversation with our spouse, for example, until it turns into heated anger. We might not see our similarity to someone because we are busy seeing them through the lens of "other." In our worst moments, past trauma and unresolved feelings can cause us to act out in our relationships.

On a global field, we see the ramifications of the mind of separation in the relational field in every instance of bullying, racism, bigotry, and war.

Deep Listening in Conflict

> Do not engage with the people you see regularly as if they were yesterday's newspaper.
>
> —Thomas Hübl

A couple I have coached for many years first came to see me at a time they were thinking of separating. They had been together for twenty years. Joan would regularly come home from work and look forward to connecting with her husband Thomas. He would be tired, checked out, and unable to engage with real interest in whatever she had to say, but would go through the motions and engage halfheartedly. Thomas was simply exhausted from his own day. But she took his behavior personally and felt unappreciated and angry. His experience was that he would come home needing to recover from the day and wanted his wife to honor the fact that he required rest and space before connecting. Her eagerness for attention, followed by anger when he was honest about his needs, caused him to shut down. Neither of them felt heard or seen by the other.

In our session, I helped them to deeply listen to one another and actually hear the other's experience with nonjudgment and openness, rather taking personally what one another shared. In the experience, they realized that they had never actually felt listened to by the other. When they came to the conclusion that they each wanted the same thing—to feel seen and listened to—something shifted in their relationship. Together they were willing to agree to a new ritual: They would greet each other and then allow forty-five minutes for rest and space apart before coming together to enjoy dinner and connect genuinely about their day. They also agreed to meditate together in the mornings for twenty minutes, which created a sense of sharing intimacy in a way that replenished them both every day. Once a week they would formally practice deep listening, taking turns doing nothing but listening to one another. What Joan and David found was that by actually listening to one another, they were able to step back from an "I"-versus-"you" stance and find the meeting place that honored "We." They were also able to start enjoying their time together again with both of their needs being met, and their interest in listening deeply to one another continued to grow.

So many of our shadows are illuminated through human interaction. Shadows can be defined as those attributes and qualities that are inconsistent with the self-concept we are trying to maintain, and thus that we often leave out of our awareness. Relational Mindfulness helps us to bring compassionate awareness to our shadows. In a world where so much collective judgment, self-consciousness, distrust, and hatred have been maintained between human beings, Relational Mindfulness is an invitation to take part in collective healing.

The act of Relational Mindfulness keeps us honest by showing us when and where it is difficult to remain present when engaging with others. Sitting alone on a meditation cushion is a wholly different exercise than social engagement, but just as the breath provides an anchor when we sit, deep listening can be our anchor in social interactions. And Relational Mindfulness provides each of us an opportunity for insight and healing, with the people we are close to and even with strangers.

How Do We Collectively Go Unconscious in Interactions?

Perhaps some of the following examples of choosing unconscious relationship will be familiar to you:

- Checking out together—making small talk or becoming intoxicated with people simply as a means of escaping discomfort.
- Being distracted and not fully available—for instance, keeping an eye on texts while conversing with a friend or child or double-tasking while conversing with a spouse.
- Assessing the person in front of you—and comparing yourself with them.
- Interacting through a mask—hiding emotions to covering up what you are feeling inside.
- Presenting yourself in a manner that you hope will receive approval, rather than bringing forth your whole self. An

example of this is a woman who presents herself as "pretty girl" in order to cover up "smart woman."

- Being unable to clearly see the person in front of you because you are putting them—or yourself—on a pedestal.
- Using "being polite" as an unconscious way of hiding.
- Maintaining control as a way of avoiding vulnerability—rather than letting go and becoming available for a co-creative or spontaneous dynamic with another human being.
- Maintaining identity—in other words, interacting through a surface identity or role you play in life such as mom, doctor, teacher, or meditation practitioner, rather than sharing your whole and unguarded self.
- Projecting onto the other person—for instance, projecting power and intelligence onto the other person rather than owning that these are qualities you carry, or projecting an emotion such as anger onto the other person, thinking that they are upset with you, rather than owning this as a fear operating within you.
- Feeding positionality—for instance, holding on to a perspective and fighting for it in discussion/conflict, "I'm right/You're wrong," rather than being open to consensus and/or mutual understanding.
- Feeding conditional love by complying with the message that "By behaving in a particular manner or complying with group standards or shared customs, you will be liked; if you don't do so, you will be rejected."
- Going along with someone rather than bringing your honest perspective forward.
- Assuming difference and "other than" based on what you perceive on the surface.
- Unconscious complaining—for instance, playing victim and unloading on someone rather than interacting in a

manner that might actually help you to step back and disidentify from the victim stance and return to center.
- Checking out and disassociating or "leaving your body"
  while in a social interaction because you are uncomfortable

Each of these habits of relating is a substitute for being willingly present and giving connection your full attention—with
another human being and with yourself. These examples can
serve as a sign that you have left presence and might want to
pause to bring your attention back to center. When we return to
well-being within ourselves, we do not need to bring conditioned
motivations to our interactions, such as fearing, hiding, projecting, seeking attention, being right, or judging. We lose interest
in feeding the illusion of separation and become available for the
genuine connection in which both parties receive.

Each time we leave presence in an interaction with another
person, we abandon both ourself and the other person. If I check
out in an interaction with a friend, for instance, when she has
said something disappointing and I want to hide or repress my
feelings, I abandon that part of me that has feelings and is in
need of attention in that moment. I disconnect from my emotional self as well as disconnecting from my friend. The commitment to staying present and paying attention in the relational
field expresses our dedication to an intact and loving relationship
with ourself as well as with one another.

How the Mind of Separation Operates in Communication

In my twenties I would often return from a powerful meditation
retreat, thinking, "Now I've found a way to access stillness and
peace of mind, but there is no way I can sustain this out in the

'real world.' How can I keep this up in social interactions, at work, talking with my boss, or in a family conflict?" I realized that there were relationships and groups I was a part of that were lined with subtexts of expectation and judgment. There were contracts I had made in the relational field that supported my identity or role in a specific context rather than truth/wholeness. The decision to become a monk was an expression of my readiness to dissolve those and any other contracts that did not serve authenticity. When I left the monastery, it was my core commitment to use the social field as a mirror for self-awareness and the dissolution of untrue contracts in a way I never had quite done before.

In the relational field, you can tell you are engaging with the mind of separation if:

- you judge or monitor yourself or others in social interactions.
- you project onto people (and even project what they are thinking about you).
- you feel self-conscious or experience social anxiety in the relational field.
- you perform, try to impress, or try to get attention.
- you put expectations on the person you are talking with or are attached to a particular outcome in the interaction.
- you put effort into being who you feel you are expected to be, rather than just being yourself.
- you engage more with the conversation in your head than with the people you are relating with.
- you feel isolated and alone while with others.
- you measure and compare yourself to others or find yourself competing with others.
- you say yes to someone when you really mean no.
- you are dishonest in an interaction.

Relational Mindfulness Toolbox

> The eye is the window of the soul, the mouth the
> door. The intellect, the will, are seen in the eye; the
> emotions, sensibilities, and affections, in the mouth.
> —Hiram Powers

We learn Relational Mindfulness through formal and informal practice. Formal practice includes exercises we can do with a partner and in groups (see appendices). These practices provide a simple and safe structure for learning the art of paying attention and deepening our capacity for intimacy. Informal practice uses our daily life as a laboratory for Relational Mindfulness. Here is a summary of how to use the nine components for Relational Mindfulness, offered in chapter two, with one another. These practices point us to freedom and authenticity in how we relate.

Intention

By committing to consciousness in the relational field and using our interactions to deepen awareness, we set the intention to pay attention. We pay attention to the inner landscape (our body, mind, and feelings) and the outer landscape (whomever we are engaging with) with openness and nonjudgment.

The Mindful Pause

We can pause before, during, and after our interactions to maintain awareness of our breath, body, mind, and feelings. If we are not aware, the stream of conditioned thought can easily disrupt our capacity for connection. Each time we pause to look within, it is like sitting ourselves down on the bank of the thought stream to come back to ourselves. Whether at a party, a meeting, in conflict, or at the dinner table, anytime we notice that our attention is being pulled away by conditioned thought, we can pause, take a deep breath, bring our awareness gently to within, and reconnect. Pausing in this way maintains our connection with spacious awareness, and intimacy is only possible when we meet one another from spaciousness.

Deep Listening

In our fast-paced, busy world, offering the gift of deep listening is an act of love. Receiving another human being without inserting one's ego into the mix is an act of generosity. Deep listening dissolves the bubble of "I/Me" in any conversation or relational interaction. In deep listening, the listener has no agenda other than giving the whole of your attention to the person you are listening to with openness and nonjudgment—not trying to fix or change anything or even be "helpful" to the other, but allowing our friend, coworker, loved one, or stranger to feel seen and heard. Listening in this way is a meditation in itself. In the words of Rumi, "When the lips are quiet, the heart can speak in every language."

When we first begin this practice, we often discover that although we believed we were good listeners, we are actually often distracted by planning our response, assessing what is being said, or some another diversion of the mind. When we practice deep listening to another human being, we cannot maintain focus on the conditioned mind.

Just as we use our breath as our anchor for staying present in meditation practice, in this practice we use listening as our anchor. Deep listening invites us to relax and listen with every cell in our body. Deep down we all want to be listened to.

Deep listening is a generous act, and we are not able to be as generous if we are always the listener or if we are always the one listened to. Some of us feel comfortable listening but not being listened to or being seen ourselves. For some of us, it is the opposite. We have to be willing to take turns being open, vulnerable, seen, and supported as well as being the nonjudgmental witness for others. Deep listening teaches us how to create a solid container for open-heartedness. We can practice deep listening wherever we are and with whomever we are spending time.

Mindful Inquiry and Clear Seeing

Deep listening means to listen beyond the words to the subtext, the energy behind someone's words, and the actual feelings of the person we are listening to. We can access much more information than we normally do through what we see, sense, and feel in this way. We can move from surface information to deeper and more essential information. We can study life with this person while it is happening. This is the nature of inquiry, and it means that while we listen, questions arise offering doorways to greater insight. Insight comes from our willingness to listen beyond the assessing mind to what is being shared. In this way, communication itself can be a pathway for awakening.

When we relax the mind of judgment, we can see what is happening (internally and externally) from a more subtly observant lens. From authentic seeing, we can have insights into another person that are incredibly valuable. If nothing else, insight helps us to be with that person and feel compassion for whatever they are caught up in. The person has an experience of actually being seen as they are. This requires going beyond being a personality, as well as seeing beyond their personality to true nature. This requires us to trust in and to recognize the inherent goodness in every human being, even when they themselves might have forgotten it.

Compassion begins with oneself and extends outward. Compassion sees the authenticity in everyone, even if it is buried underneath layers of defense, self-hatred, or pretense. It requires us to patiently be with ourselves and with others through the dust storms of personality and emotionality, which cloud up authenticity, until the dust settles.

Questions we might ask ourselves in any moment in which we are willing to pause are:

- What am I present to right now? Who is here?
- What am I feeling . . . In my mind? Body? Emotional self?
- How can I relax even more fully to receive this moment and this interaction?
- Is there anything I need to acknowledge to myself for the sake of honesty?
- Is there any part of my experience in this moment that I am not in acceptance of? Is there anything I'm resisting and can I meet this resistance without any judgment, allowing it to be?
- Aware of my thoughts, what do I want to contribute to the field of human consciousness?
- What do I want to bring to this interaction? If I allow this pause to be a reset, what choice is now available to make from a more centered place?
- Skillful inquiry prompts can help us to take a step back from our suffering and return to center.

Turning Toward Rather Than Away

Relational Mindfulness requires us to be aware of how often we shut down, space out, or distract ourselves when an interaction becomes too uncomfortable. Having a practice requires us to learn to turn toward, rather than away from, what is uncomfortable.

It sounds easy enough, but if you've ever been in a relationship (or if you've ever just sat down on a meditation cushion), you know that when the messy stuff arises, a part of us wants to scream "Never mind, I'm out of here!" Most of us have habitual escape routes in place in our lives so that we can take the exit door whenever we feel uncomfortable. If we are willing to have the kind of relationship where we don't have the back door open, where we can see the desire to escape as resistance to growth, we are well-positioned for success.

In Relational Mindfulness, each time we notice ourselves beginning to contract rather than remain open with another person, there is helpful information for us. When we bring awareness to all of the places we tend to shut down and leave the field of connection, we are given an opportunity to heal our triggers and the past traumas that created them.

Not Taking Personally

There is so much fodder in human relationship for taking things personally, but if we keep our feet grounded in the purpose of self-awareness throughout our interactions, we are much less inclined to take conditioning personally. Everything that arises simply becomes an opportunity for deepening practice, rather than something to react to.

Rather than bring habit and reactivity to our interactions, we can bring curiosity and a willingness to see clearly. We can focus on the process rather than content of our interactions, and all of our interactions become more interesting and illuminating. It is not always easy to "not take personally," but the more we realize how liberating it is, the easier it becomes.

Taking Responsibility

By not taking other people personally, we support ourselves to take responsibility for all our patterns and triggers. Even if we are interacting with someone who is acting out, even if that person is acting like a five-year-old or playing the victim, it is still our job to take 100 percent responsibility and to show up as a compassionate adult to the interaction. This might mean meeting the person with acceptance and letting go of wanting them to "shape up." This might mean finding the compassion within for what they must have gone through or be going through to be acting in such an abrasive way. This might mean taking care of ourselves and attending within so that we do not need to be triggered by the other person's "stuff" and so that our "stuff" does not add to the fire. This might also mean staying for just as long in that interaction as we can before we need to take a break or set boundaries, which is a means for taking responsibility for our own limits. It is not always easy to be an adult and take responsibility for our "stuff," but it is always gratifying.

Transparency

Authentic connection has everything to do with our willingness to be transparent with one another and to share ourselves with one another as we are, no more, no less, no shield required, and no need to hide. We live in a world with so many different messages about what is acceptable and what is not. The conditioned mind continually points out ways that we are different, other than, not enough, and separate—making it seem much more frightening than it actually is to just be ourselves.

Every time we allow ourselves to be honest and vulnerable with one another, however, the illusion of judgment dissolves. We then remember that our present and naked self is more lovable and interesting than any image we thought we needed to project. Transparency asks us to stop role-playing in relationships (the good girlfriend, the strong man, the worker bee, or the helper) and risk just being ourselves.

When we are transparent, we give the person we are with the gift of seeing us unguarded, and we give that person permission to be unguarded back. Transparency can be taken on as a daily practice, the practice of cutting through pretense and simply sharing ourselves as we are.

Compassionate Action

Hurt people hurt and healed people heal. If we bring our hurt self to an interaction, the interaction is bound to get messy. If we bring our whole self to an interaction, we can nurture peace, even during conflict. Our choice in every moment is to nurture peace rather than cause harm. Peace is not at all a flat or necessarily passive state, and it is not something we find by turning the other cheek. It is an expression of unity rather than isolation. By remaining open, engaged, and connected with ourselves in an interaction, we have the chance to affirm honest, clear, satisfying, and well-intentioned communication.

Compassionate action might arise as an insight about what the person we are with needs to hear, an insight into a problem they are having, or another gesture or action that comes from interconnection. When we stop trying to fix or find solutions for people, we can allow insight to come through naturally. We can relax and trust that the words we need to speak will arise from authenticity, rather than plan what we want to say. It can take time to trust compassionate action to arise in the moment. And even when it does, we do not always know what the outcome will be. But we can trust that presence will guide us, over time, deeper and deeper into authenticity. And authenticity is the most powerful contribution we can make to the relational field.

Accountability for Relational Mindfulness

Just as there is a balance required in meditation of receptivity and expressiveness, the same principle applies in social meditation.

At a Relational Mindfulness workshop I taught in North Carolina, I worked with a man named Henry, a psychotherapist who had done a lot of inner work. Henry was very surprised at the level to which he was uncomfortable being listened to. It was relaxing for him to be the listener. He felt compassion and tenderness as the listener and enjoyed subtly honing his listening skills.

But when it was his turn to be listened to, his body would tense up; he felt self-conscious; and he wanted the exercise to end. By staying with it, Henry had an insight arise that was life-changing for him. He realized the extent to which he had positioned himself as "the listener" not only in his career but in every relationship he had, so that he could avoid the possibility of being seen himself. He had multiple memories of being seen as vulnerable and judged as a young boy, and he had taken on a behavior to make sure that would never happen again. As a result, though, he often felt lonely, even in his close relationships. By being willing to move beyond his comfort zone and risk allowing himself to be seen more, Henry was able to find out that the past was in the past and it felt deeply rewarding to allow people to hold space and listen to him in the way he did for others. The nourishment of being seen was something he had deeply longed for but had been habitually pushing away.

If we are committed to ending suffering and seeing through our own ego habits, we can use every interaction as a mirror. Deepening our capacity for freedom and authenticity in how we relate is a lifelong endeavor. The core practices—Intention, The Mindful Pause, Deep Listening, Mindful Inquiry, Authentic Seeing, Turning Toward Rather Than Away, Not Taking

Personally, Taking Responsibility, Transparency—can be practiced formally with a partner or as a group endeavor. These practices can also be brought into daily life practice in every informal interaction we have with another human being. It can be helpful to maintain a journal while establishing a Relational Mindfulness practice to support us in seeing through our barriers to intimacy, and in holding ourselves accountable to our deep heart's desire for remembering interconnection through all of our interactions.

Please refer to the appendices in the back of this book for Formal Relational Mindfulness practices.

• • • • • • • • Mindful Inquiry • • • • • • • •

By whom have you felt deeply listened to in your life? How do you feel in this person's presence?

To what degree do you listen deeply to others?

What do you enjoy about listening? What is possible when you offer someone an accepting and attentive space to talk, without intervening?

What mind habits tend to pull your attention away from listening?

How do you take things personally in the relational field? Things people say? Things people do? An expression on someone's face?

When do you shut down in interactions? What is the experience of shutting down like?

• • • • • • • • Daily Practice • • • • • • • •

Today . . . Set the intention to practice deep listening in at least one interaction.

Begin by relaxing a taking a couple of conscious breaths. Listen from patience and spaciousness, with no agenda other than giving the person your full nonjudgmental attention. Set the intention to listen with your entire body. As you listen, be softly aware of your body, feelings, and mind, and if distraction arises, notice what pulls you away from listening.

Then gently bring yourself back.

Notice the qualities that deep listening illuminates within you.

Notice how the person you are with responds to it.

8

Transparency: The Courage to Be Seen as We Are

Make your transactions transformational, not just transactional.

—Patti Smith

In March 2012, I packed my car and drove along Highway One up the spectacular California coastline, making the move to Portland, Oregon. I had told myself that when I had fallen in love with Los Angeles and made my peace with the challenges it presented me, I could move on if I wanted to. After five years, although I had created a beautiful community in LA, I felt that my inner work there was complete and it was time to relocate to a place where I did not feel like I was swimming against the stream. I chose Portland for its deep green landscape, progressive politics, gentler economy, and creative social climate.

I arrived to four months of gray skies and pouring rain. The impact of the move on my physical health was dramatic, and I had the greatest flare-up of illness I had ever had. The Lyme disease I had contracted from a tick bite while a monk created physical, emotional, and mental distress for me thereafter. In Portland, insomnia and inflammation gripped me. With only three hours of sleep at night, I woke up exhausted every day. This made for an incredibly challenging experience of life in a new city. I did not have my familiar social or family network. I was not financially supported and could not take a break from working. I had to navigate the dynamics of establishing myself in a new environment while addressing poor health and feeling incredibly fragile. My vision for creating a new life that expanded on the beauty I had established while in LA crashed, and I entered into a dark night of the soul. I often think back on this period of life as The Great Doubt, because every day was leaden with questions about my basic security and self-worth.

Up until this point, I had become very comfortable in my skin and at peace with my perfectly imperfect self. I no longer felt a need to monitor how I was perceived—yet I was also accustomed to being perceived in good light and was considered a bright light in my community. In Portland, I did not feel like I had access to the basic level of well-being that I had developed, and I felt utterly exhausted, in physical pain, and alone. Being in a new place and invited to meet new people every day, teach at new venues, and start a new sitting group while feeling at my worst was difficult. It was in this most vulnerable time that I had to face deeper fears and subtler habits of self-consciousness and self-protection. It was when I was the most ill and lacked support that life offered me a deeper teaching in transparency.

I had no external place to rest and wanted to climb into a cave and hide. I also knew that I could not heal in isolation and what brought me most to life was sharing the teachings and being part of community. So I was forced, kindly by life, to learn to bare and embrace the parts of me I had not yet embraced and to find out what parts of me I still did not feel safe exposing to others: the weakest one, the ugly one, the tired grouch, the one with no energy, the sad one, the sore achy one, the insecure one, the poor one, and the one who doubted her entire path. I was forced to let go of the good front/appearance that I usually had to rely on, and to engage from the "worst" parts of me in full transparency and trust.

I showed up to teach a group of strangers one evening when I was particularly exhausted and began my presentation by sharing more of my experience than I typically would. "Tonight, I'm foggy, depleted, exhausted . . . and it's easy to feel that I'm inadequate to meet all of you. I'm aware of the vulnerability of sharing myself in such a fragile state." The group responded with gratitude for my honesty. I learned that the simple act of meeting my worst self with nonjudgment and giving others the opportunity to do the same strengthened the field of connection and trust. I found that my best teaching came during that time of feeling the most vulnerable and speaking about it in the most open way. I let go of long-held expectations for how I was supposed to look and allowed my heart to speak in a much more candid way. I learned to do this in the social field at the same time and was met with a level of kindness and receptivity I had not expected. I began to relax into a deeper understanding of self-acceptance. In sitting meditation one day, these words came to me and they became my guide for that time: I am the freedom of transparency. I allow myself to be seen as I am and loved.

To trust my lovability and wholeness even when it was difficult, to remember that, from presence, I had something valuable to offer in every moment, strengthened my trust in life. This new awareness allowed me to release my attachment to being perceived a certain way. I know that I would have held on tightly to this need if I had not been completely broken down.

Through aging, illness, injury, and loss, this is a lesson life offers all of us. Our outsides and circumstances change throughout life. Our beauty and confidence come from our presence or essence rather than from what we present on the surface. This basic understanding brings a level of freedom that allows us to interact with one another by sharing our always-present and unconditional inner beauty and seeing one another's inner beauty. To share one's inner beauty requires no effort rather than being present and willing to bare ourselves. Our inner beauty is there on our good days and still there on our darkest.

The Freedom of Transparency

We all have a dividing line within us—one that solidifies our relationship with conditional love. We accept ourselves when we are on one side of the line; we reject ourselves when we are on the other. We accept people when they fit into the "decent person" rules we have created, and we see them through the lens of "other" when they don't. Sometimes we are not even aware that this line exists, particularly if we've done a lot of work around acceptance. But then, something happens. Someone acts or looks a certain way or life presents us with something far outside of our circle of acceptance, and we have to face our own dividing line.

Practice invites us to courageously dissolve this line and to meet the relaxed, loving, and accepting presence that is who we are beneath the facade. Transparency means to give the person we are with the gift of our self as we really are and to give ourselves the gift of not having to coat anything in a different finish that is than it already has. When we are transparent, we give the person we are with permission to let down their guard and step entirely beyond the realm of judgment.

This is the revelation that is needed in our world—that when we take away all of the false fronts we use to be acceptable and look good, we find that wholeness embraces every single part of us—nothing and no one left out.

Transparency also asks us to move beyond the habits of self-aggrandizement or self-deprecation into humility. From humility, we do not get attached to either looking good or the possibility of failing. From humility, we can interact from the steady and reliable power of our presence rather than the false power of our ego or personality. From transparency, we trust that there is nothing to prove to one another . . . and nothing to hide from one another.

Transparency Holds Us Accountable to Wholeness

It is the first night my new partner, Mark, is cooking me dinner at his house. After an incredibly enjoyable evening of laughter and rich conversation, I feel that throbbing in the palm of my hand that means I'm falling in love. I have felt it before. It is an overwhelming reverberation of sensation and emotion, and a desire for complete intimacy with this person. At the same time I feel terrified, based on the last time I fell in love, and my body is shaking. From transparency, I say, "I feel incredibly attracted to you right now and I'm also really scared. I feel overwhelmed and need to go home and get clear about my feelings." It feels good to us both for my vulnerability to be voiced, and it allows Mark to see me clearly and compassionately in my delicate state. Even though the date ends with me leaving, the next morning, we have an honest conversation about our feelings and acknowledge that we are falling in love with each other, we are both scared, and we are both willing to take the risk.

Transparency also holds us accountable to living from wholeness, because it takes away the urge to hide or isolate ourselves when facing challenges, working with our shadows, or investigating our egos. Isolation is always motivated by self-judgment, fear, or assumed separation. Transparency asks us to demystify perfection and remain engaged with another even when we are our most imperfect. In pursuit of wholeness, we allow others to support us through the process. We ask for support with our challenges, especially when we want desperately to keep them hidden. This doesn't mean that we must disclose everything to everyone. It simply means that we allow there to be people in our lives to whom we can turn to for help as we investigate the inner landscape, rather than do it alone. We question our desire to withhold essential information because we assume that it is too unacceptable to be shared.

Transparency supports us in living in a shame-free and judgment-free reality, and reminds us that we are all facing the same human challenges. We are all human beings who get confused when we listen to the mind of separation and think that we are our ego. We are all inherently lovable underneath our ego. Transparency helps us to remember that we do not need to take the ego personally. There need not be any shame when we understand that ego is not us. Transparency affirms that we are already whole and allows us to remember this wholeness more deeply, rather than forget it.

One of the first steps we take in a practice group is to invite people into a safe space for personal sharing. This means that the principles for deep listening and authentic seeing are respected.

Many people have grown up in a culture in which certain topics may be discussed and many others may not. When such people participate in a practice group, they tend to feel a deep sense of relief and delight that absolutely anything can be talked about. They appreciate the depth of discussion that ensues, with the qualities of honesty, presence, respect, and nonjudgment as context.

What Does Transparency Look Like?

The point of transparency is not to be revealing for the sake of being revealing or to be intentionally edgy. It is just to affirm wholeness and to live in a world where we can be more open, honest, and intimate with one another. Here are some examples of practicing transparency in my life.

I am teaching on a sick day and I say, "I'm happy to be here and I am struggling with illness today. I may inadvertently drop a word while speaking, so if I do, I invite you to meet me with the same quality of acceptance that my partner meets me with when this occurs." My body relaxes. I have invited myself, and everyone else, into a safe, honest, and accepting space, and I have welcomed a vulnerable part of me.

I am with a group of relatives I have not seen in a long time, and it would be easy to keep things superficial and light, but I sense an opportunity for deeper connection. From a transparent place, I feel free to say, "Seeing all of you, I feel both happy and aware that a lot of pain has happened in our family. It feels like acknowledging it and talking about it a bit would be more honest than not. How would that feel to you?" Without knowing exactly what needs to be said, I invite the voice that is just under the surface to speak up. I trust the moment, and my relatives are open to talking because of my sincerity and gentleness about it. In this example, I trusted myself and the people I was with enough to bring up some discomfort.

I am telling a colleague that I will no longer be working on his project, and it is freeing for me to just state my honest reasons for this decision, from my heart, without having to dress them up feeling sorry to disappoint someone. In this way, I am respecting the colleague enough to be honest and intimate with him, and I am allowing him to respect me and know me more deeply. I am bringing wholeness rather than apology to my choice.

It is the last day of a group experience, and I've felt attraction to a man the whole time. I'm not certain of the nature of the attraction but it feels strong, and the habit of discounting it is familiar. In a moment of transparency, self-acceptance, and letting go of the outcome, I am able to be honest and say, "If I were to die tomorrow, I would regret not having the courage to tell you that I find you deeply compelling as a man." These words open up the door to knowing one another more intimately, and while this does not turn into a sexual relationship, it turns into an exciting and inspiring friendship.

In all of these examples, it is important to note that anything can happen when we are honest. We may receive a welcome response, or someone might turn away from us. There is no way to predict the outcome; however, I have never felt regret about being transparent. I have never personally summoned a response I did not want in a moment I was transparent. The purpose of transparency is maintaining integrity with ourselves. When we know there is something that needs to be said and we withhold it or candy-coat it, we diminish ourselves and leave integrity behind. Transparency is a gift to oneself, and a gift to those we are with. Being open to whatever we encounter is part of the dance.

Taking the Risk

> Truth-telling is like oxygen: it enlivens us. Without it we grow confused and numb. It is also a homecoming, bringing us back to powerful connection and basic authority.
>
> —Joanna Macy

Transparency practice is, I believe, needful for spiritual maturity. Cutting through pretense and sharing ourselves as we are is a daily practice. Transparency also requires discernment. It does not mean that we need to bare ourselves continually and let our insides hang out. It's about saying what is so for us moment-by-moment and acknowledging the simple magic of honesty. Like every other tool for conscious relating, it begins by learning to be transparent with ourselves.

If ego gets ahold of transparency, then we might be transparent with the agenda of "being edgy" or confrontational, appearing as the good meditation student, or unnecessarily involving those around us in every aspect of our internal process. This is not the point. The point is to remain centered and connected with ourselves, and then express ourselves freely and from presence, in the name of connection with others.

It is very important to make sure that transparency does not fall into the hands of separate self. If I am experiencing a challenge with my partner, for instance, a part of me might want to use transparency to air my frustration. Instead, I might investigate the issue internally first, and then later, at a time that feels ripe and when I know it serves connection and growth, I will share it with him.

Some inquiry prompts that help us to access transparency within ourselves:

- What am I present to right now?
- What would feel both generous and freeing to share right now?
- Is there any judgment, pretense, or projection that needs to be dissolved in this interaction?
- If there was no fear of judgment, what would I share here?
- Is there any part of me I am being talked out of voicing?
- Am I attending to only what's in my head, or also to what's in my body? What is happening in my body right now?
- Am I blocking my feelings in any way?

- Is any part of me feeling left out here, any part of me I need to acknowledge?
- Is there a kind risk for my heart to take here? Can I access the courage to take it?

One way to discern how to use transparency is to remember that ego tends to choose "what I want right now" or "what would serve me right now," thus seeking short-term gain and perpetuating an "I"-versus-"you" mentality. In contrast, becoming centered can help us see what would serve the whole, and what action would result in genuine connection and long-term benefit. Becoming centered helps us to interact from a "we" rather than an "I"-versus-"you" perspective.

We can still find ourselves, from time to time, in situations from where transparency feels like the most frightening thing in the entire world. The point is, if we are not willing to risk it, we'll receive what we've received before: less than the real heart connection we need to thrive.

As with all forms of spiritual growth, we can approach intimacy with sincerity over seriousness. If we can see intimacy as an endless process of discovery, we can stay connected to the playful, innocent, curious, childlike explorer in us rather than the agenda-filled, serious adult, who gets in the way.

Telling the Microscopic Truth

One formal practice for transparency that can be woven into informal interactions once you learn the basics, is telling the microscopic truth. (See appendix 2.) Telling the microscopic truth means to speak from the moment, sharing exactly what one is aware of on the level of body, feelings, or mind, without adding any extra meaning, explanation, or spin. It means to report directly from awareness. You can practice this with a partner, taking turns speaking and listening, and then once you have learned it, bring it into informal interactions. This practice invites you to move your awareness between the words you are speaking and what you are present to inside—in body, mind, and feelings.

Telling the microscopic truth may not be something you would do with just anyone; however, as long as there is a basic sense of safety and commitment to listening, it is useful. It is a useful aid for communicating about and navigating issues where you need support or where there is emotionality. It is useful for finding insight and also for negotiating conflicts.

Telling the microscopic truth involves a movement back and forth from speaking about a particular issue and naming what you are aware of in the moment that you are speaking about it. It is a simple means for bringing something out of story into presence, or moving from the head to the heart. Here is an example of telling the microscopic truth. You might begin by saying:

I need to make a decision about whether to join my relatives on a trip they are planning and I'm feeling confused and unsettled about it. While I speak, I'm aware of tension in my forehead, a queasiness in my stomach, and a general lack of clarity.

They really want me to go and are still disappointed I didn't join them last time, but I have a lot on my plate and my finances are challenged. A big workshop got canceled last month, and it's really impacted my financial situation. I'm present to feeling some sadness while I speak, and there is heaviness and heat in my forehead. I sense some anger that they hold an expectation that I will go. If I don't go, they will be let down.

Bringing awareness to this issue, I can see why it feels loaded, and why I'm having a difficult time deciding. I'm starting to

feel more self-compassion about this decision and feel a softening in my chest. I can understand why this simple decision has
been challenging, and I feel more tenderness than tension in this
moment.

In this practice, we go back and forth between speaking
about the issue and speaking about what it is like or what we
are aware of, internally, as we speak about the issue. Just by telling the microscopic truth, and having someone deeply listen to
us, we are invited to listen to ourselves more deeply, thus finding true transparency within ourselves. This can help to open
up space around an issue we feel caught in and allow insight to
drop in.

Transparency in Conflicts

In 2013, I faced the most difficult conflict with a friend that
I had ever experienced. This was not just a friend, but one of
my very best friends for twenty years. The conflict was painful,
surprising, and heartbreaking to us both, but the hardest part
was trying to understand why it was happening. We had begun
a project together that we believed would be fun, easeful, and
life-affirming, and instead our personalities had deeply clashed.
We were both "conscious people," doing our inner work, so why
were we having such a hard time with one another? We were both
willing to look at the shadows that it brought to surface for us;
however, at the same time, part of me wanted to distance myself
from her and that was not easy for either of us. Because we were
willing to stay present and be transparent with one another, even
in the face of the most difficult conflict we had ever experienced
together, we were able to maintain a field of respect and kindness.
We positioned ourselves to move with awareness through what
felt like a divorce. Thus staying connected to the consciousness of
"We," we were each able to use what was arising for growth and

deepening practice. We listened deeply to one another and told the microscopic truth even when it was difficult. Even as I said to her, "It feels really hard to say this and I'm aware of sadness and tension in my jaw, but I need to back out of our plans this year," there was integrity and respect in our communications. There was understanding, even while I said "I love you and I need to take space from communicating with you for a period of time." This allowed us to honor our painful feelings and to give the conflict all the time that it needed to resolve. It positioned us to accept and trust what was happening.

Our Feelings Carry Medicine

In another scenario, Mark and I were purchasing tickets for a trip back East that we had been planning for a while. I was going to be teaching a weekend workshop on this trip, visiting a beloved relative, and spending time exploring the beautiful landscape. I was surprised when Mark said he'd changed his mind, that the timing felt wrong for him, and that he did not want to spend the money. While the adult in me understood that he had had a change of heart, inside I felt the severe disappointment of a five-year-old whose long-awaited trip to Disneyland has just been canceled. I felt abandoned and lonely and hurt. I felt disappointed. I was also surprised by the strength of my feelings and the fact that tears were welling up in my eyes.

Hearing my inner five-year-old, who was really disappointed, use an adult voice I told him that it was okay. I was trying to be understanding and to grasp more fully how he came to this conclusion. I heard myself speaking from a place that sounded mature and heady, yet it completely discounted the presence of the disappointed five-year-old. I noticed myself projecting anger rather than honoring my sadness, and I noticed the interaction causing distance and separation between me and my partner.

And then I paused, took a deep breath, and allowed the little girl to speak freely with my authentic voice. I told him that I was feeling sad, that I was feeling abandoned and disappointed by my best friend. I told him that I was sad that I would not get to introduce him to my relatives. And at last I said, "I thought this was our special summer trip."

Hearing me speak honestly with sensitivity and without editing my feelings impacted him. He felt compassion for the disappointment I felt. This conversation brought us together rather than creating distance. It allowed me to acknowledge and let go of my attachment to how I had imagined the trip would be.

The next morning, I woke up feeling peace and renewed excitement about the new plan to take the trip on my own. My partner woke up feeling a clear and renewed commitment to and enthusiasm for taking the trip with me. He told me that I had responded to his resistance beautifully. He did not feel judged or attacked. He told me it helped him to really understand how I felt at a deeper level.

We were both reminded, in a culture that suggests we hold back, that our feelings when shared carry medicine.

Loving Fearlessly

To love fearlessly is a revolutionary act. It requires us to relax into self-acceptance over constant self-improvement. We spend a great deal of time seeing ourselves through the lens of what could be fixed or improved, afraid that we might not measure up. We reward ourselves when we "make the grade" and berate ourselves when we don't. All this needless activity keeps us busy and feeds the underlying myth that love is conditional—that parts of us are lovable and parts are not.

Intimacy begins with our willingness to erase this myth and see through the eyes of love. We have to learn how to "be with" the pretty and not-so-pretty parts of ourselves without needing to do, fix, or change anything. Fearless love asks us to stop striving, let down our guard, and find out what is possible between two human beings.

This begins by seeing ourselves through the eyes of love, rather than through the busy surface activity of our conditioned mind. When we explore a new landscape with the eyes of awareness, we see everything as it is and can also observe the larger beauty in all of it: not just the beauty in the blooming, brightly colored flower, but the beauty in the decaying detritus in a garden . . . not just the beauty of two lovers kissing, but the beauty of two lovers being present with one another through a difficult day.

A Fearless Love Story

After two years in Portland, during which I gained a lot of practice in transparency and finally felt at peace with my time there, I led a retreat in Ojai, California. I have always loved Ojai and its vast desert landscape and tree-filled canyons. On this retreat, I gave a Dharma talk about practicing with illness and my healing process. At the end, I shared a personal desire: that now that I was healthy and in a happy body again, all I wanted to do was meet my life partner—someone who was available for the level of intimacy I was—and dance.

I had a strong and powerful dream that night that I was to move to Ojai, and I woke up feeling that the dream was calling me. I also knew that when spirit spoke to me, it was my job to listen. But moving again at that time did not make any logical sense to me. My life was now established in Portland. Then later that day I received a phone call informing me that the home I had rented in Portland was being sold. Almost simultaneously, a friend in Ojai offered me a six-week housesit. I knew that this would be the perfect way to spend some time in Ojai and also work on my book, and so I went with the dream.

A month later, on my second day living in Ojai, I saw a flyer on the wall of a café advertising a conscious dance class/gathering that Friday night. I made note of it and invited a couple of girlfriends to come with me to dance. That night I met Mark, the facilitator of the space. I appreciated his down-to-earth, honest, kind presence and felt that there was something refreshing about him. The first time Mark and I sat down to get to know one another, I was struck from the start by how relaxed, open, and unselfconscious Mark was. Mark was just himself, he wasn't performing, and I didn't feel like he was seeking any validation or other agenda in our conversation, so we could really talk.

He began telling me how unsatisfied he felt dating.

"I wish I could go on a first date," he said, "and just name my faults and shortcomings up front, so it was all out there and there was no fear. That would be so refreshing."

"And what would you list?" I said. "I'd like to hear."

As he openly listed every one of his self-perceived shortcomings and quirks, without editing, I softened, relaxed, and thought, Wow, here's a man who knows what real power is . . . vulnerability. Here's a man who is not afraid to be honest. Here's a man I could really love and bare myself with. My heart melted, one thing led to the next, and a soft, deep, sweet, passionate, radically honest relationship began.

· · · · · · · · **Mindful Inquiry** · · · · · · · ·

Consider . . . What masks do you wear?

Are there parts of you that you tend to hide, diminish, or discount? What is the impact?

What messages did you receive growing up about what conversation topics are welcome and what are not?

What do you gain when you are willing to risk transparency?

What do you receive when others are transparent with you? When have you been moved or relieved by someone else's willingness to be radically honest?

Think of a situation where you are not practicing transparency. What is the impact of not being fully honest and open in this situation?

What stands in the way of you being willing to be transparent? What are you afraid of? And what would support you in taking the risk?

Can you think of a time when someone's willingness to give you honest transparent feedback about yourself was helpful to your growth? Or a time when your willingness to give someone else honest feedback brought you two closer?

• • • • • • • • **Daily Practice** • • • • • • • •

Today, bring awareness to the masks you wear, and notice what happens in your body, feelings, and mind when you put on a mask.

Take one risk each day in the name of transparency, a risk that allows you to be more honest and to be seen as you are.

9

Being of Service Has Little to Do with Being Helpful

All that is required is that you pay attention with kindness and neutrality. Compassion is not something to do but something to be.

I remember a trip to Los Angeles during which I received a visit from a friend who had just found out that he might have a life-threatening illness. He felt like he had been hit by a tidal wave and did not know what to do. At the same time, there was a chance the illness was benign. He was nervous and scared, and there was nothing to do but wait. I could have reassured him that everything was going to be okay. I could have told him about the people I knew who have had that illness and what they did to respond. I could have recommended healers or books. I could have offered advice and told him what I did the last time I had to wait for possibly difficult news. Or I could genuinely listen and give him my full attention—not needing to fix what was not mine to fix and not needing to cheer him up artificially. I softened my body, settled into stillness, and allowed my heart to open.

We moved together into the shared field of vulnerability and not knowing that we naturally share as human beings. My friend felt deeply seen, supported, and at peace, and I feel the nourishment of having met him with full presence.

How do we respond from presence when people are in need? How does Relational Mindfulness help us to act skillfully in times of crisis? How can we truly be of service to others when life offers us opportunities to help?

What most of us need, in any moment that we suffering, is to be seen and listened to by a compassionate and nonjudgmental presence. I have spent a great deal of time in my practice learning how to discern between authentic service and "being helpful." Service has been a koan for me both because my heart knows the priceless reward of care expressed in action and because I have also experienced the regret of my ego interfering in situations without seeing clearly. True service comes from compassionate action and noninterference. In the attempt to be helpful, however, we often interfere in other people's situations to the point of causing harm.

Much of the time, to be listened to and know that we are not alone is enough to allow us to find our own clarity. But we have all experienced the friend who tries to fix us instead of be with us in our pain, or have seen a parent override a child's opportunity to find out they are adequate to a new challenge by stepping in to do it for them. There are endless examples of situations where unexamined "helping" has the opposite effect. Our every action impacts the world around us and as human beings. We can rarely foresee the full consequences of our actions. Seeing clearly requires that we allow our hearts to guide us, rather than our heads, as we can never control the whole outcome of any form of action or interference.

Authentic service nourishes both the receiver and the giver, and in a sense erases both roles. Distinguishing between service and "being helpful" is an art—not a science—and it begins with inquiry. Many of us were conditioned to be "helpful" and to "fix" as a survival mechanism. Many of us have experienced difficult situations, problems, or conflict led to a major loss, and those memories arise within us in times of difficulty, impeding our ability to serve others in a clear and centered way. Mindfulness allows us to show up from a clearer and more generous place.

Service stems from observation and discernment. Some of the questions we can ask ourselves are:

- What is the underlying motivation beneath my desire to be helpful in this moment?
- Am I paying attention and listening deeply to the dynamics of this situation in order to respond appropriately? Or is ego seeking to insert itself, by bringing in its agenda, offering advice, or clinging to a certain outcome?
- Am I approaching this situation from a place of acceptance or from the assumption that "there is something wrong"?
- Am I coming from effort or noneffort? And am I responding consciously or playing a familiar role of "helper" or "savior"?
- Am I coming from fear and control or love and trust?
- Is my intention to be "nice" or to be kind?
- If I am helping another person, am I assuming that they are adequate to their life experience in this moment? Or that they are not adequate to meet what is arising, and I need to intervene and "save" them?

In the world at large, there is no shortage of examples of the shadow side of ego trying to be helpful: the junkie who is enabled in his/her addiction by the parent who is trying to protect them. The farmer who introduces toxic chemicals into a river to ensure a better harvest. The governmental organization that steps in to "help" an indigenous culture without foreseeing the psychological impact of helping rather than empowering people to help themselves. The ill-advised introduction of organisms into an ecosystem in the name of "biological control" without enough examination, resulting in the alteration of the entire native bio-diversity in an ecosystem. In the 1970s, during the green revo-lution, in the guise of helping farmers in developing countries improve their crops, hybrid seeds and pesticides were introduced into villages all over the world. This led to the loss of centuries of biodiversity and the pollution of rivers and soil.

There is a benevolent desire in each of us to be of service to one another and to our world. Service affirms the interconnected self. Serving strengthens our sense of belonging to something larger than ourselves and the understanding that we are "in this together." It always feels rewarding when we are able to be of service. However, there is deep conditioning in the human psyche that can compromise our capacity to act in beneficial ways.

We are given opportunities every day, all day long, to meet life in an attentive way and to make choices that have long-term benefit or that cause harm.

I am with a friend who is feeling depressed because a new romance just took a downhill turn. In an effort to be helpful, I might console her and get her to "lighten up." But I hold space and just listen. The last thing she wants is for someone to tell her to be positive or offer the kind of sympathy that makes her feel worse. I can see this. She is confused by all the layers of her experience and needs someone to simply listen while she allows more clarity, emotional release, and insight to arise. I relax my body, give her my unwavering attention, and just let her speak. From time to time I reflect something she says back to her to express my willingness to fully be with her.

After about ten minutes, she has had a breakthrough and has come to renewed peace about the situation. All she needed from me was to hold space while she explored her feelings.

How We Become Confused

How do our good intentions get confused? What are the clues that we are coming from conditioned helpfulness rather than from authentic service? How can we bring more awareness to this?

Our underlying confusion is identification with a separate self who believes that "Something's wrong" and "There's something I've got to do!" If we are coming from the assumption that something needs fixing, we are likely to approach a situation from fear and urgency rather than presence and wisdom. It is indeed likely that we will choose to act from confusion and therefore cause more harm by affirming the notion that there is something wrong. In those moments, which we all have from time to time, compassion requires that we forgive ourselves for going to sleep and reset our intention to be present. As a general rule, only acceptance can guide us in loving action.

Please bring the spirit of nonjudgmental curiosity to the following questions:

When someone you care about comes to you in pain or with a problem, do you check in with how you feel about them being in pain before you act?

Do you ever feel that it is your responsibility to fix or solve someone's problems?

Do you ever find yourself so uncomfortable with something painful going on that you move right into advice offering?

Have you ever said something unhelpful or shallow when responding to someone in pain in order to cheer them up?

Do you ever put on the "helper" persona simply out of habit?

Being of Service through Inward Focus

Service stems from observation, beginning with observing ourselves. When we are willing to step back from the thinking mind's agendas and our attachment to problem solving, we enter the field of interconnection and acceptance of what is. From this place, we can be of service not because we are trying to fix something but because we feel genuine compassion for the other person. From compassion we avail ourselves of insight and information available beyond the thinking mind.

A world of information comes through attunement, listening, and sensing—information that is available only in the present moment.

Whether we are engaging in the interpersonal field or working with a living landscape, as soon as we embody present moment observation, we are positioned to work with rather than separate from life. We can receive guidance that comes from a place larger than our ego. A loving presence willing to bring calm and grounded compassion into a challenging situation can have a tremendous impact on another person for the better. The following is one example.

I am talking with my partner Mark. He is having a challenging month at work, and I am becoming a little affected by the self-doubt that is stirring in him. I watch my mind begin to come up with solutions: You could do more promotion. You could give a talk. You could write a book. And as I attend within and notice each of these thoughts feeding the notion that "there is something wrong," I relax, come back to my breath, and realize that I have left my center. I return to a feeling of well-being. In reality, his work is simply experiencing a two-week dip and that is hardly reason to panic. He needs my neutral and trusting presence. I consciously let go of my worries rather than projecting them onto him. I say nothing of my fearful thoughts and simply listen to and reflect his feelings. Having someone just listen to him helps him to come back to gentle equanimity. The doubt quickly passes and within a week his professional practice picks up and again is in full swing.

Being of service requires that we first find our own center before taking an outward action. We have to release our own conditioning so that we have something to offer. Presented with another's troubles, we might notice that we are emotionally triggered by, uncomfortable with, impatient with, or panicked by the situation. We might also notice that we really want to make someone we love or care about happy so that they appreciate us. If we act from this stance, we are actually serving our own ego rather than addressing the needs of the other person. The first step to serving is to examine honestly what is going on inside ourselves.

Generosity requires us to be radically honest about our motivation. If we are going to intervene or offer input, we must do so from a base of clarity and insight rather than from the busy mind. We might offer a "solution" based on our own past experience, but even this can be ego's way of relating the person's problem to our own experience rather than fully honoring theirs.

Compassionate action cannot come from an idea or concept about what compassionate looks like. It comes from an in-the-moment experience of what compassionate feels like.

Remembering the Bigger Picture

When a "problem" presents itself, it can be easy to forget the bigger picture. Conditioning tends to zero in on problems and stir up so much drama about them that a molehill can quickly become a mountain. Practice invites us to be mindful of our mind's capacity to create story and drama. It invites us to experience what is with acceptance, rather than to assume that there is something wrong.

If we remember that we have no idea what the outcome of a situation will be, what is ultimately best for someone else, and what will happen next, then we can position ourselves to be of service to the larger unfolding, rather than to ego's agenda in any given moment. If someone we care about is struggling, there can be many components to the burden. The balm might be as simple as the passing of time to heal a loss or a wound. For others, challenge and adversity can become life-changing, as the person suffering redirects the course of their entire lives for the better as a result.

We must bring along humility when approaching any perceived problem. If I am talking with someone who is struggling with a repeated pattern, for example, and I can see clearly why they are doing so, I might want to point that out to them and show them what it is they need to see. But deep within, I know that my understanding of the problem does not matter. The person who is struggling must see it for themselves, and my pointing it out to them could actually interfere with their natural process. If instead I meet the person with kind neutrality and deep listening, the odds are that they will feel heard and acknowledged, allowing them the space to come to it on their own.

Acceptance is inherent to the field of present moment awareness. It is not something we have to "do." It is who we are when we are present. Awareness does not hold concern or fear or doubt. It does not perceive anything as a problem. Awareness does not even actually care, but awareness is inherently caring. It is the field of kind spacious neutrality. It is the state in which, through paying attention, we are attuned and able to meet life with care.

Flags of Conditioned "Helpfulness"

Here is a summary of some of the differences between authentic service and conditioned "helpfulness." The most important thing is that we bring nonjudgment to ourselves as we learn how to discern between being "helpful" and being of service. We will make mistakes. We will identify with the mind of separation. The point is to become a compassionate presence in the world and to start by bringing this compassion to ourselves as we learn.

The markers of being "helpful" can be one or more of the following.

- Being "helpful" usually comes from the mind of separation and the belief that "there is something wrong."
- Being "helpful" can be a way of avoiding feelings we are experiencing in the face of another's pain.
- Being "helpful" can be an attempt to escape discomfort, rather than be with it long enough to honor a situation.
- Being "helpful" is often a way of finding a short-term solution to a problem, so we can feel better right now ("Let's go get ice cream!") rather than serving the long-term and bigger picture.
- Being "helpful" can be a way of inserting ego's agenda into a situation it has nothing to do with as a way of serving ego rather than the situation.
- Being "helpful" can cause harm when it comes from the belief that something has to be fixed or changed about the person or situation we are working with. It can support the sense that the person being helped is not adequate to his/her life experience.

In contrast, the signposts of service encompass the following:

- Being of service comes from acceptance and nonseparation. In other words, when we accept what is and stay present to all that it stirs in us, then we can find a response that does not come from urgency or judgment but rather compassion.
- Service begins with listening and observing in a receptive way.

- Being of service comes from immediacy rather than urgency.
- Being of service supports the knowledge that the person struggling is completely adequate to their life experience.
- Being of service puts us in touch with a genuine willingness to meet adversity with loving presence.
- Being of service comes from willingness. When we are willing to serve, this means dropping our own idea or projection of what the situation needs and finding out what is really needed.

Burnout and the Shadow of Conditioned Helpfulness

The helper sees through the lens of "me" and "you" rather than the lens of "We." Helpers can easily find themselves outside the circle of life they are serving and may end up feeling depleted by helping others. Being of service requires that we include ourselves in the circle of life we serve. From this orientation, it is possible to acknowledge clear boundaries and needs and offer our support to others at the same time. If our needs get sacrificed along the way, this is not a true expression of compassion or wisdom.

It is not unusual for those who have a practice to go through a period of time where there is confusion between service and helpfulness. As we open our eyes ever more to the suffering in our world, we begin to see the endless gifts our practice has to offer. We feel needed and desperately want to share our practice with others. Sometimes we want to heal the people in our lives or we want them to experience exactly what we have received, without knowing if it is their true pathway. Sometimes, we simply agree to respond to everyone who comes our way with a need, at the cost of our own well-being. Part of spiritual maturity is learning to trust that our practice gets shared most generously when we keep our focus simple. Our only job is to attend to the quality of presence that we embody, while allowing this to naturally radiate out.

The world does not need saving—yet the world does need a great deal of care. So do our bodies and our minds, our friends and family. Even strangers and stray dogs, as well as our soil and oceans, need care.

Taking care, moment by moment, is the essence of being of service. Only when we get out of the way and give our attention fully, without agenda, to a situation, can we receive clear insight into how to bring care to a situation, right now, in this moment.

• • • • • • • • Mindful Inquiry • • • • • • • •

What is a situation when someone stepped in to offer advice or solve a problem when you truly just needed someone to listen? How did it make you feel?

What is a situation when you stepped in to offer advice or to problem solve for someone else, rather than generously listen? How did it make you feel?

In what relationships is it hardest for you to stay centered when someone is having a struggle?

Think of someone in your life who is struggling with something. How does it make you feel that they are struggling? Are you able to attend to and take care of yourself in the face of their pain?

• • • • • • • • Daily Practice • • • • • • • •

Today, notice each time the desire arises to help, fix, offer advice, or problem solve for someone.

Pause . . . turn your attention within . . . and notice more subtly what is happening inside of you. Take a couple of deep breaths, and take a moment to find center. See if there is any self-compassion needed in this moment.

Turn your attention back to the other person. Practice refraining from helping, fixing, or problem solving, and allow yourself to simply listen.

Trust that being a compassionate listener is the best service you can offer. If an insight arises as to what this person needs to hear, it will enter through the doorway of listening, rather than trying to solve.

What do you notice?

10

Mindful Sexuality: Healing the Divide between Sex and Spirit

Human sexuality is another area where we can either hide out in the guise of separate self or access freedom from the mind of separation. If we pay attention, eros can be our greatest ally in reclaiming the sacredness of being alive and in unity.

When I first arrived in Los Angeles in 2007, after eight years of celibacy I was excited to explore the realm of human connection, but sexuality was not a realm I felt ready for. I suspect I was subtly under the spell of some of the same illusions that pervade our society: the notion that sexuality is more charged than other aspects of life and is therefore more complicated. This being so, I felt it might be too much to open that door.

I had two experiences during my first season in LA that motivated me to step forward. One of my great loves is dance as a form of creative expression and meditation. Even when I was a monastic I had an agreement with my teacher that I could have a weekly personal dance practice in my hermitage in the middle of the woods with headphones on and music my brother sent me. I hoped to find a dance class that resonated with me in Los Angeles, and the receptionist at my chiropractor's office recommended a class just down the block from where I was staying. It was a class only for women, she said, with soulful music that celebrated the body.

She gave me the address—but failed to mention that it was a pole-dancing class! And so, when I arrived to the door with my shaved head and yoga clothes and entered a room painted crimson red with sultry lighting and stripper poles throughout the space, I was more than a little surprised. While that might not have been my first choice for a dance class, my practice is to meet every experience with beginner's mind, so while at first I thought, "How on earth did I get here?" I endeavored to drop any associations I had with pole-dancing, opened my mind, and decided to have a fresh experience.

The woman who greeted me had the wholesome wallflower energy of a librarian, and when she began moving in a way that felt powerfully erotic and genuinely uninhibited, I began to cry. It was the most beautiful thing in the world to witness a woman move from her true unconstricted expression of eros. She was not doing it for a man's attention nor curating her movement in any way to please, but moving for her own enjoyment and expression of life force. It was cathartic for me to be invited to reconnect with my own sexual expression in this forum. It appeared to be so different from the monastery on the outside, and yet, it fit well my intention of cultivating freedom.

After that experience, I enjoyed a few months of pole-dancing practice until I decided I had received from it what I had come for. From there, I moved on to another form of dance, one that was a guided awareness practice through movement.

Around the same time, I went to a yoga studio to meet with the head teacher about starting a weekly meditation group. The man behind the desk, a yoga teacher himself, was good-looking, intelligent, and had an uncanny sense of humor. I could tell that he had a long-term practice of some kind, and he radiated a magnetic energy. We got into a rich conversation, and I left feeling the kind of inspiration one experiences when developing a new crush. It was fun to be turned on by a man for the first time in years, and I was grateful that I would likely never see him again. "I am not ready to meet the realm of attraction quite yet," I told myself.

However, life surprised me. I had been housesitting for a few weeks while looking for a permanent place to live. I responded to a Craigslist ad for a single room in a house of spiritual practitioners, meditators, and yogis in Silverlake, a creative neighborhood in East LA, the same neighborhood where my sister lived. It sounded great to me and I had a positive first meeting with the host of the house, who introduced me to the rest of the housemates. It was then that I reconnected with the man from the yoga studio.

I felt trepidation and doubt when I learned that the man I'd found attractive would be my housemate. It was already a new experience to be moving in with a group of strangers, and I needed my home to feel like a sanctuary. But the pull was not so strong that I felt off-center, and I decided to use the situation as a practice opportunity and to trust myself to stay present. Pretty quickly we developed a dynamic friendship, and over time my crush grew. Eventually we decided together that when I was ready for it, he would be my new "first" sexual experience post–monastic celibacy.

The Divide between Sex and Spirit

When we are committed to living from wholeness, there is nothing to keep hidden or compartmentalize. This doesn't mean that we need to be vocal about our sex lives. It just means we can align our sex lives with our larger intention for awareness. Sexuality, while being a pathway for love, intimacy, healing, and ecstasy, is one of the aspects of human life where humans carry the most conditioning, shame, judgment, self-consciousness, and violence.

In my own training in meditation and mindfulness, sexuality was too often left out, as if it were uniquely separate from awareness practice. In so many circles, and certainly in Buddhist and other religious traditions, there is a divide between sex and spirit—a belief that sexuality is somehow so highly charged, dangerous, and complex, it is possibly an impediment to real practice. There is a widely held misconception that spirit is separate from the physical body. Therefore sexuality needs to be transcended in order to access enlightenment. The unique crucible of human consciousness that sexuality offers is simply avoided.

The education I received growing up also perpetuated the view that sex is too loaded to be addressed in a conscious way: "Navigate sex yourself but first memorize this nonverbal sex manual full of conditioned beliefs, rules, judgment, and contradictions." This "manual" included a list of right versus wrong, shoulds and taboos, that did not easily match the natural curiosity, nuance, and even contradictions I experienced as a budding sexual being, and there was very little actual guidance to navigate my exploration. As a result of this subtle, or not so subtle, messaging, sexuality and spirituality are often divided and we are not empowered to connect our sexuality to our inner guidance and our erotic intelligence.

The larger ramifications of this divide are a horrific level of sexual abuse, trauma, violence, shame, and wounding in the human psyche. We see examples of sexual abuse in every religious tradition, even in Buddhism. Because the religion is historically primarily male and monastic, there has been a history of sexual scandals and unacknowledged abuse. For any teaching on meditation or mindfulness to hold integrity in the context of the modern world, it needs to address sexuality in an integrated way. The sex-spirit divide does not serve enlightenment, and it does not support the consciousness of interconnection.

Erotic Awareness

> The soul should always stand ajar, ready to welcome ecstatic experience.
>
> —Emily Dickinson

Eros is a fundamental part of any honest exploration of presence and aliveness. It was a rich part of my experience as a monk, but in a more universal way than we usually think about eros. As a monk I explored eros through the subtle energetics of awareness, the human body, and the body of the natural world. I lived in a state of deep intimacy with life. When I moved to the city after being celibate for eight years, I felt like a novice exploring a foreign land. My intention in that time period was to bring compassionate awareness to aspects of myself that had not been fully engaged for many years.

The gift was that I had a fresh "beginner's mind," a commitment to present moment curiosity and to freeing myself from delusion. I had no interest in meeting conditioned stories or standards, of which there are so many around sexuality. I saw layers of conditioning in this realm (externally and internally) but was not sure where to look for guidance on how to navigate consciously. I had to face head-on collective conditioning around sexuality while observing remnants of conditioning alive in me. How was I to find my truth in this maze of allure, distortion, projection, and hormones?

As I began my exploration, I realized the degree to which the society I lived in was missing out on true intimacy. Everyone seemed to carry some confusion or drama around sex, and among my thirty-something peers, people seemed to be more interested in game-playing than true intimacy. Men and women played out the roles of predator and prey. There was a consumer marketplace approach to sex and dating, where people judged one another by marking off a checklist. People were made to feel disposable through online dating apps. And in bed, people seemed to focus more on goals than sensation, connection, and flow of energy. It appeared to me that the mind of separation had completely colonized the field of human sexuality. It used the field of sexual attraction, with all of its power and potential, to lure people into further distraction, distortion, and disconnect rather than unity, shared power, healing, and sustained pleasure.

I also sadly witnessed the extreme objectification of women, especially in a city as monopolized by Hollywood as Los Angeles. As a monk, I had lived completely free of this dynamic for many years and had happily forgotten that reality. As much as men objectified women, the objectification of women seemed to be perpetuated even more by women themselves. Women's choice of dress and the hypervigilant attempt to present themselves as sexy, manipulating their bodies and even their voices, appeared to be an obsessive pursuit. The desire to present an image that grabbed attention but would never lead to the intimacy they wanted seemed sad to me. The delusion of "power over" male attention through appearing sexy was a poor substitute for the real power of a woman knowing her wholeness. In the name of sexiness, I witnessed women do things that harmed their bodies— from walking long distances in eight-inch heels to injecting toxic chemicals into their pores. I saw women competing, judging, and being hateful of other women in the name of objectification.

The Duality of Repression and Explosion

Everywhere I looked, sexuality seemed to be marred in the duality of repression/explosion. People either positioned themselves with sexual repression, discounting and clamping down on eros to some degree, for religious or other reasons or they broke "free" into explosive sexuality that they avidly advocated to others. Neither repression nor explosion felt authentic to me, as they both carried ideology and a field of dogma. As long as we take a position standing on one side of duality, we remain in constant relationship with the conditioning that creates it. We are not free to find our authentic middle way or to allow that middle way to evolve and grow as we evolve. We let ourselves be guided by outside ideas rather than the intelligence of eros and the human heart.

I found spiritual teachers either preaching celibacy or recruiting people into sex-glamorization, promoting polyamorous explorations, "edginess," and techniques for orgasm rather than erotic intelligence. There was nothing wrong with any of this, but from the perspective of consciousness, it appeared deeply limited. It capitalized on conditioning's appetite for distraction and drama. It did not necessarily connect people with their subtle body or their authentic self. I also noticed books and marketing that essentially promoted the message that we could learn the "secret" to sexuality and ecstasy or become successful in relationships not by something within ourselves, but by looking somewhere outside of ourselves. There was a plethora of marketing that targeted people's fears that as they were, they were not enough. As sexual beings, we are told that we require access to a magic potion, pill, certificate, exotic concept, or special costume to access ecstasy and connection. We alone, as we are, can never be enough.

I didn't buy any of it. There is no secret "out there." There is nothing we need outside of our natural intelligence. The key lies in staying present and embracing our erotic intelligence so we can meet life with vibrant aliveness, whether we are on the meditation cushion, at work, in traffic, chopping carrots, on the dance floor, or in bed with our lover(s).

No one seemed to be modeling a third path or teaching people how to connect with their authentic sexuality and erotic intelligence, free of dogma and ideas. The choice beyond the duality of repression/explosion is an option that does not come dressed in belief. As with all aspects of life, "It's not what we do, it's how we do it." Whether someone is gay, straight, queer, playing the field, or in a monogamous long-term relationship, what matters is the process and motivation we bring to our sexual conduct. The process is what determines the level of intimacy, satisfaction, and pleasure we experience. Are we fully present and open to real connection? Where is it easy to stay present and at what moment do we check out or shut down? Are we paying attention? Are we acting from authenticity or trying to get an unconscious need met? Are we aware of what ego brings? Are we operating from erotic intelligence or the conditioned mind? Are we affirming wholeness and unity or fear and separation? Are we giving and receiving love in the spirit of generosity or selfishness?

Eros is not just about how we relate in bed. It is also about how we engage from and with our whole being. It is also about our overall willingness to relate and show up for one another with courage, love, passion, and honesty. The tragedy of a society disconnected from eros is manifested by a tremendous amount of disembodiment, sexual violence, and abuse, but also loneliness, isolation, and self-loathing. On a day-to-day basis, the loss is people not being connected to their own life force and vitality as they engage in all of life's activities. Beyond the thrill of seeking chemical stimulus, sexuality is about the pleasure of connection.

Connection—to one another and to our own life force—is what we all want deep inside.

Healing the Divide through Relational Mindfulness

During a couples' workshop on "Attention, Awareness, and Intimacy" after a day of guiding people to practice deep listening with one another, I invited people to do a simple practice. The practice was to spend ten minutes meditating and then to lie down, set the timer for ten minutes, and receive tender touch from their partner (fully clothed). The assignment was to simply pay attention more subtly to the experience of being touched and the experience of touching. Rather than inviting sexual arousal, the exercise was a sensory exploration of awareness, attention, and touch. I invited people to give touch with no agenda other than paying full attention and to receive touch in the very same way. People were asked to share with their partner afterward what they experienced on the level of body, feelings, and mind.

As we debriefed, people began to share experiences that were much more profound than they had expected. Through permission to give their full attention to touch and receiving touch,, people experienced a sense of deep peace and intimacy. People realized how often they were not fully present while exchanging touch. Many people became aware of how often they did not allow themselves to receive.

A young man in an open relationship had a revelatory experience. He admitted that sex had become a form of addiction, rather than an experience that he was actually present for. He had developed an identity as a "player" and affirmed this through sex. While it brought momentary pleasure, it never brought the tenderness, satisfaction, or experience of peace that he received in that exercise. The exercise revealed how numbed out and on autopilot he had been in regards to touch. He never brought his authentic self to sexuality and certainly never allowed himself to experience tenderness with his partners.

Another student shared that he had so much fear of intimacy that he had given up entirely on dating, and was meeting his sexual needs through online pornography. This man, while talented, successful, and good-looking, found face-to-face intimacy far too confronting. He had cut his sexuality off from the rest of his life and found a way to compartmentalize and get his needs met, but he felt extremely lonely. In the exercise he felt compassion for himself for the first time as he remembered the possibility of safe, tender, and pleasurable touch. He realized that real connection was something he yearned for, something that screen-based sex could never provide.

As more students began to chime in and express the disconnect they felt in their sex lives, it was evident that a majority of people had a more intimate relationship with the mind of separation than with their actual bodies and erotic selves. As more students began to ask for guidance on sexuality, I decided to offer workshops and retreats on the subject. A group of people would gather, typically in a yoga studio, for a day of meditation, mindful inquiry, reflection, and facilitated discussion on the topic of mindful sexuality. I created a down-to-earth space for acknowledging and unraveling conditioning, helping people to reconnect with their erotic intelligence and use it as a guide through the complex terrain of their conditioning. I learned that people were facing a barrage of messages louder than any other aspect of human engagement. It was no wonder people were struggling with sex and intimacy.

Some of the unique influences that we are up against today that create disconnect in the realm of intimacy are:

- the sexualization of everything from yoga to breakfast cereal
- standards about "sexiness" and physicality that hold weight in our consumer world
- the notion that sex is a pass/fail performance
- the notion that orgasm is always the goal of sex
- overexposure to pornography disconnecting people from any chance at knowing their authentic erotic self
- fear of intimacy
- the extreme objectification of women
- cultural expectations for men to not be emotionally vulnerable
- women and men trading their authentic power in for a limiting substitute of appearing "sexy"
- a cultural habit of people disconnecting from their bodies in order to "get things done"
- the expectation that one "knows how" to have good sex and therefore does not come to it with "beginner's mind"
- a lifestyle that perpetuates high levels of stress and information overload
- legacies of sexual abuse throughout human history and healing needing to take place for generations past, present, and future that we are all invited to take part in healing

The more I mentor others, the more I realize how helpful training in Relational Mindfulness is when it comes to sex. People are relieved to learn that, when we invite our conditioning to quiet down, our natural intelligence remains and offers clear guidance with regards to our sexual choices and expression. People are grateful to learn that regardless of what they have experienced in the past, there are practices to help us remember the intimate connection that is our birthright. If we want deep, alive, open-hearted, passionate connection, we need to be able to stay in touch with the subtle energetics of our eros and the human heart.

The Invitation of Mindful Sexuality

Consider how the practice of Relational Mindfulness might apply to your sex life and could guide you to deeper intimacy and pleasure:

- *Intention* invokes our willingness to stay present and curious while we engage with one another, rather than going on auto-pilot or checking out. With our intention we acknowledge that we are not just having sex for chemical stimulus but for the pleasure of real connection, whether we are engaging with a long-term partner or in a one-night stand.
- *The Mindful Pause* invites us to relax, slow down, and pay attention. Our erotic intelligence is only available to guide us if we are willing to stay connected—within and without.
- *Deep Listening* helps us to stay in touch with our needs and desires through sex while attuning to our partner. Through Deep Listening we can remain present to the actual sensations and flow of energy in our body during sex, as well as our emotions, rather than be distracted by ideas, agendas, or stories about how sex should be.
- *Mindful Inquiry and Clear Seeing* help us to step back from and dissolve conditioned stories as they arise. Clear Seeing is the means for keeping our conditioning out of bed, which is the last place it belongs. But when it does arise, then we have tools to not judge it but to investigate what is getting in the way. If the performer arises in bed, for instance, and in your heart you really crave deep connection, then inquiry can help you to step back from performing and drop into vulnerability.

- *Transparency* enables us to be courageously honest about sex. Transparency helps us to dissolve any false separation or a tendency to hide, especially in those awkward or triggering moments around sex.

Relational Mindfulness allows sex to be another opportunity for deepening our capacity for presence and generosity, both on the giving and receiving end. There is nothing exotic or technique-y about bringing mindfulness to sex. And there is absolutely no standard for how mindful sex should look. Mindfulness simply helps us to remember and enjoy our innate capacity for loving connection, without the disruption of the mind of separation. It helps us to commit to non-separation and possibility in a deeply enjoyable aspect of human life.

Erotic Intelligence

Erotic intelligence is our expression of wholeness as sexual beings. Erotic intelligence is the force that knows a true yes, the boundary of a no, unselfconscious enjoyment, the courage of vulnerability, and caring in-the-moment affection. Erotic intelligence is the foundation of honesty and trust that must exist in order for there to be intimacy. It is the celebration of our animal bodies without causing harm. Even in moments of sexual confusion or being pulled between our heads and our hearts, erotic intelligence can welcome that confusion too as part of the sexual journey. If we leave our sex lives out of our investigation of consciousness, I believe we are doing ourselves a great disservice. Given that human beings are wildly divergent in our needs and tastes sexually, it is a shame to trade in one's truth for society's made-up rules and manuals of behavior. In a world of sexual distortion, we each have an opportunity to turn towards, rather than away from, eros, and to be part of the healing of generations of distortion. The reward is deeper love, integrity, trust, pleasure, joy, and connection.

I often wonder, how we as a society navigate this realm of life without awareness as our guide. Without a commitment to cutting through the delusions as they arise, we are mired in thousands of years of human conditioning around sex. This aspect of life—so full of possibility for intimacy and reverence for life— has become tragically burdened with limiting beliefs, pressures, expectations, and judgment. The mind of separation has deeply infiltrated into this realm of natural human activity. I believe we have an imperative to take part in this healing.

In a world with so much distortion around sexuality and so little support for bringing compassionate awareness to the realm of sexuality, I have never met anyone who could not benefit from the tools of Relational Mindfulness.

A couple in their late forties, Mira and David, came to a weekend workshop I taught in Portland, Oregon. They had been married for ten years and their relationship was in a rocky place. After a day of meditation and Relational Mindfulness, I suggested an evening practice—that they meditate together and then take turns touching one another's body, as if it were their first time. Their homework assignment was to bring beginner's mind to the activity of lovemaking. I suggested that they follow this by making love with each other as if it were their last time. The first round brought them into a place of innocence, and curiosity. It provided a space of reverence and receptivity that they did not often make time for. In the first part of the exercise, they realized that a basic ingredient missing for them was the gift of attention. Their attention was so often on other things that even when they found time for making love, they were distracted. With some regret and grief, they both realized that they have been "going through the motions" for the past five years and taking one another for granted. In the second round, Mira and David were brought directly back into a depth of love and passion for each other they had not felt for years. With the added reminder of impermanence in their awareness, they remembered their deep love for each other and gave themselves permission to meet one another with greater generosity and immediacy through that awareness.

In retreats exploring erotic intelligence, men and women are supported to courageously release layers of conditioning. Some examples of this are:

- a young man admitting that he has not brought nearly the same level of mindfulness and integrity to his sex life as he has to other aspects of his life because none of his teachers have encouraged this; it just got left out of practice
- a forty-year-old woman feeling her own sexual power for the first time, not a power over, but the wholesome empowerment that comes from finally letting go of seeing sex as a performance and enjoying her own erotic self
- a young man realizing that he had spent so much time engaging in empty pornography that he had lost touch with his sensory curiosity in sex; he realized curiosity was a vital element of both his mindfulness practice and his sex life
- a young woman realizing that she has been participating in polyamory for years because her partner prefers it and her friends all do it, even though, deep down, she knows that a monogamous relationship is her true pathway
- a sexual abuse victim, getting in touch with his subtle body for the first time, in a mindful eating exercise aimed at putting people back in touch with their senses
- an executive realizing he's always been attracted to women outside the conventional body type of his culture, but that

he's always repressed that and chosen women he is not
really attracted to

We each have our own unique path to travel in the realm
of sexuality. With the tools of Relational Mindfulness we can
help ourselves become empowered and positioned for even more
beauty and depth in relation to eros. The work always begins
with a question, and the questions I find vital at this time are:

- What is possible when we choose to meet life and practice with the innocence of erotic curiosity as our guide?
  What do our senses have to offer us when we pay full
  attention?
- What is possible when we bring the stillness of mindfulness practice to the dynamisms of sexuality?
- What is possible when we are willing to trust our erotic
  intelligence over any conditioned beliefs, especially those
  we don't know we have?
- What is possible when we are willing to meet lovemaking
  from our ordinary self and sustained presence rather than
  romanticizing the orgasm?
- What is possible when we are willing to embody transparency and vulnerability over fear in the realm of physical
  intimacy?
- And what is possible when we invite our animal bodies
  back home to be integrated with our spiritual life?

Life happens now. Awareness practice invites us to embody
freedom in our lives, not someday in the future when we are
"healed," but now, today, when we shift our lens and acknowledge
the authenticity that is who we are beneath what we have been
conditioned to believe about ourselves. Relational Mindfulness
can offer a framework for healing the sexuality/spirituality split
in our culture.

Bringing Relational Mindfulness to the realm of sexuality invites us beyond duality and beyond roles, into authenticity: beyond the dualities of repression/explosion, good/bad, beyond predator/prey, madonna/whore, you/me—beyond all the other dualities we bring to this ordinary and sacred realm of life.

On a deeper level, how we relate to eros is how we relate to life force, to creativity, and to the natural world. My hope is that more people will choose to bring wholeness to this realm and learn to embrace their ordinary extraordinary selves. It is time to let go of any desire to be "expert" in this realm and bring beginner's mind to asking the questions that can liberate us through our sexuality.

• • • • • • • • Mindful Inquiry • • • • • • • •

How have you been impacted by the divide between sex and spirit? The duality of repression versus explosion?

To what degree are you at peace with your sex life and yourself as a sexual being?

Are there any conditioned messages you struggle with within the realm of sexuality?

What helps you to stay present through the field of attraction and sexuality?

How do you objectify other people? Yourself?

Do you carry or feel shame in your past or current relationship with sex that you have not addressed?

How have you been impacted by a culture of pornography? Has pornography had any impact on your approach to lovemaking?

What gifts and teachings have you received from your own erotic intelligence?

How do you accept and celebrate your erotic awareness?

As you bring more awareness to your sexuality, is there any forgiveness you need to do? Of yourself or others?

Do you feel called to bring more generosity to your role as giver or receiver in sexuality?

What is an aspect of sexual distortion in our world that you want to be part of healing?

· · · · · · · · **Daily Practice** · · · · · · · ·

Today, begin to bring awareness to how the divide of sex and spirit impacts you. Notice if there are any manifestations in your psyche of separation between your animal body or erotic self and spirituality. Bring nonjudgment and compassion to how this divide impacts you.

See if you can find one enjoyable way today to savor your connection with eros, through connection with each of your five senses. Consider that we connect with eros when we are relaxed and when we are paying attention.

11

Releasing the Lens of Other

Whenever you hold someone above or below you,
someone is being diminished.

—Anonymous

I am writing this just four days after the 2016 shooting
of Philando Castile by a police officer in Minneapolis,
Minnesota, while he was sitting in his car with his girlfriend
and child; two days after the killing of three officers in Baton
Rouge, Louisiana; and one month after the killing of forty-nine
people at a gay bar in Orlando, Florida. At the same time, the
news is reporting that gun sales skyrocketed the day after the
bar shooting.

As I walk into the market, someone pushes past me with
their cart, bumping into me in their hurry. As I leave, people
are arguing angrily over parking spaces in the parking lot. That
same day, a student calls me asking for support to help him to
understand and navigate through his feelings about the gun
violence. Knowing that I myself am trying desperately to integrate my feelings about the craziness out there, I encourage the
student to honor this pain as sacred feedback from the web of

interconnection. I hear myself asking him to commit to taking responsibility for his part in the disease of "othering" with a dedication he has never before known. "We're all part of the 'problem,' as long as we haven't addressed it within ourselves at the subtlest level," I hear myself say.

I hear the words coming from my mouth, and I know that, like most of us, I have subconsciously integrated the symptoms of racism and judgment into my being. Even though I have never viewed myself as racist and am deeply committed to a life of service and equality, I know that I have moments in which I am unaware of my discriminatory reactions toward others.

I know deep down that the very fact that I am a white person, who thus has more power in our culture than others, means that I could be taking a more proactive stance against racism and discriminatory behavior in the world around me. I know that every one of us needs to step it up and open our hearts even more fully during this time of intensifying divisions between people. I feel the desire to be part of a movement taking passionate responsibility for digging out the seed of discrimination within. I know that I must do so, because I am privileged.

At the same time, I have experienced marginalization in my own way, through being a petite female in a male-dominated world, a Jewish Buddhist teacher, having a chronic illness for many years, at times struggling to survive financially, and even through choosing an unconventional lifestyle. Despite knowing marginalization myself, my skin color grants me extreme privilege in a society of indoctrinated and institutionalized racism. Some of these privileges include:

- sleeping well at night knowing that my brother, partner, stepdad, and nephew, who also have white skin, are not likely to be targeted by police tomorrow
- having other white people judge me as "acceptable"

- not having to carry the history of slavery in my family directly
- having certain laws and housing policies that provide for me more support to succeed than for people of color
- as a white woman, my sexuality not being judged as easily as a woman of color
- the privilege of living in an industrialized country where I have access to resources that most of the world does not
- the privilege of education and work opportunities
- the privilege of feeling comfortable in white environments
- the privilege of access to the wilderness and outdoors
- privileges I am not even conscious of

I practice engaged meditation, using life as a laboratory for waking up to the ways I am still in the trance of the mind of separation. I see that at this moment in history, we have a unique and beautiful opportunity to bring awareness to the collective healing of -isms—including racism, classism, ageism, sexism, and elitism, to name a few. Although we might not have ourselves felt victim or perpetrator of oppression (though most of us have at some point in our lives), and even if we do not see ourselves as part of the problem or have devoted our lives to being allies to those who have been marginalized, there is a more active role for each of us to take. That role includes helping to heal the myth of separation as it relates to race, class, sex, culture, age, and physical/mental capacity.

At the time the Buddha taught, he engaged, in general, with a culturally homogenous population, primarily men rather than women, and people who had a similar cultural perspective. He simply did not face the questions of global diversity and oppression that we face today—although even in India at that time such forces were present. The fact that humanity's tendency toward oppression, domination, and subordination has gone so far as to threaten the future of life on this planet is perhaps the inspiration we have always needed.

Those of us who are privileged enough to have our basic needs met, have an invitation to participate in the collective healing of our world, and this opportunity for human evolution is phenomenal. If we acknowledge that we have a role to play in the healing of a long-held distortion in the human psyche, then we begin to see the golden invitation that Relational Mindfulness offers to us.

Relational Mindfulness invites us to take our place as conscious participants in the web of interconnection by releasing the mind of separation and living from the consciousness of "We." It invites us to bring a beginner's mind to our personal role in racism, sexism, and gender-based discrimination, and to do so at a time when it is more popular to take an all-knowing expert stance on oppression. The practice of Relational Mindfulness can ignite in us a curiosity about the unconditional nature of interconnection. It inspires us to continually look into corners of our lives where there is something to illuminate and something to release. Relational Mindfulness supports us in ending discrimination by:

- Taking joyful responsibility for owning the effect of privilege in ourselves, rather than being unaware of it.
- Allowing self-awareness to humble us, rather than excuse us
- Learning to bring cultural humility to all of our interactions, rather than to impose what we think we know.
- Releasing the lens of "other" that is the core of marginalization as it exists in the human psyche—and supporting a lifelong endeavor to prioritize this in ourselves and in our world.
- Opening ourselves to the consciousness of equality, unity, shared power, and mutual respect.

Being Conscious of Privilege

I have never thought of myself as racist, sexist, or any other form of -ist. As someone who is honest with herself, however, I don't believe that anyone is truly free of the conditioning that comes from growing up in a world of -isms. My own upbringing was immersed in multiculturalism, and, as a Dharma teacher, I have participated in diverse communities and multiple diversity trainings over the years. I have also witnessed a small part of me sometimes subconsciously devalue the impact of these trainings on my conscious self, with a subtle sense of conclusion: "Now I have a set of rules and language that I can follow, so I can stop thinking about this issue," or "Now that I have done a training on . . . , I can stop inquiring into my own behavior and perceptions."

The point of practice is to pay attention, and when we pay attention, we see opportunities to wake up continually, through every interaction. When I pay attention, I can name numerous moments every week, when, either triggered by a past incident in my life or identified with the mind of separation, I watch my mind evaluate in some way "other" beings who are different than me. For example:

- *I am watching a political debate on television and hear myself say of the other party, "These people are utterly insane. They are truly hateful."*
- *I am on a walk seeking solitude and feel annoyed when I come upon people in my path playing music on a nature trail. The mantra in my mind says, "Unconscious people . . . they're everywhere . . . you can't get away from them . . . I just wanted to be alone."*
- *After leaving an evening workshop I have taught, I am walking to my car alone and pass an alleyway in which a group of dark-skinned men are hanging out. Although they pay me no attention, I feel vulnerable and quicken my pace.*

In workshops about "Releasing the Lens of Other," students give countless examples of how humbling it is to catch in action their own unconscious habits of judging and seeing people who are different as "other." One student names it well. "I see myself as a conscious and kind person, but my ego is 'othering' all the time." Some of the examples they relate are:

- At a gathering, choosing to talk to a young and "interesting-looking" person rather than to an older person
- A male student choosing to partner with attractive rather than unattractive women in class exercises, not because he is looking to date, but because he habitually judges attractiveness
- A student who is poor and considers herself "a good spiritual person" regularly judging those who make a lot of money
- A student who is an activist hating people from the corporate world who are "the problem"

In the broader scale, the very nature of the mind of separation to categorize and compare humans and other forms of life is flawed. It is a delusional lens. There is no freedom whatsoever for any human being until this lens—of separation—is dissolved. From the reality of interconnection, there is nothing true about holding people above or below us. The motivation beneath this lens—one of protecting and defending the separate ego out of fear—is revealed as a distortion.

When we identify specific ways that we judge and "other," we do the work of asking the following inquiry prompts, with fascination and nonjudgment:

- Who do I become each time I view different as other/less than?
- How does it feel in my body and in my heart when I do this?

- What is the impact on the relational field that I am part of?
- How does this habit cause separation and fracture even within myself, rather than affirm my true nature?
- How does this kind of spiritual laziness impact my soul and capacity to open my heart more fully?
- How does it keep me from seeing the unique beauty of those who are different than me?
- What would it be like to free myself completely of hierarchical judgements?

Cultural Humility

Don't make assumptions.

When we are identified with the mind of separation, we continually make assumptions. We make assumptions about other people, about situations, and even about ourselves. To live a wakeful life means to live a life devoted to both humility and curiosity. Instead of entering the conditioned mind, we enter a space of open compassionate presence. From beginner's mind, we are willing to relax into the innocence of present moment awareness.

Even with those we might connect with daily, we impose limitations and assumptions from the day before onto this same person over and over. Our ability to actually see and hear the person in front of us is impeded. Intimacy is not possible when we interact with someone through a projection of who we think they are, rather than seeing their true being.

The impacts of this interpersonally are immense. Without consciously realizing that we are doing so, we make assumptions about people of different races, religions, social status, physical ability, appearance, age, sexual orientation, and political view. This habit is enslaved by the conditioned mind. By its nature, the relational field cannot be accessed through surface entry. It is the consciousness of oneness that lies beneath all superficial judgment.

Cultural humility is a term I first heard from Dharma teacher and activist Larry Yang. It is an invitation to take responsibility more subtly for all the ways that we unconsciously impose erroneous knowledge about someone from another culture or life orientation, when we might actually know nothing. Inquiry prompts we can bring to this area, with kindness and nonjudgment, are:

- When I enter a space, how often do I notice myself making assumptions—subtle or not—about strangers?
- What do I base these assumptions on? Appearance? Dress? Age? Body posture? Voice? Make of car?
- Have I had the experience of judging someone and finding out, in hindsight, that I was completely wrong? Deep down, how did that feel?
- How often do I project that others are judging me based on superficiality? Do I give more energy to the surface they are seeing than to sharing my inner being?

"Othering" in the Name of Consciousness/ Spirituality

> Personal change and the ability to bring about social change are linked. There is no use striving to implement principles such as nonviolence or justice in public affairs as long as one neglects them in one's personal life.
>
> —attributed to Gandhi

"Spiritual people" are hardly immune to the habit of othering. After I left the monastery, I became close friends with a healer and shaman in Los Angeles whose organic approach to healing resonated with me deeply. He invited me to meet his teacher, an elder shaman who had been practicing for a long time and had students around the world. I was to meet them at a chiropractor's office. I sat down in the waiting room on the day of the meeting to wait for my session with this "wise shaman." Feeling a mix of nervous excitement and "specialness" about the encounter I was about to have, I chose a seat near an unassuming older man dressed in athletic clothing. He wore a baseball cap and had a disposable coffee cup in his hand. I said hello and then opened my book and began to read while I waited.

Someone sitting across from the man engaged him in a conversation about football. Not being interested in sports myself, I subconsciously and superficially brushed the men off as sporty types with whom I had little in common. As the time for my session approached, my friend came out into the waiting room and called me in. The old man got up as well and introduced himself to me. Although he was the shaman I was waiting to meet, I had subconsciously created an image of him in my mind of someone far more exotic and certainly more "spiritual-looking." I consider myself to be someone who values conscious connection, but I brushed sports talk off as something separate from the realm of conscious connection. I learned a real lesson that day and vowed to never again dress spirituality in special garb.

Even in the name of consciousness, we tend to subconsciously label those who follow a different path than us. I have experienced this in the Buddhist world, the Judeo-Christian world, the alternative healing world, the health food world, the activist world, the yoga world, and in fact, in almost every conscious privileged group I have been part of.

In Relational Mindfulness workshops with people from all walks of life, I have explored the question, "When have you been made to feel 'other than' or 'less than' in situations where you least expected it?" Some of the responses have been:

- "We get this look from people every single day . . . when they come into the restaurant we work in or when they walk past us on the street. To be honest, it is a look of disgust."
  —A group of Latino inner city teenagers in a training program at an organic food restaurant in Los Angeles, California
- "I was a vegan for twenty years, and when I began to consciously eat meat again for health reasons, I received hateful comments from many people at my health food co-op."
  —A student living in Portland, Oregon
- "When I started dating a man, after ten years as a lesbian, I felt judged and rejected by most people in my community." —A forty-year-old meditation practitioner
- "After having a facelift, a decision I brought a lot of inquiry to, I received harsh verbal judgment from most of the women in my community." —A sixty-year-old meditation practitioner

It is important to remember that the mind of separation can hide out in our psyches in the most unexpected places. Its job, ultimately, is to separate and fracture, rather than to affirm wholeness. Its job is to distract us from the possibility of interconnection with all beings.

If we find ourselves perceiving someone through the lens of separation, we can look at the result of our thought patterns and see what they have produced. In the example of my meeting with the shaman, I believed the illusion that my judging mind can be trusted to assess people based on their appearances. The fact that this meeting had been arranged in the name of my spiritual growth made my behavior even more embarrassing and humbling for me. Ultimately, I was completely transparent about how foolish I'd been, had a good laugh, and received a potent lesson on spiritual snobbery, something I never would have thought existed in myself.

This is why cultural humility offers such a profound teaching. It invites us to open our eyes and see how we might at times be perpetrators of the problem. To judge, compare, and come to a conclusion about someone else based on something we think we know about them is a distortion.

Using Our Privilege for the Benefit of All

When I was twenty years old, I was given the incredible opportunity to spend a year traveling the world studying with various leaders in the sustainability movement. The year was heart-wrenching and heart-opening, as I witnessed the same dynamics of the economic machine created by the myth of separation, impacting cultures, indigenous peoples, and pristine landscapes around the world.

I had intellectually understood how privileged I was before this, but I recall one particularly eye-opening moment during my travels. Having visited various villages in the Northern Himalayas with the Indian activist Vandana Shiva, witnessing villages where people were ravaged both by poverty and the impact of multiple earthquakes, hearing their pleas for help, the inequity inherent in them having nothing while I had so much became unbearable. The realization that I had benefited my whole life from being an American, living in a country whose economic, commercial, and agricultural conglomerates have had such negative impacts on so many diverse cultures on the planet, hit me harder than it ever had—and I broke down. It was that moment that I realized that I was, in fact, one of the perpetrators of the problem.

In distress, I called my mother, an activist herself, waking her in the middle of the night. Through my tears, I told her that I could not continue on my journey meeting people whose lives were so difficult and who were struggling daily to barely survive, because I felt responsible. She said, "You are not the cause. Your privilege allows you to use your voice for change, to speak when others cannot. . . . Use your voice to honor those whose voices are pushed aside and cannot be heard."

My mom's words were not just inspired and heartfelt, but I knew them to be true. At the age of thirty-eight, motivated in part by feelings of helplessness in the face of so much that was wrong in the world, she became a lifelong social activist devoted to addressing poverty and homelessness and, in the process, affirmed her solidarity with the well-being of all people everywhere on our planet.

We could all be asking ourselves these questions:

- What does my level of privilege and well-being allow me to offer of service to the world?
- Is there any way I use my privilege to justify "othering" people?
- How does being of service to the whole serve my liberation from suffering?
- How does my taking subtler responsibility for my actions on the level of cultural humility and oppression serve our shared liberation?

We are truly privileged to be able to participate in the healing of oppression. Because our basic needs are met and we have the golden practice of compassionate awareness, we can bring love and fascination rather than fear and resignation to the process.

Processing Pain about -isms

If we are not willing to feel our pain over the oppression in our world in the short term, we are depriving ourselves of the possibility of true healing in the long term. If we do not honor our pain and respond, we continue to perpetuate the problem. Our pain helps us to remember that life is a shared field. Peace is not a passive state. There is nothing about meditation that teaches us to become numb to or transcend our outrage. Meditation teaches us to step back into a field of awareness, where we can hold and meet our outrage with love and compassion. This does not negate nor dilute our feelings. It honors our outrage fully, and when an emotion is honored, it can be transmuted into wisdom and courageous action. We cannot honestly witness oppression without feeling the wound ourselves.

We need not be afraid of our anger, nor should we add fire to it. When we are feeling broken, outraged, and in despair or when fear and aggression are screaming loudly, we can turn toward the eternal balm of stillness. Stillness is an energetic rather than physical state that grounds us in our deeper knowledge and gives us instruction on the way of peace. Simply by giving our pain and outrage to stillness, we can begin to experience ourselves and one another from a place that connects rather than separates us. We allow our hearts to remain unguarded and courageous in order to heal our collective wounds. The practice of stillness is one step we can each take toward the healing of hatred and violence in our world today. We can allow our pain for the world to be transformed instead into compassionate action.

Working with People with Whom We Do Not Agree

> Knowing others is intelligence; knowing yourself is true wisdom. Mastering others is strength; mastering yourself is true power.
>
> —Lao-Tzu

On retreat, a student always asks, "What do I do with those people with whom I truly disagree—those people whose behavior or opinions drive me crazy?" We all are driven crazy at times by

others—whether it is someone we are close to or a political figure
we are listening to on a news channel. The first step in dealing
with a situation of this nature is to turn our attention within to
examine our own reactions or responses. We can ask of ourselves
the following:

- What is it about this person or situation that is so difficult
  or repulsive to me?
- How do I really feel (in body and in mind) and who do I
  become in reaction to this person or situation?
- Am I willing to step back from the rigidity of my reactions
  and into a more spacious awareness and consciousness of
  "We"? From this new place, can I either
  - own the projection I put onto this person or situation
    and see what that illuminates in me; or
  - seek to better understand this person or situation and
    his/her way of being? Can I find the place of compas-
    sion within myself for this person's life experiences as
    I have done so for my own?

Honoring the consciousness of "We" requires us to learn
how to discern between humility and meekness. There is nothing
necessarily passive about compassion.

Sometimes compassion carries an action. Sometimes, when
we see someone acting inauthentically, we must be willing to
speak up. This might take the form of calling out an act of harm,
or telling someone something difficult for them to hear, or setting a strong and firm boundary with someone. Sometimes, the
compassionate action is to turn the other cheek and let go. The
point is to align our actions with the motivation of "What is best
for all?"

Please see appendix 4 for guidelines on Bringing Relational
Mindfulness and Cultural Humility to Group Interactions.

· · · · · · · · · **Mindful Inquiry** · · · · · · · ·

How have you been made to feel "other than"?

How have you made people to feel "other than"?

How does it feel in your body and in your heart when you view different as "other than"?

How does this habit cause separation and fracture within the relational field and even within yourself?

In what situations do you make assumptions about people based on the superficial?

Do you ever "other" people in the name of consciousness?

In what situations could you bring more cultural humility than you do?

What feelings do you carry about living in a world where so much marginalization exists? In what ways do you see yourself as part of the solution?

Is there a way you feel called to step it up in releasing the lens of other? Do you need to ask for support or accountability from anyone in your life in doing this?

How would it nourish your spiritual growth and freedom to fully release the lens of other?

· · · · · · · · · **Daily Practice** · · · · · · · ·

Today, bring more subtle awareness "to the lens through which you view everyone with whom you interact. Notice how and when your mind makes assumptions about other people, especially those who are different than you. How does your mind talk you into believing assumption and "othering"?

PART THREE

Cultivating Mindful Relationship with the Planet

This section is an invitation to cultivate a relational immersion in life. It is about healing our relationship with our planet, as well as the profound role of the natural world in personal healing. We see the impact of our separation from nature on the state of the biosphere as well as on the human psyche and health. Reconnecting with nature is not a privilege but a necessity for our survival and awakening.

The consciousness of "We" does not extend only to humanity, but to all living systems on our planet. The same principles of cultural humility explored in the last chapter can be brought to the natural world. We have an innate capacity to engage with all forms of life through a deeper means of respect, sensing, listening, communicating, and cooperating.

This section offers a new paradigm of partnership with nature, which is about remembering how to work with rather than against nature. Sustainable living goes hand in hand with a personal inquiry into what actually matters and what we have been taught to value over the undisputable worth of sustaining life on planet earth. There are aggressive commercial forces marketing particular lifestyle choices, and Relational

Mindfulness encourages us to take personal responsibility for our lifestyle choices. Particularly for those of us practicing in the context of the modern world, which tends to view the human sphere as the only sphere or dominant sphere, it is vital to question this limiting premise and to perceive the possibility of partnership with nature.

12

Partnership with Nature

Lessons from the Zen Gardener

People think they understand things because they become familiar with them. This is only superficial knowledge. It is the knowledge of the astronomer who knows the names of the stars, the botanist who knows the classification of the leaves and flowers, the artist who knows the aesthetics of green and red. This is not to know nature itself—the earth and sky, green and red. Astronomer, botanist, and artist have done no more than grasp impressions and interpret them, each within the vault of his own mind. The more involved they become with the activity of the intellect, the more they set themselves apart and the more difficult it becomes to live naturally.

—Masanobu Fukuoka, *The One-Straw Revolution*

n an important way, my first Zen teacher was the living soil in which I learned to garden. In 1991, at age nineteen and in search of sanity in the modern world, it seemed highly sane to learn the ancient art of agriculture. Something about putting my hands into the earth and learning to do something timeless, honest, physical, and co-creative with nature made sense to me. I had recently left the densely populated and highly consumptive city of Los Angeles, but was not quite over my teenage angst about the state of the world, nor was I sure about how I was going to move forward with my life in a way that would be meaningful. I began the study of organic farming as both a creative endeavor and a political act.

Living in rural Massachusetts at the time, I participated in a grassroots local community garden project. Thus began a love affair with gardening that led eventually to my involvement in urban gardening projects with a social justice mission, running a CSA (community supported agriculture) in Arizona at Arcosanti, an urban ecology project, and apprenticing at Green Gulch Farm Zen Center in Muir Beach, California. Eventually this path drew me to the monastic life, and there I developed and supervised the gardens which grew most of the monastery's produce.

Ever since my initiation into meditation, which occurred during the time that I sowed the first seeds into the soil in New England, I have been struck by the shared teachings of these two disciplines. Both teach us how to work with rather than against nature, approaching life through the consciousness of unity, rather than from separation. Both offer a gateway to moving beyond the cocoon of the human sphere and honoring the vital intelligence of the natural world.

Even though, growing up, my family always had a small garden, I generally perceived soil as "dirt" and overlooked its undisputable value. Soil or dirt was something unwanted, to be cleared away and cleaned up. In learning to grow my own food in the topsoil that makes up the exterior layer of earth's crust, my perception shifted and I became wildly enamored of soil as a brilliant and vital living ecosystem. Witnessing again and again the transformation of seeds through the synergy of clay, air, water, microorganisms, and worms that comprise soil, I came to revere humus as the seat of life regenerating. *Humus* comes from the same root as *humility* and *humble*, and gardening taught me that when we step down from our human-centered orientation, we are humbled by how small we are and how intelligent the intricate systems of the living earth are.

Observation

> In my case Pilgrim's Progress consisted in my having to climb down a thousand ladders until I could reach out my hand to the little clod of earth that I am.
>
> —Carl Jung

The first teaching in Zen is also the first instruction for an organic gardener: to show up with the attitude of nonjudgmental observation. As a student of sustainable design, I was encouraged to spend an entire year observing a landscape before planting or building anything—noticing the flow of water, wind, and patterns of sunlight, noticing the habits and trails of wildlife and insects, noticing the quality of the soil throughout the seasons, and noticing the intersection between all of the components of a garden or homestead. Patient observation allowed life to inform me, as a participant in the field of interconnected consciousness, of patterns and relationships.

The quality of observation I am talking about is not that of a student taking notes in a classroom seeking to draw conclusions. It is observation that carries the quality of deep listening with one's full body: a subtle and attentive awareness that is only available when we surrender our thinking mind in order to sense more deeply. It is the sensing of a tracker, of a mother tuned in deeply to her child, a healer listening to their patient, an artist immersed in painting on a canvas, or a lover tuned in and fully present to the beloved.

Every morning as a gardener, I would rise early, put on my overalls and work gloves, and trek out into the crisp morning air. Whatever my task was, my job was to put ego's agenda aside to be of service to the soil and plant life with which I was working. I would walk down the dirt path at the farm, gather my well-cared-for tools, and show up, no matter what state I was in, to the simple tasks that the garden communicated needed to be done.

Sometimes a crop would begin to flower sooner than expected and needed trimming. Sometimes an insect larva showed up and required attention. Some mornings I would spend hours weeding, feeding, aerating, and raking the earth until it was ready for new plantings. Some mornings my task would be to sow seeds, one after another, after another, after another, making the best use of space, and with great attention to detail and depth. At other times, my task was to harvest, gathering sweet peas in the wintertime, beans in summertime, round, hearty squash in the fall, and fresh broccoli in the spring. The point was to spend enough time in quiet observation to actually be of service to life.

The role of the organic gardener is to enter a landscape that is a collaboration between human and nature and listen to nature in its own language. This requires ceasing to impose ideas onto the garden and learning the art of paying attention.

Upon receiving insight from the plant world, the task is then not to translate it into our own language, but to simply listen. This is the most useful attitude we can bring to working with nature and working with ourselves. In the modern world, we no longer value spending time "being with" nature. We do not teach young people the art of paying attention. Instead, we teach them to move fast, multitask, be productive, jump to conclusions before investigating, and go for "bigger" and "more" over wiser and conscious. We teach people to use force rather than attunement.

We have forgotten how to work with life on behalf of life. We have dampened and numbed the energetic receptors that keep us responsive to the signs nature gives us, and this has impacted both human and planetary health.

Cultivating the Inner Garden

Start with one bed and tend it well.

—Alan Chadwick

The role of the organic gardener is not actually to grow plants but to "cultivate healthy soil." From healthy soil comes healthy plants. From healthy soil comes the right plants for that time and place, with the proper nutrients, and that soil ecosystem can be cultivated over hundreds of years.

The second lesson in Zen and in farming is to focus on process over product. This means to focus not on what we do but how we do it. When the focus is on healthy soil, all beings are benefited, from the soil microorganisms to the beneficial insects and pollinator species to the water source and air of the region to the human being who is harvesting. This is the wisdom of traditional agriculture, and this is the wisdom that has been dishonored by conventional farming.

A conventional farmer approaches agriculture with the mission of growing "the most, the fastest, and the cheapest." The ramifications of this approach can be seen everywhere in our failing food system from the poor nutrient levels of food grown in depleted soil to soil loss to the outrageous increase in pesticide use since World War II.

On a personal level, when we approach life with an agenda to achieve "the most, the fastest, and the cheapest," we justify abandoning ourselves, abusing our bodies, and disobeying our natural feedback system. As I learned to pay attention and serve the garden, I became more curious about how I approached my own life with agenda as well.

When our life focus is outward and on product, we fail to ask important questions, such as "How can I apply myself in the brief time I am here to becoming the most vital, healthy, resilient, and kind presence that I can be? How can I create the soil within that is necessary to live a good human life? How can I create within myself the capacity to meet the natural ups and downs of life from wisdom? How can I take the next step with compassion and trust what emerges from that step? How can I release the illusion of a separate self and reclaim the interconnection that is my birthright?"

The questions for the organic gardener and land steward and the questions of the Zen practitioner are essentially the same: "How can we get out of the way and allow life to find its natural, organic expression? How can we choose that which is life-affirming over that which supports depletion and violence?" "What points to compassion and what points away from compassion?" is always the primary question for us to hold. This question provides the context for every endeavor that we approach in life.

Nature knows how to make life on planet Earth work. Nature's ecosystems are self-organizing, adapting, and resilient, and operate through cooperation, communication, and network-building. It is possible to work with nature to cause the least amount of harm and keep the larger picture in mind. It is possible to approach every act aware of our impact on the whole. Through farming I learned that the joy that comes from a focus on process is far greater than the joy that comes from attaining product and imposing my own agenda onto life.

Our time here is measured; when we understand that our actions are not to be taken casually, we see the greater opportunity for cultivating compassionate process—step by step through our actions in our lifetime. In the words of Japanese farmer/visionary Masanobu Fukuoka,

> When it is understood that one loses joy and happiness in the attempt to possess them, the essence of natural farming will be realized. The ultimate goal of farming is not the growing of crops, but the cultivation and perfection of human beings.

The Deeper Teaching of Working with Nature

My actions are my only true belongings.
—Thich Nhat Hanh

Most of us have grown up in a world where we turn on the tap and receive as much water as we want to consume; we flip a switch and get all the electricity we need; and we have access to multiple kinds of food products at the market, with no connection to where that food might come from. Most of us have a category in our mind for spending "time in nature" rather than living our lives immersed in the nature of everyday life.

The impact of this lifestyle separate from nature includes:

- isolation and a sense of emptiness that many people are not even aware of
- a disconnection from the principles of sustainability and a lack of understanding in how to live harmoniously with the living systems of our planet.
- a human-centric approach to life, where people are desensitized to the inherent value of the natural world beyond providing for our needs
- an attitude of "power over, conquer, colonize, dominate, and control nature" that pervades everything from land

use policies to how we treat insects in our homes and gardens
- a modern lifestyle, built environment, and products that reflect economic interests rather than support the well-being of both the human species and of the planet
- a misalignment between our hearts and our collectively accepted lifestyle
- guilt over being part of a species that has caused so much harm to our planet

To participate in a lifestyle that poisons and depletes our own shared resources impacts us deeply. Even if it is subconscious we feel pain when we disregard mother nature. It is not possible to wake up from our sleep without recognizing our innate oneness with every form of life we encounter. It is not possible to find wholeness within ourselves without taking responsibility for how we treat our planet. There is no point in any pursuit of enlightenment today without addressing this challenge.

Nature Can Hold Us Accountable

Living in sustainable community for years, whether I was in an eco-village in the desert or at the monastery in the foothills, I was aware of the accountability my environment held me to. We always had only a measured amount of water to use, so that is what we used. Because we lived by solar energy, we turned off the lights at dusk. We grew our own food and used the resources of the land to feed our gardens. We made do with what we had, yet experienced what felt like tremendous abundance. I found great delight in being able to live so simply, with so few resources—yet to experience such abundance. This abundance came from an experience of true sufficiency, being perfectly content with exactly what we had, free of the thought that "something is missing." We did not need anything "more" or "different."

My years living on the land taught me invaluable lessons about how easy it is to have my human needs met by living simply and embracing the spirit of sufficiency. Living on the land allowed me to let go of my attachment to the human sphere and recall from deep within a greater consciousness than human-centrism.

The experience of putting my bare hands into the layer of topsoil every day, being intimate with the insect, animal, and plant life on the land on which I lived, and spending time immersed in the elements was my greatest ally in learning to trust the purity of my existence free of story. The nourishment of the elements gave me so much satisfaction that the lull of the conditioned mind finally became less interesting. My hunger for story gradually diminished as my soul's thirst to be awake was met through deeper connection with all of life around me.

When we become more present to the world around us, there is no confusion about what is real and what is not, what matters and what does not. There is no confusion about interconnection or our willingness to protect and steward the earth. There is also no confusion about the fact that we require a lot less to live in abundance than we think.

Relational Mindfulness invites us to bring more reverence and curiosity to how we relate. It invites us to learn to interact with a forest landscape or a honeybee through deep listening rather than imposing the assumption of separation. It invites us to engage in the world we live in with a more attentive and sensory-based awareness. It also invites us to meet the natural world and choose to relate to our resources from a place of oneness.

Even living in an urban environment, there are endless ways to live a more earth-honoring paradigm. It is much easier than we think to align our lifestyle with the spirit of sufficiency and sustainability. Here are encouragements for connecting with the earth more in any environment:

- Take on sustainable living as a spiritual practice and discipline; this empowering act dramatically increases one's embodiment of interconnection.
- Bring awareness to your use of water, energy, and resources each day.
- Actively express your gratitude for the natural world and the resources you use each day, whether you live in the countryside or in an urban environment.
- When the weather allows, practice walking meditation barefoot rather than in shoes.
- For a period of time give up the consumption of something that you normally do not question having.
- Be aware of the thoughts that lead you to wanting "more, different, and better."
- Question the assumption that you need to buy a food or product that does not support sustainability.

Reconnecting to Nature as Ally, Equal, and Partner

The most vital way to nourish essence is by spending time in the natural world. I have never met anyone whose heart does not soften when they take time for nature. I have never met anyone who does not benefit from fresh air, green trees, and the sound of running water. Doing so helps us to remember our deep sense of belonging. The more we inhabit an artificial environment, one that both requires and relies upon the consumer mentality, the less we feel connected to essence, and the smaller our perspective becomes.

As balm to the modern world and its demands, its technologies, its sense of urgency, our minds need time in that suspended state of fascination that nature avails to us, becoming aware not so much of our thoughts but of our animal bodies, sounds and color, leaves and light, and time to experience our sensory connection with it all. The natural world reconnects us to the spaciousness within.

The human sphere is changing faster than it ever has in the history of humanity, so this is, in fact, the time to ground ourselves in a consciousness that it is deeper than this ever-altering landscape. If we do not ground ourselves in relational immersion in life as we continue to rapidly evolve our technological capacity, I fear that we will become more and more disconnected from actual reality. The human sphere is not the only sphere. We are made whole by realizing our relationship with the biosphere. It is time to integrate the practice of relational immersion in life into our culture as modern human beings. It is not enough to engage with the nature world through a screen. It is vital that we relearn to relate through our senses.

What Partnership with Nature Is

> You are not an observer, you are a participant.
>
> —Thich Nhat Hanh

It is springtime in Ojai, and I am out with my partner, a flower essence therapist, who is seeking new flowers to make medicine from. We begin our trek by greeting the land, sharing our intention, and walking in silence along the path. Weaving through forests of manzanita and chaparral, I am struck by how engaged and attentive he is to the landscape. I see this both in the lightness of his footsteps and the rhythm with which he moves, as if he is in a deep meditation. We are aware of the individual plants we pass, our physical bodies as we move, and the animals and insects that dwell on this land.

From time to time we pause to observe something in our path, but generally our focus is spacious, beholding the entire landscape around us. At some point, as if we've had the same intuition, we turn down a smaller path, which leads us to a rare yellow violet. We sit down beside this plant and approach it with gentleness, asking for permission before trimming off only a few petals, which we place in a glass bowl of water in the sunlight to alchemize while we go to rest in the shade. We return three hours later and, after meditating beside the plant, we each taste the medicine and "sense into" our response. We each notice strong sensations in our throat and in our heart and sense that this plant is about unblocking communication. Later, we research this flower further and find out that it is traditionally used for relieving communication blocks and for giving people the courage to speak from authenticity. Although this flower has been written about by other practitioners, my partner will continue to spend months and even years investigating it experientially and taking the essence himself so that he can observe, listen, and sense into its entire healing properties. He will take as much time as needed to listen deeply as the plant communicates its healing properties.

I share this story to make a point. There is nothing new about the notion that we have a far greater capacity for communication and partnership with the natural world than we have been tapping into. There is actually nothing esoteric about the foundational understanding that we are a part of, not separate from, nature. There is nothing radical about the notion that we might learn to coexist as equals with the natural world around us rather than in a relationship of domination/subordination. Many indigenous land-based cultures have been modeling this for thousands of years. But it is time to remember this capacity within us. What is radical is the possibility that humans are ready to set down our egos and domineering approach with nature to learn what it actually means to live in co-creative partnership with nature.

Giving Our Pain to the Earth and Releasing Isolation

> Because the relationship between self and world is reciprocal, it is not a matter of first getting enlightened or saved and then acting. As we work to heal the Earth, the Earth heals us. No need to wait. As we care enough to take risks, we loosen the grip of ego and begin to come home to our true nature.
>
> —Joanna Macy

At the end of every workday I have a ritual: I acknowledge the purity of intention my heart has brought to the day, regardless of life's ups and downs, and I let go. I acknowledge everything that has gone on that day and imagine that I am giving it back to the earth. I feel my whole body relax. I surrender my concerns about the human sphere or the outcome of my efforts on that day, and give it to the earth. I imagine the earth composting the happenings of the day and working its magic. This helps me to step back into the bigger picture, knowing that life is supporting me and inviting life to support me. In this way, I acknowledge my right place in the bigger scheme of things. This helps me to remain humbled, to trust the bigger picture, and to allow myself to feel fully supported by life.

The most famous story about Shakyamuni Buddha is the story of his enlightenment under the Bodhi Tree in Bodghaya. As the Buddha sat in meditation, committed to seeing beyond and through the tangled confusion of the human mind that he knew caused all human suffering, Mara, the spirit of suffering, showed up to challenge him.

First, Mara tormented him with every fear and anxiety-inducing image and thought she could muster. The Buddha sat in stillness and well-being and did not budge. Then Mara brought on hatred. The Buddha did not budge. Finally, Mara brought on lust. The Buddha did not budge.

Enraged that the Buddha was not responding to the same cues for suffering that Mara used to torment all of humanity, Mara finally exclaimed, "Who are you? By what authority do you disobey me? By what authority do you access clarity, no matter what I throw your way?"

The Buddha responded by taking the palm of his hand and placing it on the bare earth: "By the authority of the earth."

This story is significant on so many levels for us today. So often we think we are alone, isolated in our illusion of separate self. We easily get discouraged and think that we do not have the power it takes to end our own suffering or to make a difference in the world. So often we forget that we are supported by the entire planet and all of the life it contains. The Buddha reminds us that ultimately our power is the shared power of interconnection. The Buddha reminds us that we have access to all of the resources, medicine, and power the Earth manifests, far beyond the illusion of isolation. At this time in history, when we have reached a peak of imbalance within ourselves and as a species, it serves us to remember our larger identity as one with the living systems of our planet. I believe that every physical act we take to affirm our oneness with the planet returns us to wholeness. We cannot do the work we need to do if we perceive ourselves as alone or separate.

· · · · · · · · **Mindful Inquiry** · · · · · · · ·

How much time do you allow yourself to spend in nature?

In what ways do you allow your lifestyle choices to honor the natural world?

How are you living ecologically and/or sustainably? How are you not?

What gets in the way? What do you tell yourself to justify the ways you are not?

In what ways do you focus on product over process?

How do you cultivate healthy soil in the inner garden? What is the impact of this? How do you take shortcuts or make choices for short-term gain?

If you were to trust that your actions make a difference, are there any actions you would take to live with even more ecological responsibility?

· · · · · · · · **Daily Practice** · · · · · · ·

RELATIONAL IMMERSION IN LIFE

Today, notice all of the moments you are reminded by nature and through your senses, of living in interconnection, perhaps through

- the food you eat
- the resources you use
- the elements you interact with: water, wind, sun, and earth
- people, animals, insects, and plants

Bring awareness to how often you are caught up solely in the human sphere and how often you experience yourself as a part of the earth.

13

Natural Beauty

Seeing with a Clear Mind

The question is not what you look at, but what you see.

—Henry David Thoreau

Stop a moment, cease your work, and look around you. The eyes are not responsible when the mind does the seeing.

—Thomas Carlyle

Finding Beauty Where You Least Expect It

When I was a monk, we lived simply and in silence, surrounded by 350 acres of pine trees, meadows, and breathtaking views of the Western Sierra mountain range. This environment allowed us to focus within and to continually develop our receptivity to the world we inhabited and the quality of presence we chose to cultivate within it.

As a nature lover, living this simple life was not new for me, and I was thrilled to be surrounded by countryside. I lived in a tiny hut (a hermitage) about a fifteen-minute walk from the monastery proper and a short hike to a creek. It was typical for me to see wild animals—bobcats, raccoons, snakes, deer, and even mountain lions. As much as I loved being in the wild, I had an experience my first week at the monastery that reminded me that it didn't actually matter where I was living, if I was not residing there in the present moment.

It was early spring and I was on a hike through the pine forest. As I made my way through the wilderness, I caught myself in a mind game that consisted of an ongoing dialogue with myself: "What is the next best thing to see? . . . The next most exquisite view? . . . The next most colorful patch of spring flowers? . . . The next pause where the forest opens up to a breathtaking meadow? . . . The sudden appearance of a deer or other wild animal?" I found myself alone in the woods, in complete and utter solitude, playing the "next best thing" game. I realized that I participated in this mind game quite regularly, and in a moment of clarity, I acknowledged that this was depriving me of the entirety of the forest experience.

While caught up in this activity, this dialogue within my mind, I was distracted from all the beauty around me. By fixating on the anticipation of "the next best thing," I was missing countless moments of beauty right in front of me. At that moment in time, I stopped, took in a deep long breath, and looked around with open eyes and a receptive gaze. I saw, as if for the first time, the subtle shades of color in a tree, the lichen on the ground at my feet, the perfection of a patch of twigs decomposing into powdery carbon, the precision of the design of star thistle leaves at a tree's base, and the intricate pollination of its flowers by pterodactyl-like insects.

As I slowly took in this natural beauty, I began to feel my entire body relax and settle into gravity and my senses become more alive. I let go of the subtle urgency that had been gnawing at me, unconsciously driving me forward through the forest. And as if remembering from somewhere deep inside the wholeness that is always there, I felt myself become fully present.

How often do we miss the beauty of the world around us because our attention is focused elsewhere? In what ways does our internal dialogue seeking something "better" in the future or romanticizing the past distract us from enjoying the moment right now? More personally, how often do we overlook the unique beauty in ourselves at any moment?

The forest helped me to realize that by fixating on "the next best thing" I might encounter in my trek through the woods, I was not able to see the beauty around me. Going forward, I changed the game. I began to practice what I call authentic seeing, looking for the sake of present moment observation, lingering long enough to take in something fully and savor it, long enough to begin to recognize and appreciate the extraordinary subtleties that I had been missing.

Over time, this new way of being caused a shift in every aspect of my life. I became much more attuned to seeing the beauty in ordinary moments. I realized that beauty is a process, a way of being that has everything to do with the lens through which we perceive it and the quality of attention that we give to it. I began to understand my responsibility to ensure that this lens is one of presence and receptivity rather than of conditioned judgment.

Most of us spend a great deal of time conversing in our minds about what we are seeing, while paying little attention to the actual sensory experience of seeing. This applies to each of our senses. When we are attending to the dialogue in our heads, we are not paying attention to our actual experience of tasting, listening, smelling, feeling, or seeing.

My experience in the forest that day began an inquiry into the nature of beauty and the power of seeing with an attentive and clear mind. By focusing on anticipation, internal conversation, and "what comes next," we can miss out entirely on the here and now. When we focus our attention and energy to internal conversation, we deprive our sensory experience of and receptivity to life in the present. In the words of Zen teacher Cheri Huber, "Nothing happens next. Everything happens now."

Beauty as Process

> The real voyage of discovery consists not in seeking new landscapes but in having new eyes.
>
> —Marcel Proust

We have been fed so many ideas about what is "beautiful" and what is "ugly" through today's mass-media culture that we no longer rely on our own direct experience. We may notice that it's gray outside and immediately label the day as "dreary"— ignoring the beauty of the dark clouds and the interplay of light in the skies that signals a coming storm. We immediately toss a bouquet of dying flowers without appreciating the natural beauty of their decay. As passive consumers, we have been trained incessantly to impose a learned perception of beauty onto the world, rather than to see through the lens of innocence. As a result, we are much less receptive to the beauty animating life in every moment.

Years ago, I had the opportunity to travel twice to a small, poor, and mostly undeveloped island in the Caribbean. The island is a colorful patchwork blend of untouched wilderness and small villages, wealth and poverty coexisting, sparkling blue waters and marine life, and a cacophony of birds and insects singing throughout the night. There are no streetlights and no supermarkets. The island carries its own rhythm and deadlines do not exist. When I am there, it is as if I have been transported to another time.

On my first visit, housesitting for a year-round resident, my travel partner and I followed a daily ritual: We woke early, packed some fruit and our snorkel gear, and explored the island's terrain—taking our time to discover its trails, the coral reefs, small herds of horses that roam the island freely, and coves where the turtles have lived for generations. We explored the island with no agenda other than curiosity—its lagoons and hilltops, the rough thickets you walk through to get to private beaches, the beautiful haciendas of the wealthy, and the poorer neighborhoods.

We ate the local diet, enjoyed traditional tastes, and engaged with island life fully. We were open to whatever the island had to offer each day and met each experience with wonder. We approached the island as we would approach a lover: taking our time, lingering, open, and playful, in touch with our creature selves. Nature's beauty was free, and there was little money transacted as we joyfully explored this wondrous place.

Because we immersed relationally with the island, we had profound experiences with the natural world and were able to fully appreciate the many miracles in the tide, the wind, the weather, the plant life, and the animals.

On my return to the island to housesit once again a couple of years later, I experienced the island in a completely different way. A friend invited me one day to spend time at a newly opened, world-class luxury resort. The weather was the definition of perfection, and I settled onto a batik cushion on the hotel's veranda, overlooking a scene of blue-gray ocean, flowering flamboyant trees with scarlet flowers, tropical orchids, and pristine blue sky scattered with patterned clouds. Pleasant music played and ice water laced with oranges and limes marinated in a glass vessel nearby. This was a stunning environment—calm, peaceful, fresh air, with the ocean in front of me—and I began work on a writing project.

As I sat amid all of this beauty and pleasure, however, I could not help but notice that this form of beauty had been imposed onto the island, rather than allowing the resort to celebrate the island's natural state. While it was a visually attractive scene, the resort was a perfect example of a passive consumer approach to the travel experience.

I noticed baskets of shiny red apples shipped in from abroad, although mangoes, papaya, and guanabanas grow seasonally and in abundance right on the island. I could not escape the subtle chemical smell each time I sank into the fashionable new lounge cushions, nor could I ignore the plastic cups that drinks at the pool were often served in. At noon each day, when the sun was high and evaporation the greatest, the resort's expansive green lawns—turf ferried in from the mainland—were sprayed with hundreds of gallons of water.

The discomfort I felt on the island that day was at core a sense of sadness that the existing wilderness and beauty, which I had explored with so much wonder before, did not meet the standards for the international traveler; it therefore needed to be manipulated and manicured, mowed and sprayed, in order to match a fabricated image of paradise. I think the overall discomfort that I felt at this resort is what everyone feels on some level when we are honest with ourselves and brave enough to acknowledge the collective denial that pervades our culture.

This is not, by the way, to say that people should not visit resorts if that is what brings them joy. It is helpful to remember, however, that we always have a choice to see the beauty in a place or person as they actually are. Beauty is a process, and it is vital to know the difference between being presented with a standard of beauty based on our expectations (the passive consumer mode) and actually seeing and sensing with mindful awareness the world we inhabit. This is true whether we are at a beachside resort or in our own backyard. In other words, paying attention to our inner landscape determines how we experience beauty. In the words of author Joseph Clinton Pearce, "Seeing within changes one's outer vision."

As sensitivity deepens, individually and as a culture, we can no longer ignore the chemical taste in plastic bottled water or the toxins in nail polish or flowers stripped from the rainforest and shipped in from overseas. We lose interest in wearing gems that have been obtained through violent means from abroad or purchasing beauty products that are proven toxic to both humans and the animals they are tested on. This certainly poses a challenge to us all, as our economy does not support quality over quantity—yet it is important to remember that we can choose where we use our money.

There is often a disconnect between the inner reality and the outer presentation of beauty in mainstream society. It is both a gift and a curse of awareness practice that we can no longer ignore such contrasts. The more we impose made-up standards and expectations onto a landscape (or person or experience), the weaker becomes our ability to recognize the beauty of ordinary moments. Society has rigid standards for, and very specific definitions of, beauty—both personal and environmental. These standards are both a symptom and a cause of our disconnect from nature. As we learn to immerse in life more relationally, the lens through which we are seeing softens and emerges from judgment into kindness. We remember that beauty is who we are and what exists around us. The missing piece is to pay attention to life as it is and to do so with an open heart.

The more we develop awareness and the ability to be with "life as it is," the less inclined we are to manipulate our experiences. We are able to see from our hearts, rather than from our minds, and our hearts see the world around us nondualistically.

The Heart Sees Nondual Beauty

The mind of separation views everything through duality: right/wrong, positive/negative, beautiful/ugly. One of the cogs in the engine of duality is the habit of taking things personally. Taking things personally not only leads to reactivity but also impairs our perception of what we see. For instance, we can view another person's garden and enjoy the perfection of its design, colors, and shapes; but when we look out at our own garden, we often find something wrong—a weed we forgot to pull or a plant that needs more attention. We perceive silver strands of hair on someone else with appreciation, but we view our own silver hairs with despair at growing old. In other words, we take it personally.

On meditation retreat, participants are invited to practice *not* taking life personally and experiencing the clear seeing of an open heart. When we experience the moment with clarity, we open ourselves up to the inherent beauty of life. The conditioned mind prevents us from perceiving beauty in particular settings, particularly those in which we take things personally. When we experience life without taking it personally, we can see the beauty in all things and in every moment. This applies to an environment or landscape, to our emotions and experiences, and to all phenomena.

Seeing Clearly through Commercial Distortion

In this day and age, the market economy exerts a forceful dominant imposition on the human psyche and disposition. People are encouraged to abandon and ignore their own beauty and aesthetic sense and adopt whatever the official dictate is at the moment about what is beautiful. We receive a barrage of messages and images every day promoting beauty trends, when in reality there exists as much diversity in aesthetic preference as there is diversity in people.

I believe that this is part of the deep conflict between our souls within and the dominant paradigm. When one's perception and sensory responses are soured by a dominant paradigm, it is possible to deny one's own sense of beauty. People inhabit spaces that are aesthetically oppressive to them. People wear clothing that is aesthetically or texturally oppressive to them. They resign themselves to landscapes that are utilitarian rather than inspiring or nurturing.

There is a trend today of environments that perpetuate alienation rather than nurture connection. There is an almost intentional ugliness in the world of design that our creature selves would not respond to without subtle indoctrination from the dominant culture. But beauty is not a human frivolity. It is a basic human need. Being driven by market forces to follow the approved aesthetic of beauty is perceived as moral superiority.

When we are present to that which is innately beautiful to each of us, our well-being is affirmed. Our nervous system relaxes. When humans become disconnected from their organic relationship to beauty, people's will to live erodes. An aching hunger develops for beauty—from within and from without.

Designing with Nature

Relational Mindfulness is about taking responsibility on the part of the individual to untangle the knots in our collective perception. There is opportunity to dismantle the conditioning that impedes our ability to see and know true beauty, and that keeps us from feeling supported by the beauty of the world in which we live. This beauty is available to us in every moment that we are willing to stay present. Our impetus to protect life on this planet is dependent on our bone-deep knowing and recognition of the beauty of the natural world.

> Beauty saves. Beauty heals. Beauty motivates. Beauty unites. Beauty returns us to our origins, and here lies the ultimate act of saving, of healing, of overcoming individualism.
>
> —Matthew Fox

• • • • • • • • Mindful Inquiry • • • • • • • •

A WRITING EXERCISE

Uncovering Our Beliefs and Assumptions about Beauty

Most of us do not question our assumptions about beauty. We are unaware of how often we are seeing life through the filter of conditioning, opinions, likes and dislikes, rather than through the vast lens of nondual or interconnected awareness. In this exercise you are invited to simply bring awareness to your habitual relationship with beauty in ordinary daily life. There is no agenda for this exercise other than awareness and illumination. Write down the first thing that comes to you, without doing any editing.

A beautiful day is _____. An ugly day is _____.

A beautiful environment is _____. An ugly environment is _____.

Attractiveness (in yourself or others) is _____. Unattractiveness (in yourself or others) is _____.

You have been taught that beauty is _____.

In order to be beautiful you _____.

What would you change about yourself or your surroundings to make them more beautiful?

An emotion you find beautiful is _____. An emotional state you find ugly is _____.

In your day-to-day life you experience beauty through _____.

The current conversation your mind tends to have around beauty is _____.

If ever you've made a purchase in the name of beautification (of self or environment) that was not in alignment with your values, it was _____.

The last time you were surprised by beauty was _____.

Does the habit of "taking things personally" get in your way of seeing beauty in the people or world around you, or in yourself? How?

• • • • • • • • **Daily Practice** • • • • • • • •

This is a simple practice for cultivating authentic seeing. There are further mindfulness exercises for going deeper offered in the appendix.

Today, pause, in an ordinary place and ordinary moment, to turn within and connect with your breath. Feel the breath moving in and out of your body and notice the sensation of the air touching your skin.

Then, soften your gaze and take a couple of minutes to fully take in what you see in front of you, without needing to label or assess. Take in the colors . . . shapes . . . tone . . light . . . and shadow in what is in front of you.

Just allow yourself to receive in this visual meditation. Continue to be aware of your breath and to meet your sensory experience with curiosity.

There is no goal to this practice other than seeing what is in front of you and softening the mind of judgment.

What do you notice?

14

Conscious Consumption

The Radical Art of Satisfaction

To know sufficiency—the place of no more, no less needed—is to know freedom.

As a monk, I owned two pairs of shoes and three pairs of pants. One pair of pants was for sitting meditation and two were for working meditation. I gave away my belongings when I moved into the monastery—and I did not earn an income for the entire time that I was there. I had chosen to live a nonmaterialistic lifestyle throughout my adult life up to that point, but letting go completely of the habit of needing "stuff" felt cleansing at an even deeper level than I had experienced before. I became keenly aware of how much that I carried around was unnecessary and even energy-draining. My "stuff" had also served to help maintain my identity out in the world—but was no longer necessary as a monk. It was a profound privilege to finally let go of the extraneous in order to experience the deeper satisfaction of simplicity.

Monastic training allowed me to let go entirely of the notion that I needed anything nonessential from "out there." My training was about stepping beyond my limited and narrow definitions of self and dissolving boundaries to oneness with life. As a monk, I received the deep satisfaction of living simply, in the moment, and free of the story that I needed something "more, different, or better." I was invited to know myself through the consciousness of "We," intimately connected with myself, with community, and with the natural elements. I ate whatever food was served each day, and my basic needs were met, which allowed me to focus on spiritual work.

Meditating and working outside every day, my cheeks were always rosy, I felt fully alive, and my breath flowed easily. Even at times when I felt challenged, there was a baseline of spiritual well-being. I learned that to invest in this spiritual well-being was the most important use of my life force.

The Transition to Los Angeles

Leaving the monastery and making the transition to being a layperson, my material world changed by necessity. There were so many things—from gas, to clothing, to store-bought foods—that felt compromising to my simple living approach. I was no longer just a monk, but now played roles that included business owner, writer/author, car owner/driver, taxpayer, renter of a home, employee, family member, gardener, and woman in my early thirties dating and attempting to have a social life. It was a different experience entirely.

As a monk, even when purchases were made on my behalf, they were always aligned with my heart. I could always find companies to support that I believed in. Living in Los Angeles, consumption became more complicated. I had no interest in a cell phone, but then I gave in. Eventually I needed a computer and then a printer and then a new jacket and then a suitcase. In order to live in the city and sustain well-being, I found that I needed supplements to support my diet, an assistant so I had time to rest, and different forms of body care to recover from the stress and intensity of sometimes hectic city life.

There was no turning back. Today I continue to live very simply in comparison with most, but I also enjoy the material world, and my partner, who only owns two pairs of shoes himself, would say that the seven pairs of shoes I own are now too many.

In retrospect, thinking about my return to the modern world, what struck me most at the time was that it seemed to offer every choice but the choice of real satisfaction. The modern world we live in today, for example, offers us a million colorful options and variations for every product, creating an illusion of wealth, but it never offers the deep satisfaction that comes from simplicity or sufficiency.

Relational Mindfulness invites us to reclaim our personal authority in the choices we make, rather than blindly following collective habits. It invites us to bring the same care to how we consume resources and products as to how we consume thoughts and participate in our relationships. Relational Mindfulness invites us to look at our personal conditioning around consumption, as well as our collective distortions in this realm.

Shopping Meditation

I arrived in Los Angeles in late November just as the holiday season began, and by my second week back, I felt overwhelmed by the frivolous consumption around me. My mother asked me to visit a shopping mall to pick up a gift for my five-year-old niece, and I was mortified by her request. I felt a strong distaste for malls. Despite my resistance, I drove to the mall and immediately found an empty bench to sit on. I then spent twenty minutes sitting in meditation, but with my eyes open, taking in all of the sensory inputs, sounds, and smells. As I observed people shopping, I slowly felt myself settling into the stillness and curiosity of my meditation practice. I then began a walking meditation across the mall, moving slowly but not so slow as to draw attention to myself. I stayed in full contact with the sensations in my feet and body and the experience of the world around me, while I moved through various stores. I held a soft gaze and just took in color, shape, and the sensory experience of each moment in the way I would in meditation. I allowed myself to take everything in through relaxed spacious awareness without needing to label anything or assess. I allowed myself to simply notice sensation, emotion, sound, and mind, the same way I would in mindful eating practice (see the exercise at the end of this chapter). In so doing, I found that I was able to keep my attention fully within while immersed in one of the most distracting, disturbing, and synthetic environments I could think of—a shopping mall!

Meditating in this way was a powerfully grounding experience for me. It was in a sense a rite of passage in which I saw how easy it was to find peace in an over-consumptive environment that triggered deep emotions within me. This experience helped me to affirm my intention as a conscious consumer. I decided that from there on out, when I did need to shop, I would do so in this way, as a sensory-based meditation. This choice not only helped me to stay clear of conditioning when I had to make purchases, but it also put me much more in touch with my intuition and inner guidance. Facing choices about what to buy, whether it was clothing or supplements, shopping as a mindfulness exercise became just another means of maintaining presence and allowing my inner guidance to direct me, and surprise me sometimes in the process.

The Role of Media and the Myth of Inadequacy

Consumption has to do with how we take—as well as what we take in, how much we take, and why we take. We make a thousand tiny choices each day about what and how we take, what and how we buy, what we eat and how much, and how we decide what is enough. There is great significance—spiritual, environmental, social, and political—in how we consume. Moment by moment, we are consuming either in ways that are life-affirming or not. We are making choices either from our hearts and sense of adequacy and sufficiency or from our conditioning and sense of inadequacy.

We are a disposable society, taught to abandon what we have at this moment and to want something more. The messages of "not enough" weigh deep on our psyches. From the belief that we are inadequate as we are and that there is a product or experience "out there" that can improve us, we make unconscious choices about what to buy to fill the gap. We might make the choice to smoke a cigarette or buy a piece of clothing we will never wear or consume a box of candy we regret. We might even make a major purchase unconsciously, like a car that we cannot actually afford.

The perception of inadequacy is held together by the mind habit of comparison. "Look what he/she has over there." "Look how much better off that person is than me. I want that." According to our minds, there are always people with more money, better looks, better bodies, better careers, and more happiness. We even project that people are more "enlightened" than we are and that if we could achieve that same enlightenment, then we would feel better about ourselves inside.

Our economy is built on the collective belief in inadequacy. We are fed the message that we continually need "more, better, new, and different." The media, TV, and social media support these patterns of aggressive market manipulation. When I turn on TV, I see a completely faux world being presented as reality. This faux world is most often a monoculture—primarily white privileged people of a certain age range, with good looks, nice cars, and makeup, who wake up with smiles on their faces and participate happily in the consumer world. "As long as I look good, I can pretend I'm not feeling bad or inadequate" is the story we tell ourselves. Despite how we are feeling, we try to prop up an image that we and others hope to see of ourselves. I have had students confide in me that even in dark painful times in life, upon waking up in the morning they post a photo on Facebook first thing to try to maintain their participation in the "happy world" they seem to think everyone else is participating in based on what they see on Facebook and other social media.

The Real Satisfaction That Comes from Sufficiency

We have come to misinterpret abundance as a continual state of fullness and excess that happy and successful people maintain. We are not taught the value and meaning of sufficiency. We see abundance as a farmers market table packed full with fresh peaches all of the time. We are drawn to things that are packaged to appeal to a part of us that values all things "shiny and bright." When we examine such packaged items more closely, however, we can't help but sometimes notice the subtle smell of rot. In other words, if we have too many ripe peaches all at once, we can't process them and they begin to decay.

The misunderstanding of affluence as "more is better" prevents us from seeing the goodness of what is just so—not too little and not too much, but sufficient. In a world of oppressive consumption, where everywhere we go and much of what we see and hear are geared to making us want more, real wealth lies in finding the freedom of sufficiency.

Sufficiency is the place of freedom from wanting and excess. As we are wildly divergent in our needs, what is sufficient for each person varies, but the joy that we each find when we come into sufficiency is the goal of mindful consumption. Finding this for ourselves is the practice. It cannot come from being preached to or feeling that it is morally correct to have a certain amount of stuff. It cannot come from measuring against those who have more or less. It can only come from listening to our authentic self and making a fresh choice beyond collective judgment.

To want that which we have is a subversive act. To remember that we are enough is revolutionary. To have a mindful relationship with consumption is a gift. Not only to ourselves—as it feeds our sense of peace, integrity, discipline, and well-being—but also to our world. To partake is defined as how we participate, and one of the antidotes to unconscious consumption or "taking" is engaged participation with life.

Mindful consumption goes way beyond the things that we buy or how much food we eat. Cultivating mindful consumption is an exploration of how we relate to what we "take in." This conscious discernment serves us across the board—in every aspect of our lives.

Conscious discernment enables us to avail ourselves of the radical art of "living in satisfaction." We learn to dwell in satisfaction and hence to enjoy our lives more deeply, rather than having our satisfaction tied in to what we consume. Part of the purpose of this book is to look deeply, candidly, and compassionately at the spiritual impact that participating in the passive consumer world has on the human soul and psyche.

Today to be a conscious consumer and not cause harm in a world completely built on the foundation of consumption requires devotion and discernment. There is a lot of pressure in conscious circles to be a mindful consumer because it is the "good person" thing to do. I do not believe that this motivation is helpful. I do not believe that people make a real shift in their approach to consumption until they see clearly in their hearts the spiritual ramifications of a passive consumer way of being.

What if we chose to remember, every day, that we are enough?

What if we did not engage the barrage of messages that we are not adequate as we are?

What if we were taught to want exactly what we have and to savor it?

What would happen if we realized that pure satisfaction comes from the spaciousness within that we only find when we stop filling ourselves and allow ourselves to "be"?

What if we were taught to remember that we have access—twenty-four hours a day—to the undeniable well-being that comes from dwelling in present moment awareness?

Are Our Real Needs Being Met?

When I was growing up, I spent a substantial amount of time in LA's Skid Row where my mother started a center for marginalized youth. I was always struck by how people found the courage to survive the dire conditions in which they lived and what they sometimes had to do to get by. Imagine that you are a child living in an inner-city ghetto—hungry, cold, and alone—and a junkie in an alley offers you really good drugs for free. You would probably say yes and take them, because you know that they will help you temporarily escape the bad feelings that come from your most basic needs not being met. When our basic and fundamental needs are not met (physically, emotionally, and spiritually), then it is no surprise that we turn metaphorically to a junkie for solace—to such distractions as alcohol, nicotine, drugs, food, shopping, porn, toxic relationships, or frenetic exercise. We respond in this way when we do not have access to the real nutrients that we need for well-being and wholeness.

We also turn to the junkie of the conditioned mind. We are more susceptible to fear-based and unhelpful thoughts. When we see the connection between being a passive consumer in society and the passive consumerism of the conditioned mind, our practice has an opportunity to deepen quickly. We see more clearly, and with compassion, the child within us who feels unsupported, and we find the willingness to step in and save that child. We see the opportunity to say no to our conditioned mind, and the authentic power that we experience through this choice can extend out into how we engage with our world at large.

The Global Impact of Over-Consumption and Its Impact on Us

We are all aware of the environmental ramifications of over-consumption on the planet. The extent of the degradation and depletion of our resources is both astounding and absurd. It's difficult sometimes to even take in such devastating information.

How do we digest, for example, the fact that our culture has contributed to half of the world's forests disappearing? What do we do with this other than put a (reused!) bag over our heads and feel guilty and depressed? What I find helpful instead is to ask, "How can I receive this information from an open and grounded heart—holding space for both profound grief and unconditional love and acceptance?"

When we respond to the destruction of our planet from the heart rather than the head, we commit to not participating in the unfolding tragedy. We realize that our most basic choices as consumers carry weight. What if learning to not be passive consumers to the human mind were the key required for a larger sustainability? In other words, what might be the global impact if we committed to applying this knowledge to our personal lives?

The Human Impact of Passive Consumerism

Beyond the global impact of over-consumption on our world, let's examine the impact of over-consumption on ourselves. Often some (or all) of the following might apply:

- Guilt
- Shame
- Powerlessness
- Teaching ourselves that our actions don't matter
- Training ourselves to turn away from what is hard and escape through consumption
- Knowing on some deep heartbreaking level that we are active participants in a global economic/consumption model that is harming the planet
- Teaching ourselves to turn to externals rather than turn within
- Teaching ourselves that we are not in control
- Feeding the notion that we need more than we do, that there is lack within
- Feeding the notion that "it's too hard" to live in alignment with sustainability
- Feeding the misconception that we cannot be satisfied without consuming
- A sense of resignation about how our cultural life is set up
- Acting with carelessness, which feels bad deep inside

Renunciation and Voluntary Simplicity

In Buddhist practice, renunciation plays a big role. While I was a monk, renunciation meant not owning anything, cutting off my hair, and not participating in any activity that might cause harm. Now, as layperson, renunciation means being willing to let go of anything that takes me away from spiritual freedom—and it continues to mean not participating in that which causes harm.

When I moved back out into the world, I knew I was not required to live off the grid nor, as I had for many years, to live sustainably. I knew that simplicity and sustainability could be practiced anywhere, but it became much more complex. It was not being modeled much around me. Although the context had changed greatly, purity of heart was not something I was willing to give up. This required great creativity.

In essence, renunciation means reclaiming our relationship with the authority within. This is revolutionary in a world of passive consumerism.

Here are some encouragements for renouncing passive consumerism and reclaiming a more enlivened and joyful relationship with our material world. Consider how the following intentions could support you in letting go of collective agreements that you are ready to let go of, and in bringing more peace to your relationship with the material world:

- My happiness and wholeness do not come from outside of myself.
- Acknowledging that I am already whole, I allow my consumption to reflect this awareness, rather than support stories of inadequacy.
- I agree to stop comparing myself to others and to see myself clearly.
- I choose to want what I have as a revolutionary act.

- I choose to make choices around consumption that honor the interconnected body of all beings on this planet.
- I choose for my material world to reflect sufficiency—the gift of not having too little and not having too much.
- I choose to pause, center, and connect with my senses and my motivations before I fill myself (with food, purchases, entertainment, etc.).
- I choose to become re-empowered to use resources, energy, and life force as a source of love and nourishment, with future generations in mind.
- I choose to support companies and products that feel more aligned with my heart.
- I choose to be mindful of the waste I create, as part of my commitment to conscious consumption.

I choose to do so while practicing nonjudgment and kindness, knowing that there is no wisdom in setting up strict standards for myself and knowing that it does not serve to "judge others" in the name of consciousness. I acknowledge that these intentions are not a set of rules, but encouragements for me to find my own Middle Way.

• • • • • • • • Mindful Inquiry • • • • • • • •

A WRITING EXERCISE

Pause and consider the day you have had thus far. Acknowledge all of the resources you have utilized today, with an open mind and without judgment: water, food, clothing, skincare, energy, fuel, media, online intake, reading, and entertainment.

In what ways do you bring care and mindfulness to your consumption? In what ways do you not?

And now consider the entire week that has just passed. What resources have you consumed with awareness and care? Mindlessly and from need? (For instance, I drank water in a moment of real thirst after exercise.)

What resources have you consumed out of habit? Emotion? Trigger? What resources have you consumed to try to get away from something? What resources have you consumed to try to "get" something indirectly? What resources have you particularly appreciated?

Where was your attention while you were consuming these resources?

How much of your energy today has gone to "wanting" something or trying to "get" something?

When was the last time you experienced authentic satisfaction? Be honest.

When was the last time you experienced the satisfaction that comes from being rather than from getting?

• • • • • • • • Daily Practice • • • • • • • •

MINDFUL EATING

Today, each time you sit down to eat, pause and notice:

your thoughts, sensations in your body, and how you are feeling

your motivation for eating (are you hungry? stressed? bored?)

Then . . . Take a moment for gratitude for where your food came from. Slow down and pay close attention while you begin to eat, feeling the sensations, temperature, and textures of your food, and feeling the sensations of your mouth chewing.

What do you notice?

EXTRA CREDIT— RECEIVING VS. CONSUMING

Right now, in this very moment, you are consuming (taking in) this book. Notice what is going on with you as you take in this book. Are you taking it in with relaxation and ease? Are you present? Or are you speed reading, trying to squeeze this chapter in before you get to the next item on your list for today? What do you notice about your process in this very moment?

15

Personal Sustainability

How we treat ourselves and how we treat our world
are one and the same.

Learning to Be in the World but Not of It

My first few months back in the city provided a unique window
of unobscured perception. I had the fresh open eyes and inner
calm of someone who had never before visited the modern world
and did not assume the same limitations. It was similar to having
traveled abroad or immersing in the wilderness for an extended
period of time, but my journey had been primarily internal. This
world felt totally unfamiliar to me, with strange customs and a
new language to learn.

My intention was and has been since to learn to "be in the
world but not of it" and to question each collective custom
from my inner being. As I transitioned to the life of a layperson,
I brought curiosity to every aspect of the urban lifestyle, from
"What is a wise relationship with technology?" to "How do I
choose to relate with money?" and "How do I wish to express

myself as a woman?" The overall question was, "How can I participate in this lifestyle while affirming the consciousness of interconnection?"

One unique aspect to living in a monastery is that there is an overall ecology of questioning. The only collective identity is a commitment to going beyond limiting beliefs. What struck me about being out in the world again was the degree of collective resignation there was, a mentality that "This is just the way things are. This is just how the world operates. I have no choice in the matter." The passive consumer mentality invoked a sense of being without choice. The agreed-upon habits too often affirm the mind of separation: to be busy, to be distracted, to be dependent on technology, to compartmentalize, to continually want "more," to consume a lot of resources, to engage in a fear-based mentality, and to live more in the past and future than the present.

Having lived in a silent sanctuary where my receptivity had exponentially deepened over the years, my body felt like an amplifier, as if it were picking up every sound, vibration, and rumble in the urban landscape. I recall many moments of what I came to think of as "everyday ordinary violence" when the pain of the experience hit my entire body like a tidal wave. At the same time, my relationship with myself had changed so much over my years of practice that my experience of Los Angeles was completely different than it had been in the past. At times I felt like I was going crazy because so much that I witnessed around me seemed to go unnoticed by other people. A mom berating her child in public, for example . . . Gossip on the news taking advantage of someone's suffering . . . A homeless man on the corner with a sign with no one stopping to help . . . The unfathomably loud ambulance siren that was an assault to the human ears . . . An anorexic woman pounding the pavement to burn a few more calories . . . One driver screaming at another in rage.

What felt so violent to me was not one particular scene but the overall lack of care that was being modeled around me. It was evident in how unkindly people treated themselves and how they treated one another. My commitment was to keep opening my eyes to the suffering I saw every day, while allowing it to deepen my own commitment to end suffering within myself.

While teaching others held me accountable in walking my talk, there came a moment when I began to slide into the seduction of the modern world and lose my focus. This seduction came in the form of the glamorization of busyness. As people responded to my offerings and teaching and my schedule became fuller, I began to find myself doing more and being less. I found myself busier, more driven, and more involved in an internal conversation around productivity and my to-do list than I had been before. I recall one morning sitting on my meditation cushion distracted by a nagging sense that I really needed to be sitting in front of the computer. This certainty that productivity was more important than my meditation practice was a red flag for me.

It was at this point that I began to realize that this obsessive doing was a direct response to receiving less and less of my nourishment from just being . . . and that this was, in some real sense, a choice.

In the monastery, I had become accustomed to spending time with myself and the natural world in a state of quietude and stillness. Out in the modern world, my nervous system was becoming more activated and my sense of well-being depleted. I was trying to compensate for this by obtaining nourishment from success in my work and the outside approval that I received as a result.

I realized that personal sustainability was the next chapter in my personal growth. I became dedicated to the practice and modeling of personal sustainability, and the more I investigated this within myself, the more I began to understand: Personal sustainability is a step to spiritual maturity that has been missing in conversation about both mindfulness and global sustainability.

How can we even begin to address global sustainability if we do not ourselves embody personal sustainability? If we want to create a kind and just world, we must learn to treat ourselves with sustained kindness. If we want ecological balance, we must be willing to choose balance and peace in our own lives. If we want to live in a world that honors interconnection, we must live our lives, moment by moment, from interconnection. We have to look deeply and honestly at the ways in which we have been trained not to live sustainably and acknowledge the conditioned mind's habits of self-abandonment and depletion.

Practice invites us to do the inner work and outer work at the same time. How can we teach our children to take care of themselves and their world—its soil, its people, all forms of life, now and into the future—if we do not model doing this for ourselves on a daily basis?

Embodying Sanity

When we do not have the modeling for balance, it can be easy to forget. Without the support of the monastery I found myself becoming depleted, but the circumstances became a perfect opportunity to deepen my own understanding of personal sustainability as an ethic in today's overly busy world.

At a facilitator's retreat with one of my teachers, eco-philosopher and Buddhist scholar Joanna Macy, a participant from Northern Canada—and an influential Okanagan activist—shared with us a perfect explanation of the imbalances of the twenty-first century, by breaking down the etymology of the Okanagan word for insanity:

First syllable: "talking, talking inside the head"

Second: "scattered and having no community"

Third: "disconnected from the land"

Fourth: "cut off from your whole-earth part" (i.e., from the more-than-human community)

According to this Okanagan translation, most of the modern world is indeed insane. People today are distracted by the conversations in their heads and enslaved by their thoughts, which repeat like a broken record. Many people in today's world feel isolated to some degree. Living as separate selves in a competitive world, they long for an experience of community support, participation, and co-creation. Increasingly, people live in a primarily human-centered and indoor world, disconnected from their bodies, other forms of life, and other forms of knowing. We can get lost, caught up in the trappings of the modern world (cell phone and laptop always nearby), forgetting that we are also simply animals and spiritual beings, living in connection with and dependence upon the land, air, water, resources, and all life forms on this planet.

If the Okanagan translation of insanity is a clear reflection of the imbalances of the twenty-first century, Relational Mindfulness offers us a true antidote:

A practice that quiets the mind and supports us to live from center.

A way to reveal and release perceived separation from one another in order to connect more deeply, and tools for conscious communication and community engagement.

Radical reconnection with the earth and practices that affirm an earth-centric consciousness that includes all forms of life.

Reconnection with our physical bodies and with other forms of knowing.

Personal Un-Sustainability

> You cannot solve a problem with the same mind that created it.
>
> —Albert Einstein

What do I mean by personal sustainability? Sustainability equates to living in balance, longevity, and from interdependence. When we look at ecological sustainability, we see principles having to do with a system's ability to thrive long-term. For example, ecological systems need to be self-regulating and able to maintain natural balance; nutrients in a system need to be continually replenished and recycled to avoid depletion; and existing energy within a system should be used to benefit the system rather than as a source for combat/conflict.

Mindfulness teaches the present-moment inquiry required to maintain our balance. It invites us to consider how sustainable our engagement with the world is on the broader level (for example, how efficient our use of energy is in our homes and how we utilize the resources of the world around us) to the more personal (for example, at work, do I use my energy focused and attentive to the important task at hand or let it drain away with unimportant tasks or distractions?). And more subtly, how much time do I spend in the mind of "doing and striving," which drains energy, versus "being in a state of awareness and receptivity," which generates energy?

Some of the signs that we are getting imbalanced are:

- we begin to feel fractured within ourselves.
- we become aware that we are more "in our heads" than our bodies.
- we feel like slaves to our "to do" lists.
- our nervous systems are less relaxed.
- we experience less mental clarity.
- we experience less peace of mind.

- we experience increased physical tension and strain.
- our circadian rhythms get disrupted.
- our relationships with others get compromised in the name of "busyness."

Sustainable Design as an Attitude of Mind

What moved, touched, and inspired me the most when I discovered sustainable design was the sweet sensibility of it all. It touched me to see the degree of care and beneficial attention humans could give to their landscape and other life forms. Rather than abuse and mistreat their built environment, sustainable design enables depleted landscapes to regenerate and helps humans find right relationship to the landscape they live in.

Rather than interfere with the natural world in the name of human cleverness, sustainable design offers a process of observing and working with nature as ally. Rather than use more energy and input than needed with minimal results, sustainable design invites us to use the least amount of energy input for the greatest amount of output. In a sense, sustainable design uncovers the intelligence that already exists in a system and makes wise use of it.

Over time I have come to experience sustainable design as an attitude of mind that can apply to how we do anything and everything. This helps us to cultivate a more graceful lifestyle in which feelings of being overwhelmed, busyness, chaos, and depletion in our lives decreases. There are five primary elements required for cultivating personal sustainability:

A commitment to being honest about how our energy gets used, setting clear intention about what thoughts and actions we give our energy to and what we do not.

A commitment to presence in a world of increasing distraction.

A commitment to valuing process over product. Only when we step back and let our focus shift from the small picture and end goal to the big picture (process) of our lives are we positioned to embody personal sustainability.

A commitment to accepting low energy as a worthy messenger, and letting it remind us to not push ourselves to depletion

A commitment to self-care and deep rest. This is the golden rule demonstrated by nature and required by nature. It is time for us to learn it and to live it.

There are so many unquestioned assumptions by which we live our personal lives that contradict the principles of sustainability and regeneration we see in nature, as well as conflict with basic human kindness. Consider that the degree of stress, striving, and low-grade dissatisfaction that many people have come to expect in life may not be necessary nor what nature intended for us. Symptoms of depression, anxiety, and chronic pain may all be messengers—the body's brilliant way of telling us that our creature self, the source for our interconnected consciousness, is being ignored.

For many of us, it is rare that we are provided the space to pause and question whether the collective agreements we have made with ourselves and with the world are sustainable in the long term. Practicing mindfulness is a way of reconnecting.

Having grown up in a big city, when I first lived off-the-grid in an intentional community, I became infinitely more sensitive to the wise use of energy and was shocked to realize how much I had been wasting, even while being aware. When I moved to a Zen monastery, I became even more attuned to wise use of human energy. Over time I have become passionate about treating all energy as sacred. I have learned that to do so, however, requires both staying awake (aware) and in mindful inquiry.

How the Mind of Separation Depletes Our Energy

Because everything begins with the mind, conditioned thought patterns shape our world and can greatly deplete our energy. Even in sitting meditation, the mind can intrude to tell us that we need to "do something" such as adjust our position, improve our breathing, or apply some imagined antidote to our busy mind. If you are saying to yourself, "But I'm perfectly balanced, I don't waste energy, I don't let energy drain by my thought patterns," consider looking more deeply into how your mind operates.

Operating from and maintaining the separate self takes a tremendous amount of energy. It's like playing a game of baseball as not only the pitcher but also the sportscaster, assessing every move in the game with our busy minds while we play. Consider . . . is there unnecessary energy going to the conversations in your head about your actions and choices? Is there energy being drained from this moment now by past and future? Is energy being depleted by the stories that "There is something wrong. There is not enough _____ (*fill in the blank*). . . . There is something I've gotta do"? What if life could be dramatically simplified by learning to navigate from center rather than from the conditioned mind?

Five Minutes of Silence—A Meditation Experiment

For this exercise, find a relaxed and comfortable position. Set a timer for five minutes. In a moment, you will either close your eyes or let them rest open in a soft gaze. Focus all of your attention on your breath, simply allowing your breath to be an anchor for staying present. Pay close attention to your internal landscape for the next five minutes and simply notice. Notice where your thoughts go. Notice where your energy goes. Focus on the experience of breathing, one breath at a time, and maintain awareness of what pulls you away from your breath. Each time you find yourself pulled away, gently let go, label what pulled you away (planning, reviewing, daydreaming, etc.), and begin again.

Consider that "how we do anything is how we do everything." We can learn a lot about ourselves and our conditioned tendencies in just five minutes of awareness.

The more we see clearly how we use our energy, the more committed we become to staying present so that our energy can be directed by our hearts and our conscious intentions, rather than by the conditioned mind and its hidden agendas. The more we see how compelling it is for us to get caught in small mind/separate self-engagement, the more we begin to feel a real and solid compassion for ourselves and others. The more we stay present, the more we treat our energy as the sacred life force it is.

Choosing Process over Product

> It's not *what*, it's *how*.
> —Cheri Huber and June Shiver, *Suffering Is Optional*

I grew up wanting to save the world. I read all the right books and took up causes where I could make a difference. I spent most of my twenties engaging in the world of environmental activism, but began to feel that there was something missing in that world. Something did not match up in terms of people's intentions to heal the world and the degree of stress, burnout, conflict, community drama, and inefficient communication with which they were living their own lives. It was sad to see inspiring communities and projects slowed or shut down by human ego. I wanted to believe that something more was possible.

Coming from a family of activists, I witnessed firsthand how the dedication and commitment of one person can change the world, but I also witnessed the phenomenal degree of stress and tradeoffs involved in the process. People burn out. Community projects fall apart. Momentum peaks and dissipates.

It was not until I came upon spiritual practice and moved to the monastery, that I began to understand the vital significance of process over product in serving the world. It was then that I experienced the possibility of a group of people doing good in the world from the inside out. I began to realize that it didn't matter what I was doing. What mattered was how I was doing it. What mattered was that my attention was on awareness (expansive nonjudgmental equanimous) rather than solely on the end goal.

As monks, we were given permission (and required) to shift our focus entirely from product to process. That was the significance of our training. If we were assigned to scrub potatoes, it was about being present to the inner and outer landscape throughout the act of scrubbing potatoes. If we were assigned to working in the wood shop, it was about expressing reverence while we measured, sawed, and sanded wood. If we were assigned to facilitate a group of students, it was about being present, in compassionate awareness, as we worked with the students. It didn't matter if I was fixing a plumbing problem or doing weekly budgeting. If I was experiencing extreme stress, berating myself, and not listening to my body along the way, my actions were not serving the whole.

What I had never understood in my activist years was finally clear: the whole included me. Therefore serving the whole required that I include myself in my circle of generosity and reciprocity.

What does this have to do with sustainability? Human beings have depleted a great deal of the planet's resources over the past 100 years. We have been living as consumers of the earth's resources rather than in partnership with nature, and we bring the same attitude of consumption to ourselves. We often deplete ourselves for whatever ego's agenda is; we use our resources to meet goals and ends while going unconscious through the means of how we treat ourselves along the way.

Sustainable choices begin with allowing life's natural feedback systems to lead the way. Only when we begin to honor the signals of our natural feedback system do we learn to make choices that do not necessarily serve the momentum and agenda of the ego. In other words, only then do we value the discipline a compassionate process of life..

Foundational Practices for Radical Self-Care

When our energy is depleted, we have less to offer others. When we allow ourselves to receive our own generosity, our ability to be generous with others expands. When we commit ourselves to radical self-care, our ability to care for every form of life we encounter grows.

The simplest practice for self-care is meditation, in which we give ourselves the gift of our own attention. Letting go of striving and being present offers us the deepest form of replenishment. Meditation trains us to tune in moment by moment to our needs as we move through our day, In addition, here are three more simple practices for bringing more self-care into your life.

Deep Rest

One simple restorative practice I have come to love is the revolutionary nap (revolutionary in our productivity-obsessed world). I pause and take a thirty-minute nap almost every day. It is a time to rest and affirm "doing nothing, going nowhere." By taking a nap, my body replenishes, my mind rests and clears, and my connection with source is strengthened. If your work schedule does not allow for taking a nap, then I recommend setting the timer for thirty minutes and picking some other form of doing absolutely nothing: not talking on the phone, not watching a video on YouTube, but allowing your entire being to relax into the mode of nondoing and serenity. You might sit on the porch, sip tea, or watch birds at the park, but the purpose of this break is deep uninterrupted rest.

Gratitude

In the Mohawk tradition, the words that come before all else are the words of thanks. Despite all the Mohawk peoples have been through as a tribe, their commitment to gratitude has resulted in dignity, resilience, and self-respect. The magic of gratitude is that it is not dependent on external circumstances. We can turn our attention to gratitude no matter what, and like a muscle, we can exercise and strengthen it. For the past twenty years, I have kept a gratitude journal that has grown over time into a collection of journals on my bookshelf. Within each book are pages dedicated to listing gratitudes from my day. At the end of each day, or as I transition from my period of work to personal time, regardless of the content of the day, I pause, turn my attention to gratitude, and record three things that I feel thankful for about that day.

My list can include anything: people I appreciate, fleeting moments of beauty, insights, surprises, gifts from nature. As an experiment, I invite you to take on this practice for at least one week, no matter what mood you are in, and see what you notice.

You might find that it is easy to record your gratitudes on some days and challenging on others. Like any writing practice, the trick is to show up to the page no matter what. Over time you will find your attention turning to gratitude throughout your day, organically. Over time this practice can change your life.

Acknowledging Ourselves

Another way we can practice self-care is through self-appreciation. Most of us have lengthy "to do" lists and receive detailed reports from our internal standard keeper about the ways we are not accomplishing fast enough and do not measure up. In addition to learning to let go of the belief systems that hold judgment in place, it also benefits us to develop a healthy habit of self-appreciation.

Consider that most of us approach our creativity/productivity in three steps. First, we get an idea of something we might do or create, and for most of us, there is no shortage of ideas. Some of these ideas make it to the next step, where we actually begin our project. The step after that (which even fewer of our ideas make it to) is completing our project. If we are lucky, we see one of many ideas through to completion. We feel good for a brief moment (yay, our project is done!) but still bear the weight of all the ideas we haven't put to fruition, and we then go back to step one coming up with more ideas.

There is another, more enlightened way to approach the cycle of creativity, and that is to add one more step at the end: acknowledging and appreciating ourselves for what we have just accomplished. In other words, we take the time to really appreciate ourselves for what we have completed and what we have put into the project thus far. We acknowledge our victories, large or small, and by doing so we realize there have been a million small victories despite the mind's assessment that we have not "done enough."

I keep a whiteboard in my office solely for this purpose. Every week, day by day, this whiteboard fills with accomplishments and victories. Some of my victories are tangible projects, for instance, "Chapter 5 completed" or "Led a successful workshop," while others are more process-focused, such as "Took a courageous risk despite fear" or "Met family dynamic with presence, though it was challenging." I watch this simple but profound practice change people's lives all the time. This is a form of "giving back to the soil." We tend to not realize how much it feeds us to be acknowledged and appreciated, because most of us are used to and more comfortable with our internal self-criticism and self-berating. Our to-do lists are long. Our "should" list weighs heavy.

When we add this acknowledging-and-appreciating step and commit to acknowledging ourselves on a daily basis, our "victories" list becomes the longest list and our sense of empowerment increases.

The energy behind the appreciation is like compost being added to the soil for the next seed to grow, for the next project to be cultivated. In other words, energy previously going to self-criticism gets redirected to an authentic, honest, wholesome "pat on the back."

My encouragement for practicing personal sustainability is to be aware of the collective agreements you are immersed in and to take responsibility for your own choices. Remember that you have a choice in every moment and especially to question the places you find yourself believing "this is just the way things are." Depending on whether you live in an urban metropolis like Los Angeles or the countryside, this will be varying degrees of challenge. Surround yourself by the support systems you need in order to dwell in inquiry and possibility.

The natural world offers many lessons for personal sustainability, but until and unless we are willing to pause and loosen our grip on this mentality of collective resignation, we will not be open to the possibilities for change.

Dare to Not Be a Passive Consumer of the Culture of Busyness

Though I have come to view personal sustainability as a gateway to spiritual maturity, my sense is that it is a doorway many are not willing to enter. In my experience training longtime meditators to be facilitators of mindfulness, I have been surprised to see how quickly people fold their facilitation practice into their already busy life, just getting busier, rather than seeing the deeper lessons and opportunity for being a mindfulness facilitator who walks their talk.

Real abundance is the satisfaction and relief we receive when we are enough and have enough in each moment. When we let go of the belief that our merit is attached to our level of busyness or engagement, we allow ourselves to prioritize well-being, rest, and spaciousness. It is deeply healing to reclaim the spaciousness that we've been told we do not deserve and to understand that this deeply serves the whole. It serves our well-being, our attunement to truth, and our health, as well as the projects and communities we participate in in the long run.

Bringing It All Together

Going back to the Okanagan definition of insanity, "Talking inside the head, Disconnected from the land, Separate from community, and from your animal body," consider your own life. Where on the spectrum of sanity are you in this moment? Be radically honest with yourself as you consider these questions:

To what degree do you have a kind and nourishing relationship with yourself?

What is the general quality of your mind? Are you at peace with your mind?

What is your experience of community on a day-to-day basis?

Perhaps you feel embedded in community. Perhaps not.

How are you nourished by community and how is this nourishment lacking?

In what situations do you experience intimacy with others and in what situations do you experience separation or isolation?

Is your community interacting as a committed team or distracted by friction and conflict?

What is your level of connection with the earth on a day-to-day basis? To what degree do you get caught up in the human-centered world?

To what degree do you stay connected with your body and your intuition?

Is there a way in which you long to be even more connected in one of these areas?

We are all in this together and have some work to do to cultivate a more sustainable world. It is time to let go of every misconception that has blocked our view of what is possible for us individually and collectively.

• • • • • • • • Mindful Inquiry • • • • • • • •

WRITING EXERCISE AND
PERSONAL INVENTORY

Every path of discovery begins with honest nonjudgmental investigation. We each have different ways of becoming imbalanced and losing our personal sustainability. How does a lack of sustainability manifest itself in you? Please take a few minutes to fill in the blanks of the following statements to begin to take personal inventory and understand your own relationship with personal sustainability.

1   Personal sustainability to me means _____.
2. One way I am sustainable in my lifestyle is _____.
3. One way I am not sustainable is _____.
4. What I tell myself to justify this is _____.
5. Most of my energy goes to _____.
6. The primary ways my energy gets drained, depleted, and imbalanced are _____.
7. My body's signs when I am beginning to feel imbalanced are _____.
8. My emotional signs that I am beginning to feel imbalanced are _____.
9. The things that fuel and revitalize my energy are _____.
10. The basic inputs I require to function healthfully are _____.
11. Am I receiving these inputs (all of the nourishment I need) adequately?
12. If not, the story I use to explain this limitation is _____.
13. How I feel about this limitation is _____.

14. I tell myself that the most important thing in life is _____.

15. According to my actions, what actually appears to be most important to me is _____.

16. If I actually lived by my most cherished values, what I would do differently is _____.

17. I waste time and energy by _____.

18. The last time I experienced deep peace and a sense of ease was when I _____.

Now take a few minutes to look over your answers. What stands out to you? If these questions brought up emotion, I encourage you to pause, take in a conscious breath, and bring gentle awareness to your experience. Let yourself settle into stillness and trust as you look with curiosity and compassion into these perhaps unexplored corners of your being.

• • • • • • • • • Daily Practice • • • • • • • •

REFLECTIONS ON
PERSONAL SUSTAINABILITY

Today, pause in the morning, mid-day, and evening for reflection.

Morning Reflection: When you woke up this morning, what was the first thing your attention/energy went to?

Mid-Day Reflection: What messages have you received from your natural feedback system (body, feelings, mind) to help you maintain balance and well-being? Have you obeyed or disobeyed your natural feedback system? Is there any form of self-care needed to replenish you?

Evening Reflection: As you reflect on the day, has your energy gone to the most important and regenerative aspects of your life or has it been drained by distraction or habit patterns? Is there any form of self-care needed to replenish you?

16

iPhone Therefore I Am

A Mindful Relationship with Technology

If you give people an open door through which to escape consciousness, they will take it every time.

As my work in Los Angeles evolved, I noticed an added pressure weighing in on me each day—keeping up with emails. One morning after meditation, I sat down at the desk to evaluate my relationship with the internet.

As I began to read and respond to emails, I set a timer to remind me to pause every ten minutes and observe my internal experience. With certain emails came attachments, links, or recordings. I soon noticed that I had a secondary job of managing my computer desktop. At the same time, advertisements began to pop up on my screen, and I felt both irritation and a dream-like pull for my attention from some of the ads. One of my emails included a Facebook link, which opened up a whole other dimension on my screen. And from time to time a text came in, adding even more complexity. Slowly, I experienced my shoulders and neck feeling tense, my breathing becoming constricted, and my mind soon overwhelmed with chatter.

In the middle of my communications, I thought of a few other people I should reach out to while online. My mind became layered with multiple conversations about the invitations, links, and news that I was taking in. My fingers began to tire from tapping on the keys; at the same time, an internal voice was saying, "You have to take care of as much as you can online before you start working with clients, so just keep going." I was present enough to recognize this voice for the conditioning that it was, so I observed it, paused, and let it go—and was thus able to reconnect fully with my breath and body. Still, there was an undeniable effect from simply engaging with the internet. The impact of staring into a screen while using my organizing and problem-solving mind, with my body completely disconnected from the activity, felt somewhat unwholesome.

I continued to observe this process over the next few weeks, and, in conjunction, I began to notice that I did not feel well physically when on the computer for more than an hour. When I was on too long, I felt a tension in my head, and my eyes would begin to sting. My wrists, hands, and fingers were becoming increasingly overworked. I wondered, "Do other people experience these symptoms or am I just more sensitive? Or are they not paying attention?" Being on the internet was like being caught in an obsessive maze that compelled me to keep looking, and looking, and looking at the screen. Looking for what, ultimately, I didn't know.

The conflict between what I thought was required in order to reach professional goals and my sense of unease with the internet/phone connection was growing deeper. I began to hear students and colleagues voice the same complaints. As I explored further, it also became apparent that some were playing out addictions online—to shopping, for example, or to sex—through the internet.

I realized that the very technology we were so excited about might actually lead at some point to our demise; it certainly compromised the quality of presence and focus that I considered foundational to well-being.

Radical Honesty and Digital Technology

Growing up in the 1970s and 1980s, no one had cell phones and comparatively few people had access to computers. We relied on old-fashioned dial-up landlines and answering machines, and there seemed to be less assumed urgency around communication. Of course, there were times when we could not be reached, but that was a perfectly natural part of life.

For all of the good that the digital age has given us, it has also brought a tremendous amount of distraction to the human sphere. A human being in the twenty-first century receives more information in one day of their lives than did someone during an entire year of life in the 1700s. The internet has increased our ability to communicate and process large amounts of information, but at great cost. It has compromised the quality of our relationships with ourselves and with one another.

Very few people were using cell phones in 2000 when I first moved to the monastery, which was also somewhat isolated from the modern world. When I returned to Los Angeles in 2007 to begin teaching the Dharma, I had multiple experiences that completely shocked me:

- Conducting a daylong retreat at a corporate business, I ask everyone to turn off their cell phones and place them on a table, in a safe place. I am met with resistance, fear, and verbal affirmation that this request sends people into an anxiety-ridden state, even though, by nature of the retreat, they are completely free of their work responsibilities for the day.

- Teaching a Relational Mindfulness workshop for families, the number one complaint I hear from every mother there is that there is no window of time, even mealtime, when their spouse is cell phone-free and when their children have their full attention.
- Out to dinner with relatives, I observe with sadness as a large family of six, including three children and an elder, sit down at a nearby table, retrieve their iPads, and each move into their own isolated sphere until their meal arrives.
- Having lunch with an old friend, I witness him maintaining eye contact with his cell phone the entire time, pausing whenever he receives a text in order to respond, and exiting our conversation completely while doing so. I feel that I am in the presence of someone who is not completely present—unavailable for real connection.

Personally, I question whether our society has the spiritual maturity required to use technology in a sane and balanced manner. Like giving car keys to a teenager, the promise of speed and entertainment can carry weight over safety and sanity. Through digital technology, we have found a way to feed the mind of separation constantly, twenty-four hours a day. In a society that already struggles with attention deficits, mental illness, and stress, this issue is not to be taken lightly. I fear that while communications technology appears to lift the burden of repeated labors, it undermines our natural processes for assimilation. And nowhere in the user's manual for technology is there encouragement to investigate the health and safety effects of technology and the internet or take responsibility for their appropriate use.

Technology is certainly not going anywhere anytime soon; however, there is a possibility for allowing technology to become our ally in living a wakeful life rather than a deterrent. If we develop a true commitment to paying attention, to setting wise boundaries with our technology usage, and to discerning between information that serves truth rather than the nonessential chatter of the conditioned mind, then we can cultivate a more compassionate relationship with technology. When I pay attention to my experience on a land-line phone, my capacity to orient myself— in my body, in space, and in consciousness—remains intact. I can stay focused, grounded, and relaxed. But when using a cell phone, as soon as calls and texts come in, my capacity begins to fray quickly. I feel that I have one foot in one conversation and another in a second. The quality of connection that I value becomes compromised, and this gets justified by a story or rationale of "saving time."

Costs of Constant Digital Connection

How can we cultivate a healthier and more compassionate relationship with communications technology? What is our body's honest response to the age of the screen and keyboard? How do we navigate communications technology while deepening our commitment to presence?

Following are some of the challenges we can learn to negotiate as we bring mindfulness to integrating technology into the evolution of humankind. As you reflect on this list, consider your own experience. Reflect on how the following costs of constant digital connection have impacted you and the people in your life:

- We have less command and focus of our attention.
- The boundaries between work and personal or family time are weaker.
- There is an epidemic of screen addiction, which most people are not even aware of. Technology has become another way to fill space and distract, although we have a desperate need for empty space to integrate all that we take in.

- We have increased the volume on the collective conditioned mind, with more distracted communications and less connected communications. More people experience less intimate and shallower connections. In other words, it becomes too easy for communication to become transactional rather than relational.
- People interact with their environment and the world around them in a less direct and engaged way. Even while walking at the beach, with the surf lapping the sand nearby, many people have their eyes glued to their cell phones. It has become another barrier between humans and the natural world or ordinary life experiences.
- The message that "more and faster are better" is in the nature of technology, thus drawing us into a world of greater speed and complexity rather than simplicity. There is no encouragement for people to find their own relationship with the world through direct and personal contact with it. There is no framework on the internet for "less is more."
- There is also collective denial about potential health and mental health ramifications from communications technology and screen use, which have not been thoroughly researched.

Command over Attention

The quality of our life is governed by the focus of our attention, and the internet encourages loss of command of our attention. As a society, we are more distracted than ever before in human history. We have given technology the authority to dictate the fast pace with which we will forever be racing to catch up. I believe it is a form of spiritual poverty that so many people have lost their ability to slow down and focus and give full attention to the moment.

We justify multitasking with stories of "urgency" and "too much to do." Our attention is directed away from what is "here right now" through the visual and mental stimulation provided instantaneously by the internet. People striving to become present find themselves instead in an inner struggle with their failure to live in the moment and engage with their senses, while at the same time being accessible to others. As a value, having command over one's attention seems to be disappearing in the surge of technology. The result is resignation to living in a world where increasing numbers of people have lost the capacity to be present—when driving, when socializing, when walking, when working, when alone, and even when making love.

Weaker Boundary between Work and Personal/Family Life

I have worked with countless families whose quality of connectedness has been impacted by the cell phone. They no longer have personal time together separate from the parent's work time. Conversations between spouses are disrupted by text messages. Children have interactions with their parents every day that are disrupted by texts or where their parents are in conversation with them and, at the same time, on the phone with someone else. Parents give their children electronic devices so that they are not bored or disruptive, rather than giving their children their personal attention and connection.

If we investigate honestly, we see a desensitization in the field of communication that is a direct result of people texting and emailing rather than having face-to-face or voice-to-voice communications. The shared field of presence cannot be accessed through disembodied texting or emails. Deep listening is not possible through this form of surface communication.

The quality of relationships has been further damaged by technology because, even when families and couples are spending time together, often one or more parties are looking at a screen. People post opinions online rather than having real conversations.

One More Escape Route

I believe that the quality of one's relationship with oneself can be measured by how content we are to be with ourselves when nothing else is going on. The capacity to be with ourselves in peace and relaxation in the ordinary or empty moments of our day is a hallmark of wellness. I see young people provided with nonstop entertainment instead, as if down time and spaciousness might be the worst experience in the world. Clients seek assistance in decreasing their obsessive use of email as a way to distract themselves from anxiety and discomfort. I feel particularly concerned for the younger generation, who have not experienced life without the internet and cell phone.

An addiction is something that we turn to when we want to escape discomfort and is characterized by compulsive engagement in rewarding stimuli, despite adverse consequences. Many people have an addiction to technology that they are not fully aware of. We now have a new means to escape the moment. We allow our devices to fill the ego's need for constant distraction and mental stimulation.

Giving Power to Collective Conditioning

Globalizing the internet has been like giving the conditioned mind a megaphone of unlimited volume and capacity. Our psyches are overloaded with large amounts of imagery and information. Much of what we consume digitally is unsavory and even toxic. Video games and news accounts are filled with stories of death, violence, Armageddon, and advertisements. The conditioned mind, which carries the messages that "There is something wrong," "What I have is not enough," and "There is something more that I must do," now has continual access to people and places across the globe. It operates at a vibration that is loud, all-knowing, and repetitive.

Technology has given incredible momentum to the illusion that the human sphere of commerce and entertainment is the primary context within which we live our lives. This distortion is not without cost. There is an increase in over-consumption, mindless consumption, and overall dissatisfaction.

Another mental habit that has been colonized by the internet is the comparing mind. Whether it comes in the form of a high-schooler comparing her photos to those of her peers, a woman comparing her looks to the airbrushed models of Hollywood, or even an indigenous farmer comparing his agrarian life to urban European life, the comparing mind gets triggered continually on the internet.

The rise of social media has also exacerbated a fear-based, externally focused story that we all carry: "There might be something better out there" or "Fear of Missing Out (FOMO)." In other words, there might be somewhere better to be, something better to do, or someone better to be with. In order to ensure that we remain aware of the array of possibilities available, we maintain an almost obsessive connection to social media of all kinds. In reality, this state of mind is a losing battle, because true well-being comes from center.

We have crowned Convenience our god and savior, an illusion that perpetuates the message that productivity and appearances are more important than everything else—our health, our peace of mind, the passing moments of our lives.

Less Direct Engagement

The disconnect between humanity and the natural world is perpetuated by the cell phone, which serves as a barrier and defense mechanism between individuals and the world around them. Instead of engaging with the world around us through our sensory experience, we are entranced by what we view on our screens. Instead of feeling, seeing, touching, tasting, smelling, and sensing the life around us, we are photographing it or texting someone about it.

Denial about Potential Long-term Effects Unknown

A sustainable society is one that asks the question, "How will this action affect people seven generations from now? What kind of world are our choices today creating for our children and for their children?" When a new technology is introduced and imposed upon us with the aim of rapid spread, it does not allow society to properly acclimate to the change and evaluate through experience and outcomes its pros and cons. If we honestly consider long-term human health and quality of relationships between people and within family units, there is a lot that we do not yet understand.

Research indicates that screen time and screen addiction negatively affect gray matter of the brain. What is happening to and within the brain is not subtle, as it causes the gray matter to shrink. This impacts the brain's development, neurotransmitters, and ability to communicate internally.

I believe we need to research more fully how screen addiction impairs psychological and emotional development. Research indicates that results can include less resilience, more anxiety, less impulse control, and diminished empathy. Most of this damage occurs in the frontal lobe. This area in the brain experiences large growth from puberty until the mid-twenties. This is a crucial time for personal growth, a time when our identity is being formed.

Encouragements for Allowing Technology to Be Our Ally

Mindfulness gives us tools for cultivating wakefulness in everyday life. Regardless of the context within which we find ourselves, awareness can help us to inform better and more conscious habits. We all have different opinions about what is right/wrong or enough/too much in terms of technology, and it is possible to develop protocols and practices that work for each of us personally. The first step is to bring observation and inquiry to our experience with technology. The second is that we set up structure and discipline in our use of technology. Some suggestions for cultivating a wakeful relationship with technology are:

- Don't do yourself a disservice by being online and in front of a screen every day. I encourage people to take a technology and media fast at least one day per week at minimum, but ideally more often. If you meditate in the morning, consider not engaging with social media, email, or your phone beforehand; communicating from center can help us to make kinder choices as we interface with technology.
- Be aware of your mental and emotional experiences as you engage with social media. Does Facebook use, for example, cause you to feel more genuinely connected or does it instead trigger the mind of separation?
- Don't assume that producers of these new technologies have evaluated the long-term ramifications of their products on health and well-being. Take responsibility for your relationship with technology, including limiting your exposure to radiation.

- Create structure for yourself so that you regain and then maintain control of your relationship with the internet and cell phone. Perhaps set up a usage schedule for yourself. Create guidelines to make emailing itself a mindfulness practice. For instance, a Zen student of mine created a rule for himself that no email ever requires more than five lines. This holds him accountable to communicating essential information in a clear way, which makes life easier and more efficient for him and for the recipient.

- Maintain a boundary between your personal time and time spent online. My own practice is to respond to emails at a set time each day, and never first thing in the morning or at the end of the day, to honor my circadian rhythms.

- Protect the field of interconnection when you are physically with others. While at meals and with your children or partner, I recommend that cell phones be turned off. While together, make time for focused, undisrupted attention and no distraction. I recommend that families and couples develop agreements about what conscious usage is for them.

- Approach texting and emailing as an awareness practice. Pay attention to the transition from what you were previously engaged in to engagement with a screen, and notice the impact on your body, mind, and emotions. Set a timer to pause from time to time in the same way that we use a mindfulness bell to remind us to pay attention while meditating.

- Find, establish, and tinker with the freedom that comes from sufficiency. Do you really need the newest "right plan" that gives you access all the time? What intensity of use would actually support your health and well-being?

- Lastly, please do not let the internet or social media be an escape or substitute for engaging fully in both the beauty and messiness of real life. If this is happening, I encourage you to turn toward the part of you that chooses this escape route and begin to investigate your real needs.

• • • • • • • • **Mindful Inquiry** • • • • • • • •

How content are you with your relationship with the internet, email, and the cell phone?

In what ways do these communications technologies support you?

What are some of the gifts communications technologies have brought to your life?

In what ways do they distract you and take you away from presence?

Has the quality of any of your relationships been compromised by the other party being distracted by phone/text?

How much consciousness do you bring to when to use and not use the cell phone?

Do you bring it everywhere you go?

Do you ever feel frustrated by the use of it around you?

MINDFUL INQUIRY
WHILE USING TECHNOLOGY

Before using your cell phone, computer, or another device, ask:

Who is here right now?

What is my motivation in this moment? Where is my attention right now?

Can I set the intention to maintain full connection with my body as I engage?

While engaging, ask:

What is the sensation of having my visual attention resting on a screen right now?

How are my hands doing with this piece of technology?

What is my physical experience right now?

What is the state of my mind?

How long does it feel good, to my creature self, to be engaged in this way?

Can I stay present, focused, and in well-being while doing this? Does my monkey mind get activated and go from thing to thing?

How much of what I'm engaging in is nourishing and how much is unsavory or even feels toxic or destructive?

Afterward, ask:

What is the state of my body, my feelings, my mind now?

· · · · · · · · **Daily Practice** · · · · · · · ·

Today, pay attention to your cell phone communications. Allow your communications to support presence and well-being rather than distract or cause stress. Allow yourself to pause before sending or responding to a communication, take in a deep breath, and check in with your body, mind, and emotions. Be willing to set boundaries and say no to communications technologies when necessary. Make notes to record the qualities that you experience while engaging with your phone.

PART FOUR

Healing Our Relationship with Global Uncertainty

Thus far, we have explored the significance of Relational Mindfulness as a path for deepening intimacy with our self, with one another, and with the planet. In this section, we will explore how these teachings can help us to address the larger issues we face as a species such as global climate change, social injustice, and the continual loss of living systems on this planet. We are all invited to be agents of change at this time in human history.

What are the lessons that Relational Mindfulness offers us as agents of change at a pivotal moment on planet earth?

How can we meet global uncertainty with a wide open heart rather than reactivity?

How do we turn toward, rather than away, from our pain for the world and allow it to strengthen us?

How do we support ourselves to continually deepen practice in the face of self-doubt and resistance?

How can we support ourselves to avoid burnout, when there is so much suffering in our world?

17

Taking Passionate Responsibility in the Face of Global Uncertainty

Grace happens when we act with others on behalf
of our world.

—Joanna Macy

On Friday, March 11, 2011, when the idea for this book was first seeded, a massive 8.9 earthquake followed by a twenty-three-foot tsunami devastated Japan, and shook the world. On Saturday, March 12, came what is considered to be the worst nuclear disaster since Chernobyl. Cooling systems failed at the Fukushima Daiichi Nuclear Power Station and radioactive material was detected outside the plant. More than 200,000 residents were evacuated and some radiation areas will take decades to clean up.

As the worldwide media began reporting on the disaster, each day the crisis seemed to escalate and become more perilous. It was as if we were suddenly being jolted awake to our collective fragility. For a brief moment in time, the world seemed to rouse from its somnolence, from "business as usual," and open its eyes and hearts to the immediacy of interdependence. And then, when the danger was reported to be somewhat contained, the world appeared to go right back to sleep.

The aftermath of Fukushima, like that of so many large environmental disasters and acts of violence, was disappointing and illuminated a collective resistance to change. Although there continues to be concern, we failed to fully address the threat of nuclear energy for life on this planet today and for generations to come.

When a tragedy like this occurs, we allow ourselves to feel the razor-sharp intensity of global fragility for a moment. Shaken up and concerned, we either consciously or subconsciously remember the truth of interdependence that we have forgotten. We re-establish in our minds that reality of how small we actually are as human beings on planet earth. As we are knocked out of our separate bubbles and fall back down to earth, we remember the solid ground of shared vulnerability.

Whenever there is a nuclear disaster, an oil spill, a terrorist act, a shooting, or another unfathomable disaster, it shocks our system that the powers that be have not made choices to ensure our basic safety and well-being. When we experience a collective trauma, after the initial moment of waking up from sleep, something else typically happens soon after. Realizing that we are in fact completely dependent upon forces that seem to be beyond our control, our collective psyche gets pulled back into the familiarity and numbness of our own little bubbles.

We do not allow ourselves to go through the full grieving process or honor our feelings communally. We turn instead to the mind of separation for false safety, and there we position ourselves. We take opinionated intellectual stances against one another. We battle about our interpretations of politics and events. We miss the opportunity to stand together in our human fragility. We extract ourselves from the vulnerability through which we might access deeper clarity and co-creativity. Instead we cower alone, often with feelings of hopelessness and despair that remain unacknowledged.

We choose one of two sides of a dualistic /divide. We either minimize our concern and return to "business as usual" or we catastrophize. To choose either side of this duality is to turn away, rather than come face to face with the vast uncertainty of life. Typical reactions we have to the state of the world are:

Paralyzing despair: "There is absolutely nothing that anyone can do to change things. We're doomed."

Anger: "I hate this messed-up world we live in. Screw the government."

Reactive fear: "I'll prepare for the worst and find a safe place to run to when things unravel."

Denial or indifference: "There's nothing going on. Let's just continue with business as usual. Whatever."

All of these reactions are understandable when a disaster occurs, but they do not inspire in us skillful action on behalf of the whole. They do not allow us to participate in the collective healing of our world.

Reclaiming Our Shared Power

An alternative to these reactions from the teachings of Relational Mindfulness would be:

To connect with others and listen deeply to our shared experience as human beings, including to connect with people of divergent perspectives

To turn toward rather than away from what is happening in our world and allow our pain and grief for the world to inform us and feed our resilience.

To contemplate the state of the world from center or the consciousness of "We" rather than from "I." From "I" we take life personally and tend to feed egoic reactivity rather than allowing a response that comes more deeply from the shared heart. From center we can honor our rage, our grief, and all other emotions without adding extra judgment and venom to the situation.

To contemplate the state of the world from the wisdom of "not knowing," which avails us to the field of all possibility, rather than clinging to conclusions and stories about what we think we know.

To take passionate responsibility for our corner of the world and our impact on the whole. This requires us to move from a sense of powerlessness to empowerment. It begins with each of us moving past complacency and asking, How does this particular issue invite me to step it up in terms of how I live my life and engage with the world? Is there a larger action for me to take?

If we are to meet global uncertainty with grace rather than reactivity, we need to reclaim our shared power. This begins with each person doing the deep work of learning how to pay attention, first within ourselves and extending it out to the field of all relations. This is how we can make a difference in how life is being treated in our lifetime. We gain power by letting go of the "I" that separates us and diving into the reality of "We." We gain power by acknowledging what is true and witnessing one another in our pain. We gain power by finding the courage to be with the reality of uncertainty.

Not Knowing

When I lived as a monk, I was given endless opportunities to practice the wisdom of "not knowing." This is a Zen teaching that brings awareness to the mind's incessant desire to know, solve, come to conclusion, and figure out. In Zen we are encouraged, instead, to meet life with spacious awareness and surrender to the experience of "I don't know." Especially in the face of uncertainty or fear, it can be deeply relaxing and insightful to settle into not knowing. The monastery was a crucible for change. One never knew when the entire schedule and structure might change. One never knew when our teacher might take a spontaneous action that would impact our lives in a tremendous way.

In the face of global uncertainty, I see people trying to draw all kinds of conclusions about the future, from Armageddon (as demonstrated in so many popular films) to the New Age. I see both as limited and human-centric. Without having to know what will happen, we can instead hold the questions in our hearts, Regardless of whether humans will survive as a species or not, how much love, attention, care can I bring to every step I take today? With the awareness that I have about what leads towards and away from harm, what actions am I inspired to take today? In this lifetime? When I am willing to let go of what I think I know and listen deeply to life, what insights arise to guide me through these tumultuous times?

The Healing Power of Grief

These are not inconsequential times and they do not allow us to turn away. Humanity has witnessed greed, hatred, and delusion for as long as we have been on this planet; never before, however, have we faced the degree of destruction, loss of living systems, and potential for global mass destruction and annihilation of an entire human species that we face today.

We no longer have the privilege of checking out and shutting down from life without grave ramifications. We must be willing to meet tragedy from openhearted presence and to let it bring us together rather than keep us apart. In other words, we must turn our reactivity into compassionate action.

We have pills to take for headaches, attention deficit disorder, and anxiety, and for almost every ailment under the sun, but we have no pill for the pain for our world. As sensitive sentient beings, we have no way to successfully escape our pain—our awareness of what is happening on our planet. There are visible signs of ecological and societal damage everywhere. The isolation that comes from pretending the pain is not there only leads to more isolation, feelings of anxiety, selfishness, and numbness, and negative reactivity.

Because nothing is healed without being touched, turning away from pain ensures that healing cannot take place. We must begin to perceive our feelings of pain for the world as valid, wholesome, and acceptable—and we must overcome our fear of them. We are dealing with planetary anguish, but we possess an ability to "be with" and to feel the suffering of our world. That is good news. Our pain for the world and our capacity to take part in its self-healing are intrinsically linked.

The Truth Mandala

At a daylong retreat on "Transforming Our Despair into Compassionate Action," participants are invited to sit in a circle, and the guidelines are set for confidentiality, deep listening, and truth-telling. The circle is considered an alchemical vessel for holding the truth. In this circle there are four quadrants and four objects marking each quadrant. These objects are the stone, symbolizing fear; dry leaves, symbolizing sorrow and grief; a stick, representing anger and outrage; and lastly, an empty bowl, standing for our need and sense of lack—our hunger for what is missing. An invocation is made to open the circle.

As in any Relational Mindfulness exercise, people are invited to relax, look within, and set the intention to stay present through the interaction. When someone feels ready to speak, they move into the center of the circle and pick up whatever objects speak to them. While each person shares, participants are asked to deeply listen—within and to one another.

A young mother picks up a bunch of dried leaves: "I am tired of fighting every day to create a nontoxic world for my baby to thrive in. I am tired of there being poisonous chemicals in nearly everything we buy. And I am tired of wondering if my child will even have a healthy biosphere by the time he is an adult."

A young man in his thirties takes the stick in both hands: "I am stunned by the attacks that are taking place right now alongside ancient rivers in the Dakotas. The pipeline project is an atrocity that if built, will have repercussions on generations from here on out. I desperately wish more people would speak out against it. I feel powerless, and I feel like I'm going crazy."

A Peruvian grandmother and immigrant with tears in her eyes holds the stone in the palm of her hand: "I recently learned about the port that is being proposed in the rain forests of Ecuador. I have spent a lot of time in the rain forest ecosystem, and the people I come from rely on the forest for all of our medicine. It is a sacred ecosystem, and yet we seem to be putting all of the world's rain forests under threat."

A mother of two sons picks up the stick and holds it above her head: "It took last week's shooting to send me over the top. I cannot believe we have not instilled gun control yet! Has this country gone mad? How am I supposed to raise my kids to feel safe and confident when they hear instances every week on the news of the shooting of innocent people?"

A young woman picks up the ceramic bowl and looks into it: "I just saw more photos from Aleppo, and I want to scream. How is this happening? How are we letting this continue? What can I do to help? I feel powerless and like I am witnessing a Holocaust occur in my own lifetime. I am hungry for sanity, and I feel empty and unable to help."

By being invited to be witnessed in honoring our pain, a powerful healing unfolds. That which we have held deep within our psyches is given a voice. By being invited to witness others, we realize that we are not alone.

At this time in history, there is a tremendous amount of suffering to be aware of and very little forum for integrating our feelings about it, aside from communication on social media. The Truth Mandala, explained in depth in appendix 2 at the back of this book, offers a powerful forum for honoring our pain for the world. After the 2016 elections, when so many Americans were struggling with shock and fear, I guided a large group of meditators through the Truth Mandala.

After the ritual, a forty-five-year-old man in a corporate leadership position said, "My feelings about the election felt like venom before this experience. Waking up every day to such difficult reports on the news . . . I was completely thrown off center. . . . Coming together in this way has healed something for me. The validity of my feelings was honored I feel like I have a much wider perspective and peace to move forward from now." The man described how sharing the experience of truth telling transformed his feelings into empowerment.

Taking Passionate Responsibility

An essential step in taking passionate responsibility in the world is an acknowledgment of the reality of death.

In many primal societies, rites of passage in adolescence help to integrate the reality of personal death as young people become adults. In the modern world, there are few forums that help young people integrate the reality of death for themselves and the potential demise as a species into the rights and responsibilities of planetary adulthood.

What if we were willing to enter adulthood with the following question: "How can I allow my pain for the world to ensure that I take more responsibility for myself and my personal healing, for the healing of my relationships, and for the health of the living systems on the planet?"

I believe that our willingness to take responsibility comes from an awareness of transience and of the inevitability of death. In other words, when we fully acknowledge how short our time on this earth is, our priorities and actions become more honest and courageous. We begin to understand how precious is the opportunity to expand our consciousness in the time that we are here, and we lose interest in playing it small. When we are done with playing it small, we begin to ask, "How can I allow what I sense and see to sober me, making me accountable to walk more wisely in this world? How can I allow what I see to strengthen my gratitude for what I have and help me exercise the power of choice that I carry?"

We must also be willing to dwell in the uncertainty of not knowing what will happen in the future to the state of the world, rather than coming to false conclusions. We must be willing to take action because we care, rather than from an effort to control the outcome or product. When we do, our actions become more courageous and more aligned with possibility. With the motivation of process over product, there is no need to know the outcome of our actions or even if humanity will survive as a species. There is only a need to be curious about what our hearts are here for and are capable of and to live each day from that curiosity.

Cultivating Resiliency

A sustainable system in nature is one that has both its natural feedback system intact and a level of resiliency to be able to absorb change and trauma. Most people are out of touch with their natural feedback system and unequipped to bounce back or to integrate unexpected challenges and crises successfully. Although we know that crises occur in our families and in our communities daily, we often pretend that they do not. Our social systems are not designed to provide adequate support in crises, and we view death and disease as unfortunate disruptions that negatively impact the status quo.

Within this environment, personal pain is often experienced in isolation. When loss or heartbreak happens, people are forced to integrate their pain somatically, emotionally, and spiritually, without support, while at the same time pretending to participate fully in life. Storms are a regular part of nature, as are crises in life, so preparing for them is an unquestionable tenet of sustainable design. A sustainable system has supports in place for any and all storms.

We can also utilize our personal traumas as contexts for growth by nurturing the compassionate presence within—the principles of deep listening, the sacred pause, transparency, turning toward rather than away, and seeing clearly. These same tools help us to respond with wisdom when challenges arise.

We can invest in resiliency through the cultivation of compassionate relationships—with our self, our communities, and the world at large. As a planet, the reality is that none of us can actually control the fate of the web of interconnection that is Life. But we can acknowledge from a place of wakefulness our true role in the web of interconnection and choose to bring to it responsibility, passion, joie de vivre, and compassion.

Mindfulness, Compassion, and Activism

Taking compassionate action can sometimes feel more challenging than leading or following the polarized actions that are so popular in our world. Ego finds the context of polarization quite familiar and safe. It requires much more of us to find a compassionate response to a political or global issue. And a compassionate response that honors the question, "What is best for all in this situation?" makes the greatest long-term impact. The invitation is to first turn our attention within, in order to face our own, often complex and contradictory, feelings about an issue. From there, we can unhook ourselves from unhelpful reactivity and direct our attention to what is real rather than to conditioned story. If we listen patiently, compassionate action may arise in any number of forms; but it will come from creative intelligence rather than reactivity. It will make impact rather than cause harm.

There are endless forms that activism can take, but compassionate action is always non-violent. It is always directed towards the alleviation of suffering, rather than towards moral righteousness. It carries long-term rather than short-term view. And it feels loving, even if it is a strong or protective expression. Compassionate action might lead us to protesting or speaking up about injustice or to starting an organization on behalf for a cause. It might also lead to no action other than silence. Sometimes amid a barrage of loud voices, silence itself is the most potent and powerful tool we have. Silence, when it is called for, can be a demonstration of giving oneself by holding a form: the form of stillness as a teaching in non-separation.

Finding the Hero in You, Finding Dignity

When I began to reclaim my personal power from the mind of separation, I became aware of a level of courage, compassion, ease, and unstoppability that I had not before known. But deep inside I had. I had, like so many of us, learned to turn away from my authentic power. I did not see a welcome place in the world around me for a genuinely powerful woman, one who stood for the shared power of "We" and the strength of sensitivity.

I had been taught that power was about "louder, bigger, better, faster, power over." But I ended up learning that the ultimate and only real power humans have is the ability to meet life with love—to give and receive love. The more courageous vulnerability I accessed, the more my striving softened, and the more humbled and patient I became with myself, the more there was love. Also I felt more power—not egoic power, but shared power. This power carried the qualities of stillness, patience, perseverance, and a steadfast compassion for our shared suffering.

I believe that each of us has a hero/heroine within, one that we have been trained to discount, diminish, and hide from. We play it small by giving our power to the conditioned mind. When we commit to a practice of presence and Relational Mindfulness, we remember our natural state as an expression of interconnected consciousness—more vast, caring, wise, and powerful than we ever imagined. We realize that we had given up our power to the mind of separation and that by allowing it to divide us from ourselves, from one another, and from the earth we had given up our shared power.

Our shared power is our interconnection as sentient beings. Our shared power does not go away. It is always there, and it will be there when we are ready to reclaim it. The point of practice is to allow the pain we feel for our world to evoke our willingness to step outside of our tiny little bubble of isolation and continually expand our embodiment of the consciousness of our interconnection. This is ultimately what love is, and this is what Relational Mindfulness teaches us.

This shift requires us to remember the hero within and to let go of playing it small.

In the words of Joanna Macy:

> The most remarkable feature of this historical moment on earth is not that we are on the way to destroying the world—we've actually been on the way for quite a while. It is that we are beginning to wake up, as from a millennia-long sleep, to a whole new relationship to our world, to ourselves, and to each other.

· · · · · · · · Mindful Inquiry · · · · · · · ·

What concerns me most about the world today is _____.

When I think of the world we will leave our children, it looks like _____ and I feel _____.

Ways that I avoid these feelings are _____.

Ways that these feelings empower and inspire my choices are _____.

Some of the ways that I take part in the healing of my world are _____.

What I find hard in the process of changing old ways is _____.

What keeps me going in this work is _____.

In talking with children about the state of the world, what I would like them to know and feel is _____.

One way I would like to "step it up" myself is _____.

I am supported and held accountable to my deepest heart's intentions by _____.

REFLECTIONS ON FINDING
THE HERO WITHIN

How have you experienced the hero/heroine within? What aspects of heroism do you carry? Courage? Command? Willingness? Tenacity? Kindness?

Are there aspects of life where you play it small?

Can you tell someone your hero's story, acknowledging at least one thing you have done in life to make a positive impact large or small, when you did not let yourself be stopped? Be generous with yourself, acknowledging that every step we take to move beyond the separate self and live more from true nature involves a hero's story.

· · · · · · · · **Daily Practice** · · · · · · · ·

Today, begin by taking in a few relaxing deep breaths into the center of your heart. Allow your attention to be drawn to a relaxed part of your body, and rest your attention there, noticing sensation, temperature, and vibration. Then, when you are ready, allow your attention to be drawn to another relaxed part of your body— taking a few minutes to simply practice relaxation.

When you are ready, pick one challenge that our world is facing and bring it into your awareness. Allow yourself to soften your body and hold this topic in your heart as you meditate, in stillness, for ten minutes. Notice all of the feelings that it brings up for you and allow yourself to simply be with and turn toward each of those feelings. Notice where those feelings reside in your body.

Now consider two different parties affected by this situation. For instance, if the issue you picked is police brutality, pick the victims and the police. See if you can find compassion for both parties in regards to the brutality—for example, compassion for everyone whose lives have been taken so unjustly and violently and those who must be carrying around a tremendous amount of trauma and fear to act so unjustly in the world. And lastly, see if you can find compassion for yourself, as someone witnessing these atrocities occurring during your lifetime, feeling affected by them every day.

Anytime you get stuck or challenged in this meditation, bring your focus back to the practice of relaxation. And when you are ready, begin again.

If it is difficult to access compassion for any of the parties, you might experiment with these words, "I see you. I see your pain. I see your suffering. I allow my heart to open to you."

18

Sustaining Ourselves
as Change Agents

Many things have to change course, but it is we human beings above all who need to change. We lack an awareness of our common origin, of a mutual belonging, and of a future to be shared with everyone. This basic awareness . . . will demand that we set out on the long path of renewal."

—Pope Francis

We can philosophize about the state of the world and how humans could make a difference, but there is nothing more direct—nor more satisfying—than embodying and aligning our actions with interconnection. With the world facing such confusion and devastation, there is something we're all being asked right now: to heal not just the symptoms of separation, but the myth of separation. Relational Mindfulness offers a grounded pathway for moving beyond the distortion that the myth of separation has created in our psyches and our communities. It helps us to listen more deeply, to move beyond the noise of surface thought and access the deeper clarity within. It dissolves the habit of perceiving people as "other than" when we are of the same source. It empowers us to stop deferring to external authority over the authority of our hearts. It helps us to remember that "this too" can be met with the loving acceptance of nonseperate awareness. And it affirms our capacity for sacred connection, a source of ever-deepening fulfillment in our lives. Relational Mindfulness returns us to the wholeness that is our birthright.

When I look back at the darkest times in my life, there was a level of disconnect that was both necessary and unnecessary at the same time. Conditioned messages kept me from seeing clearly. By choosing to open my eyes to the darkness and perceive in a new way, I learned to see beyond that conditioning. This inspired a process of awakening in me that will continue for as long as I am on this earth. It began by being willing to risk going beyond what I thought I knew was true—and I took that risk again and again.

By being willing to turn towards our shadows, we learn to question the barrier between light and shadow. By being willing to be transparent with one another and share our vulnerability, we remove perceived obstacles to the heart that is already open. By being willing to honor our pain for the world, we affirm tremendous shared power. By being willing to rest in the vulnerability of "not knowing," we allow our habit of controlling life to soften into trusting life. Relational Mindfulness is a pathway for love in the largest sense. Every part of our human experience, enjoyable or painful, becomes a teacher of that love—and we become its devoted students.

Moving Beyond Resistance

Even when we are willing to awaken to interconnection, there are aspects of our psyche that continue to resist and make the process much more difficult than is necessary. It is helpful to understand that resistance in all its forms—fear, procrastination, or attachment to victimization—is just a false protection against the all-powerful force of love. We can face this resistance both firmly and with a light heart, like a parent mentoring a growing child.

It can seem difficult to let go of our addiction to suffering for three reasons:

1. Suffering has a lot of momentum. We have believed the myth of separation for a long time. We come up with excuses to delay practice. We insist that the problem is "out there" and not within ourselves. We tell ourselves that others may be able to wake up, but for some reason we are different.

2. Suffering, as painful as it can be, has at least given us the illusion of comfort because we have become accustomed to it. Letting go of "subtle incessant dissatisfaction" is freedom for the heart, but for ego this equates to death. Habit gives us somewhere seemingly solid to stand amid the mystery and the vastness of life. When we realize that the part of our psyche that is terrified of letting go of the separate self is trying desperately to maintain itself, our fear begins to dissipate, and we access the willingness that is required for awakening.

3. Suffering gives us a false sense of belonging that we can be afraid to trade in for real intimacy. In other words, it can be frightening to release our conditioning on our own, when our family, friends, and culture may not be ready to let go. We sometimes hold on to toxic relationships or contracts with others, instead of cultivating a conscious relationship with ourselves.

Following are some of the most common misconceptions that people reveal as they begin this path of letting go:

- If you live from your authentic self, you won't be able to fit in, succeed, or survive. To be a member of society, you just can't live from authenticity all the time.
- Productivity is what makes you valuable as a person, and authenticity is not productive.
- Meditation and Relational Mindfulness take time, and there is not enough time.
- If you are in a state of "just being," you are actually being lazy.
- People don't deserve to receive compassion when they make a mistake; they deserve to be punished.
- Interconnection sounds good and all, but survival is really how we are wired.
- Someone has to lose in order for someone else to win.

Collective Conditioning

As we expand our awareness, we may encounter beliefs and assumptions that society is deeply immersed in. We don't have to take them personally—and we don't have to live under their tyranny. But it is vital to understand that we cannot change the world outside without releasing these misconceptions that we carry within.

As we practice, we also run into conditioned fear-based messages. Think of FEAR as False Evidence Appearing Real.

- If I release my suffering, something dangerous or life-altering will happen. If I become more aware of how the mind of separation operates within me, I will have to face that which I've always pushed away.
- If I start questioning my conditioning, my existing relationships will be threatened, and I'll end up alone.
- If I stop participating in activities that aren't aligned with my true self, I'll lose my friends.

We also run into resistance in the form of self-doubting messages or issues of self-worth:

- This can work for other people, but not for me. I am different.
- I don't believe I'm worth it, and will express this belief by saying that I'll show up to practice but not following through.
- Things can't really change. People can't really change.
- I am already conscious. I don't have to do the work.
- I just don't have time to practice awareness.

As with all conditioned thoughts, we can notice these limiting thoughts arise, and ask ourselves, "Is this actually true? How do I know this?" We can bring awareness to the degree to which we have invested in this thought, and be willing to question it. The more we question our habits of thought and identity, the more inspired and courageous we become to keep questioning.

What We Have When We Have Nothing Familiar

> A journey makes us vulnerable, takes us from our more secure environments and commits us to the unknown. Perhaps this is why the journey has so often been our basic metaphor for life itself.
>
> —Thomas Merton

For all the ways that turning within served me, there came a moment when it was time to close the chapter of my life as a monk and depart from the spiritual community I had been part of for so many years. Even as a monk, I had the safety of identity. I had a chosen both a role in life and a conscious community. The more in touch I became with my authentic self and the authority within, the more I sensed that it was time to release the known and move into completely unfamiliar territory. I sensed the growth that could only come from stepping deeper into the mystery. I began to feel a soul urge to serve others in a larger way and expand beyond the life of a monk.

From time to time during my seven years in the monastery, I had dealt with inner conflict about the choice to remain living as a monk. Each time such conflict arose, I made the choice to make monastic life my expression of love and service. When I first separated from the monastery, it felt to me like leaving a familiar shore for open waters without seeing the next shore in sight. In the beginning, it was utterly heart-wrenching. Yet I had metaphorically left the familiar shore time and time again, in every instance of letting go of my past ego-centered orientation to life, and I knew that I would continue to do so.

Out in a world where no one shared my experience as a monk, I felt alone, and it was not easy. But I knew I had the tools to take one stroke at a time and to swim out into the unknown. As long as I was guided by presence, I trusted the bigger picture and kept swimming.

As I moved forward, I slowly became aware of a veil of separation I had placed between the monastery and the world to which I had returned. I began to understand that this was a false separation between the consciousness dichotomy of "those who are on the path" and "those who are not." It was an invisible line placed between the sacredness of spiritual practice and the sticky messy world in which we all live. When this dividing line was revealed to me, I knew it was inherently false and realized there was a thick layer of arrogance in it. It was a form of seeing through the lens of "other," and I sensed the treasure to be found in dissolving it. I saw evidence of the myth of separation all around me in the city in which I lived. The more I made myself available to serve, teach, and participate in community in the larger world, in many diverse contexts and environments often outside my comfort zone, the more I affirmed the essential truth of interconnection. I could bring the practice of Relational Mindfulness into any context and find intimacy and unity—no one and nothing left out. The reality is that the human heart is always open, and Relational Mindfulness helps to remove the distortions that get in the way of remembering this.

The Resources for Resilience

When we have nothing familiar to hold on to, we have the choice to turn deeply to our inner resources and see that even when we feel naked and alone, our well of resources within remains intact. Finding center is a choice we can make in any moment. For those of us who view ourselves as change agents in the world to whatever degree and in whatever realm we are working, there are moments when all that we have access to are the resources within. For each of us forging a new way of being, pioneering, and letting go of our entanglement in an old paradigm, there are moments when we cannot see the path clearly because it has not yet been forged.

The path of awareness tests and strengthens our inner resources every day that we show up to practice. It strengthens our relationship with ourselves. Imagine a companion at your side at all times saying, "I am with you. I love you, and throughout everything that might appear as an up or down, an expansion or contraction, a victory or a loss, I will help you to remember who you are. I will help you to remember the boundless and steadfast quality of awareness. You are not alone, and I will be here with you no matter what."

Practice affirms our sense of belonging/interconnection with others. By taking responsibility for our shadows and showing up to the relational field with vulnerability and honesty, our sense of belonging and being a part of the larger landscape that is our world is strengthened.

It deepens our connection with the planet we inhabit, and with all beings of the past, present, and future. By engaging more intimately with the natural world and treating it as an extension of ourselves, we become less confused by the myth that we are the small solitary bubble of ego.

It deepens our trust in presence. If there is one mantra to carry into all dark places, it is this: I trust presence to guide me. I trust presence to guide me through navigating this life, moment by moment, with love.

Whether or not we can know the ultimate outcome of our survival as a species at this time, we gain shared power, joy, and fierce compassion within by committing to being vessels for change and sustaining change in our world.

This Work Is Fed through the Nourishment of Joy

A bone-deep joy begins to weave itself through the fabric of our life as we allow interconnection to permeate all parts of our human experience. Those of us who are privileged to be giving our time and energy to creating a kinder, saner, more sustainable world know that it is a full-time job. It requires taking responsibility and letting go of old ways of being. It requires commitment. It requires a fundamental shift from product to process. It requires time to be with life in spacious awareness, meeting whatever life presents with deep listening. In a world that glamorizes busyness and survival mode, it invites us to see busyness as the surface habit that it is. It is not a job in the sense of "work," but it can be hard work nevertheless.

This work can be approached most successfully with the spirit of joyful responsibility. It is joyful in the sense that spending time in awareness, free of delusion, offers deep contentment. It is joyful in the sense that it deepens our access to vitality and creativity as we set our egos aside to be of service to the larger whole. It is joyful in light of the intimacy and tenderness it gives us access to.

At times we can become caught up in stories that seem overwhelming, such as "this work takes too much effort and perhaps I'm not up to it," or "opening my eyes more fully to how the mind of separation operates in me is painful at times," or "I'm feeling immobilized by how much cleaning up there is to do on this planet." It is therefore imperative to stay connected at all times to the underlying point of practice.

By returning to the consciousness of "We" over "I," the entire world becomes a more compassionate place to be. We have a compassionate presence as a guide and we now realize that we are never alone.

Whenever I become overwhelmed or doubt my ability to choose love, I seek support from the consciousness of "We." I do this through sitting in meditation and allowing myself to be held in the spacious awareness of presence. I reach out to someone I trust to listen to me. I spend time in silence or in the deep green sanctuary of the woods, or give myself fully to dance, forgetting the mind entirely. I let go of whatever nagging thoughts have my attention and turn instead to the deep knowing of the awareness. That enables me to say no to all that is nonessential. I turn to my body's innate ability to relax and remember that awareness does not judge or react. Awareness is a boundless refuge that we can come home to as long as we are willing.

The task at hand does not actually require a lot of *doing*. It comes more from *being*, and addressing our personal, interpersonal, and transpersonal way of being, so that we can participate in an undoing of the collective myth of separation. I cannot think of anything more pertinent than returning our authority to the heart. It is deeply rewarding to get ego out of the way, and to see

302   HEALING OUR RELATIONSHIP WITH GLOBAL UNCERTAINTY

what is possible when we operate from our natural intelligence rather than from conditioning.

Essence is totally unaffected by our conditioning. The natural world is totally unaffected by our conditioning. The relational field is totally unaffected. Our minds become lured by the myth of separation—but we are much more than our minds.

Nonnegotiable Basics for Sustaining Ourselves as Change Agents

It is important to remember that we cannot participate in the release of the myth of separation alone. Our communities are here to remind us. Our body is here to remind us. The wind, sunlight, and rain are here to remind us. Human laughter reminds us. Our own and others' children remind us. We can support ourselves and restore ourselves by some of the following:

- following a nonnegotiable healthy routine
- spending periods in the timeless realm of being rather than doing
- asking for help when it is needed
- choosing simplicity and sufficiency
- spending time immersed in nature
- enjoying music, art, or dance, any form of creativity that gets you out of your head
- engaging in laughter, play, and spontaneity
- receiving bodywork or energy work
- doing conscious movement
- finding ways to be of service to the world
- accessing beginners mind as often as we can
- relaxing the mind and trusting the wisdom of "not knowing"

When we reside in whole mind, we avail ourselves of a much broader range of support. We no longer cut ourselves off from experiencing direct support from other forms of life, plants and animals, our ancestors, or other levels of consciousness. When we are not stubbornly holding on to belief systems, we do not push away realities that may not fit with our old beliefs.

As we allow our awareness to expand, we naturally receive information and insight that comes from places we did not have access to when we identified as separate self. This is not arcane information. Quite plainly, when we identify with the separate self holding on to conditioned beliefs, we close out entire venues of information in the vast universe in which we live.

The more we choose to experience life through whole mind awareness, the entire universe shows up to support us. When we identify as a part of earth consciousness, rather than focusing on the human sphere, we can call in all of the forms of support— from the medicine of plants to prayer—to help us to live each day on behalf of "We." And in so doing, we co-create new pathways for humanity to live in partnership with the planet.

The You of the Future Is a Resource

In my most challenging times as a monk, I would ask myself, "What would the me of the future do in this situation? If I could reach far into the future and have a conversation with her, what would she have to offer me right now?" Even when I felt stuck or could not fathom why life was offering me such a great challenge, I had faith that my future self would have moved beyond this challenge. I trusted in the person I would become, even if I was immersed in a fearful, messy, or awkward moment in my own development. In this way, I learned to get out of my own way and trust the guidance of the compassionate presence within. Asking this question and then patiently awaiting an answer, I was able to step beyond whatever small perspective I was caught in, and gain access to insights that came from my larger self. This helped me to remember, time and time again, that my whole self was already here. The me of the future was actually here in present time. All I needed to do was adjust my attention away from my conditioning and turn toward my essence.

Participating in Life Wholeheartedly

At the monastery where I trained, the daily schedule was built around working meditation. We did not do working meditation in order to "get things done" or for approval. We did working meditation to participate wholeheartedly in life, deepening our capacity to pay attention and meet life with presence as we worked. Whether baking bread, driving the tractor, digging in the garden, or doing carpentry, we received nourishment just by showing up fully. I (like all of us) showed up fully whether or not "I" wanted to, letting go of ego's agendas and stories, and making myself available to serve life.

The most easily sustained satisfaction I experience in life comes from present moment participation in life. Relational Mindfulness invites us into full participation. Through bringing greater presence to our daily interactions, our own stories which may have carried great momentum in the past begin to bore us. Although our lives have often been directed or controlled by our stories, there awaits tremendous relief in letting them go.

The gift in the spirit of repetition is that, as we continue to show up to practice, to surrender to and give ourselves fully to the task at hand, we support the organic dissolution of the separate self. When we show up wholeheartedly for the sake of bringing a present quality of attention to a task, over and over and over, in a sense we learn to "get out of the way" and become one with the task at hand. This serves us in all of our activities and relationships. The spirit of repetition allows our work to become a mirror for self-awareness above all else, and gradually allows us to cultivate the qualities of humility and dedication.

• • • • • • • • Mindful Inquiry • • • • • • • •

It is vital that as change agents, we place ourselves in a field of regenerative support and reciprocity. How do you give yourself the support you need? Which of the following are part of your support system?

- a daily meditation practice, even if it begins with five minutes of meditation per day
- time to immerse in the natural world
- "deep time" to spend in the timeless realm of being rather than doing
- deep rest and replenishment
- creative expression
- a community or circle of friends who nourish you deeply
- a body-based practice such as dance or tai chi
- people you trust to listen and to hold you accountable to your deepest intentions
- people you can turn to when you are facing challenging times
- connection with plants, animals, or other allies from the natural world that support your true nature

What I have to offer/give/model/share in this time of change in our world is _____.

A perceived limitation I am willing to let go for the sake of the whole is _____. (Or, if I am not ready to let go of it, am I willing at least to investigate it?)

What challenges or fears are currently in your way?

What would it take to cultivate courage in the face of these fears?

What steps would you take to contribute if there were no perceived challenges?

What qualities or process do you wish to bring to your work in the world (for instance: courage, peace, ease, presence, joy, fortitude, trust?)

Is there any way that you need to ask for help or accountability from outside of you?

Lastly, what is one step you can take this week to affirm you alignment with this vision?

· · · · · · · · **Daily Practice** · · · · · · · ·

CONVERSATION WITH YOUR FUTURE SELF

Today, take five to ten minutes to turn your attention within and meditate, inviting yourself to relax into the spaciousness of awareness. You can do this meditation either sitting or lying down.. When you are finished, with your eyes closed, take a moment to reflect on where you are in life, reflecting on what you are grateful for and what challenges you face. When you are ready, invite connection with your future self. Imagine that your future self has access to even more life experience, wisdom, and courage than you do now. Your future self is an even more embodied expression of your authentic self. Have a conversation with the you of the future.

Ask your future self, "Is there any guidance you have to offer me today? About my life? About a particular question I am holding? About my contribution to the world? Is there any encouragement or reassurance you have for me today?"

Allow yourself to simply listen and to patiently wait for response.

When you are finished, please turn your attention to your breath and take a minute to be still. In your jounral make any notes that you find helpful.

Please note that this exercise may call forth a sense of possibility and imagination. It calls for recognition that linear time is not the only time we are connected to, but that the heart has a much more expansive knowledge of time.

If you wish to take a next step with this exercise, you can write a letter from your future self to your current self. The purpose of this letter is for your future self to express gratitude for how you are living your life, how you are meeting life's challenges, and for all the ways you are giving your energy to consciousness. Writing and later reading this letter can be a deeply nourishing and profound experience.

Appendix 1

Helpful Guidelines for Working with a Partner or a Group

If you are reading this book with a partner or group, it is important to uphold

safety

confidentiality

structure

honesty

compassion

With a partner or group, it is recommended that you read this book over an established time frame, such as one chapter per week, or one chapter per month.

After each individual answers the inquiry prompts in writing, take five minutes each to share what you learned and any insights you have had. Pick one person to be the listener, who just pays attention without asking any questions or making any comments, and then switch and allow that person to become the speaker while the other person just listens.

Then do the practices offered, in pairs. Follow this with a period of reflection on what you noticed.

If holding a discussion group, it is important to maintain a container of deep listening. You can either take turns speaking, perhaps using a talking stick (any object you choose to pass around noting who is speaking and inviting everyone to give their full attention to that speaker), or you can take turns facilitating the group if members have facilitation skills.

You can also schedule a personal or group workshop/retreat taught by me or a facilitator trained to guide these specific practices. Please visit deborahedentull.com or mindfullivingrevolution .org for more information.

Appendix 2

Formal Relational Mindfulness Practices

These are some formal practices that can be experienced with partners or in groups. As vulnerability and compassion are foundational aspects of each of these exercises, it is important that they be practiced in a context of safety and presence. Please note that while anyone can do the partner exercises, the group exercises, such as Circle of Transparency and Truth Mandala, require someone in the role of facilitator. These practices can be profound gateways to intimacy, and they can also bring up discomfort. The point is never to "get it right" or "achieve a state" with these practices. It is simply about showing up and paying attention. Please follow the guidelines and steps offered. They are in place, after all, for a reason.

Deep Listening

This is a simple practice to do with a partner using any of the inquiry prompts offered in this book. Before beginning, both participants are encouraged to take a moment, to pause, close their eyes, take in a deep relaxing breath, and check in with their body, feelings, and mind. Then the practice begins. Decide who will speak first and who will speak second. The person speaking first has the responsibility to remain as present as they can while sharing whatever arises in response to the question asked. The person speaking second is the listener with the simple job of asking the question and listening to their partner share without adding anything. This means no questions, no comments, and no problem solving. It means to rest one's full attention on the person while they share. A timer is set (or a facilitator can ring a bell). Usually three to five minutes is enough time per person. After the share, both people pause to once again take in a couple of conscious breaths and turn within to notice their experience. Then they switch. At the very end of this practice both people might want to share with each other how it was to just listen, what they observed inside, how it felt to share, and what they received. This practice can be followed by noticing and processing how it was to be the listener and give someone your complete attention, and how it was to be listened to and to receive someone else's full attention.

Open Sentences

This is a partner exercise. Before beginning, both participants are encouraged to take a moment to pause, close their eyes, take in a deep relaxing breath, and check in with their body, feelings, and mind. Then the practice begins. The first person will ask the partner a question, and the person responding will answer the question in whatever way feels authentic in the moment. He or she might answer with one word or an entire paragraph. The point is to allow whatever arises naturally to arise and not do any editing or preparing. Then the person listening will say thank you, which helps the listener to stay present and will ask the same question again. Just as the breath is our anchor in meditation, in this relational meditation the anchor is to rest one's attention fully on the other person and listen. The same question then gets repeated, and the speaker again answers in whatever way feels authentic in that moment. This process will get repeated a few minutes until it is time to switch. Beginner questions for open sentences can be:

What brings you joy?

What is something you are no longer afraid of?

What are the qualities of your essence? Tell me about your essence?

What takes you away from your authentic self?

Transparency Exercise 1: What Are You Present To?

This is a partner exercise. Decide who is going first and who is going second. Before beginning, both participants are encouraged to take a moment, to pause, close their eyes, take in a deep relaxing breath and check in with their body, feelings, and mind. Then the practice begins. Partner A will ask partner B: What are you present to? or What are you aware of in this moment? or Tell me what you are present to. Partner B will simply have an opportunity to speak from the moment. For example: I am noticing the touch of air on my skin, the sound of a bird chirping, the weight of my body relaxing into gravity, the presence of a set of eyes watching me as I speak, the question in my head, "Am I doing this right?" After the first person shares, both partners can close their eyes again to pause and turn within for a moment. Then they switch. There is no need to come up with clever responses in this exercise or to fill up space. It is an opportunity to share the field of pure awareness with another being. Be sure to maintain eye contact while doing this exercise.

Transparency Exercise 2: Telling the Microscopic Truth

This is a partner exercise. Decide who is going first and who is going second. Before beginning, both participants are encouraged to take a moment to pause, close their eyes, take in a deep relaxing breath, and check in with their body, feelings, and mind. Then the practice begins. The point of this exercise is to have an experience of speaking about a topic that is alive in your life while having the opportunity to attend to the inner landscape at the same time. Partner A will speak while partner B just listens. Partner A will bring up a topic and then from time to time partner B will ask: What do you notice in your body while you speak? What are you present to while you speak about this? How does it feel to share this with me? What emotions or feelings are you noticing? What sensations are you present to in your body while you speak? After the first person shares, both partners can close their eyes again to pause and turn within for a moment. Then they switch. For more information on this exercise please revisit chapter 9 on Transparency.

Reflective Listening

This is a partner exercise. Decide who is going first and who is going second. Before beginning, both participants are encouraged to take a moment, to pause, close their eyes, take in a deep relaxing breath, and check in with their body, feelings, and mind. Then the practice begins. The instruction for this practice is to deeply listen to the person who is speaking and to reflect back to them, in their own words, what they are saying. The speaker might say a few lines or a few paragraphs, but it is important that the speaker pause from time to time to allow the listener to reflect. The listener's job is to then say back to the person the gist of what they have shared without changing the words or offering their own spin. This helps the speaker to hear more deeply the issue that they are talking about. It helps the speaker to come to deeper insight around the issue they are looking at. Example:

> I've been feeling excitement and fear about my upcoming move . . .
>
> So what I hear you saying is, you've been feeling excitement and fear about your upcoming move.
>
> Yes, but right now I'm much more aware of the fear. I'm afraid of leaving my community. I'm afraid it will be too cold. And I'm afraid of how it will impact my work.
>
> So you are afraid of leaving your community, afraid of the cold, and afraid of the impact on your work.
>
> Yes. Hearing you say that, I think the biggest fear is leaving my community. I feel . . . (The person talks for a while and ends with the sentence, "It took me a long time to establish community here and I'm not sure I'm up for doing it all over again.")
>
> So you are not sure you're up for establishing community all over again.

This practice is a way of being a compassionate presence for the other person. It helps the speaker to hear themselves more clearly and therefore gain insights. It is also very useful in conflict. This exercise also helps the listener to stay present. In other words, when there might be a pull to react to something being said or to come up with a solution, this structure, simply reflective listening, holds the listener accountable to being present.

Circle of Transparency

This is a Relational Mindfulness exercise or game for a group of people. It is derived from a practice traditionally called Hot Seat and a beautiful way to invite people to engage in the moment with one another and to experience the power of transparency and vulnerability. In order to hold a safe container for this exercise, it is necessary to have one person act as the facilitator or guide. Once everyone is in a circle and has taken a moment to settle into presence together, the facilitator can set guidelines and then ask for a volunteer to come into the center of the circle. The main guideline should be everything that is said is held in confidentiality.

The facilitator will call on people who wish to ask a question, so that there is some order.

Everyone stays for the duration of the exercise in order to not disrupt the space.

As a relational practice, everyone's intention is to stay as present as they can and to bring awareness to their experience.

All of the other participants are invited to rest their gaze gently on this person sitting in the center of the circle as in a meditation. The person in the center is now in the position to receive questions from anyone in the group, which they are invited to answer with transparency. The facilitator can call on members of the circle to ask these questions in order to ensure a safe space. The first person might begin with simply asking: How does it feel to be in the center of the circle? or What inspired you to volunteer first? The instruction for people asking questions is to stay as present as they can and follow their curiosity. Following their curiosity means to ask questions that intuitively arise and to listen for the openings or clues in a person's response that might invoke the next question. People are invited to ask questions from the heart and with respect. People are welcome to ask provocative questions, but discouraged to ask questions with an agenda of "being edgy" or to try to analyze the person in the center. The person in the center of the circle is welcome to pass on any questions they do not wish to answer.

At the very end of the exercise, when the facilitator begins to feel that it is time to bring it to a close, the facilitator will ring a bell to announce that it will soon be time to close the circle. Final questions can be asked, and then at the very end, the facilitator will invite appreciations to be offered to the person in the center of the circle. Appreciations can be as simple as, "I appreciated your openness and your vulnerability," or "When you spoke of your family's challenges, I saw how big your heart is and I felt absolute solidarity with you." It is helpful to end this exercise with a couple minutes of silence.

Truth Mandala

This Relational Mindfulness practice comes from The Work that Reconnects and is published in full form in the 1998 book *Coming Back to Life* by Joanna Macy and Molly Brown. I find it a beautiful way to bring people together in a field of Relational Mindfulness to honor our pain for the world. This is a ritual for speaking out about our pain for the world and recognizing the solidarity that speaking truth can bring.

People sit in a circle, guided by a facilitator. The circle is divided into four quadrants and each quadrant holds a symbolic object: dead leaves, a thick stick, a stone, and an empty bowl. The dry leaves represent grief and sorrow for what is happening in our world. The stone is for fear. The stick represents our anger and outrage. The empty bowl is symbolic of our hunger for what is missing. Hope is also represented, by the very process itself. The exercise typically begins with a dedication and invitation for people to settle into deep listening. A few guidelines are set: for instance, that everything is held in confidentiality and that no one leaves in the middle of the ritual.

After a short meditation for people to settle in to presence, people are invited, one by one, in their own time, to step into the circle. They are invited to pick up an object that holds the emotion they want to honor and to speak their truth about the pain for the world, while everyone listens. It is fine for a person to pick up more than one object. The group rests their full attention on that person as they are speaking, and at the very end of each person's share, they say the words together, "We see you. We hear you."

Participants are invited to stay as connected as they can to their body, feelings, and hearts as the ritual proceeds. When the facilitator feels that it is time to bring the ritual to a close, the facilitator often invites people who have been holding back or waiting on a signal to step up if they would like to do so. Then the facilitator guides a closing moment to honor the truth that each person has spoken and the support that each person has given.

It is helpful for the facilitator to take time to debrief the participants about this experience and to support people to integrate it.

Appendix 3
Seeing with a Quiet Mind

Practices for Connecting with Ourselves and the Natural World

Here are three exercises to practice awareness through the senses and cultivate "seeing with a quiet mind" in today's busy world. These practices relate to chapter 13.

Three Mindful Steps

Allow yourself at least ten minutes for the following meditation. You can do this meditation anywhere—outside in nature, in your backyard, or indoors—but it is useful to have some degree of quiet to help you to focus.

Take three mindful steps and STOP. Close your eyes and bring your awareness first to your sense of hearing and listen to the sounds surrounding you, without any need to label what you hear. Simply receive. Then take another breath and shift your attention to taste, followed by smell, followed by touch, simply noticing the feeling of the air touching your skin, without internal commentary. If there is commentary, notice it without judgment, and direct your attention back to your sensory experience. Lastly, bring awareness to your vision, looking around you and seeing with a quiet mind, without any need to label your experience. Then pause, take a deep breath again, and take three more mindful steps. Repeat the process.

This is one of my favorite meditations. I always find that it heightens my senses and expands my awareness. It helps me to tune in fully to the beauty that is surrounding me, wherever I am. Sometimes the experience is subtle. Other times, at the end of this meditation I experience what we might call an altered state of awareness. Paying attention to our sensory experience is a radical act in a society that encourages us to numb out. This can be a helpful meditation to practice on a regular basis. What do you notice when you tune into your senses in this way?

One Activity at a Time

Pick a time of day to practice "one activity at a time." If you choose to listen to music, simply listen without any other distraction, and see if you enjoy the subtleties of listening more fully. If you choose to prepare a meal, simply cook, turning off your cell phone and the TV and focusing entirely on the sensory experience of washing, chopping, tasting, with your full attention. Consider the countless opportunities in a day for fully experiencing the pleasure of the moment without distraction. Pick something ordinary, like washing the dishes, cleaning your car, or brushing your teeth. What would happen if you turned off your phone and allowed yourself to wholeheartedly give yourself to that one activity at a time, not trying to reach any particular goal, but simply paying attention to the process of what you are engaging in? What would happen if you invited into ordinary activities the spirit of "just being present"? What do you notice?

Seeing with a Quiet Mind

Turn your attention within, take a deep breath, and bring gentle curiosity to your moment-by-moment experience.

This is an invitation to cultivate a richer, more three-dimensional life experience and to turn to your own experience to teach you.

This is a visual meditation practice to help you explore seeing with more awareness and receptivity, free of agenda and free of your mind's interpretations or expectations of your visual experience. This is a simple exercise. You can do this exercise either indoors or outdoors. Pick any scene or object. Begin by closing your eyes and turning your attention to your breath, fully feeling the air as it enters your body, fills your body, and leaves your body, not trying to get anywhere with your breath, but rather fully receiving and enjoying your breath.

Then gently open your eyes and take a moment to allow your eyes to relax in their sockets, taking on a soft rather than a hard gaze. Begin to observe the object or scene in front of you, paying attention to the experience of seeing, without any need to label what you see or to listen to your mind's commentary about what you see. Just look without labeling and return again and again to your authentic visual experience. Notice the subtleties of what is in front of you and the space around it. Imagine that it is your first time seeing this object or scene (which it is, if we consider that every moment is a fresh moment).

As you look, notice the experience you are having in your body. Allow any physical sensations that are there to be there. Notice the sensations and muscles around your eyes as you see.

Take your time. When you notice the thinking mind begin to label your experience, STOP and focus on bringing your attention back to your breath and to your authentic experience of seeing. Bring awareness to your eyes as you gaze, noticing how effortless it is to simply see. To the best of your ability, stay connected with your experience of seeing rather than to the commentary about what you are seeing.

Now do this a second time, and this time allow yourself to label your visual experience in the most bare-bones way. In other words, you can label exactly what you see while looking out a window—light, gray, curving shape, pointing angle, moving shadow—without going into the meaning (gray clouds, winter sky, pine tree) or the associations and stories we attach (depressing weather, cold and wet, another winter's day in Portland). What did you notice?

When we are not fully present, we often look at something through the filter of association. The mind immediately labels whatever it is we are looking at and we jump to our association with that object, rather than staying present to our fresh in-the-moment experience of it. For example, when you look at an apple, an item you probably see regularly, do you really see it? Do you notice the subtleties in color, texture, shape? Or have you seen so many apples that your mind labels it "apple," and turns to your mind's interpretation of "apple" rather experiencing this particular apple at the moment, in all of its beauty and perfection or imperfection? When you look at the people you see every day, do you allow yourself to see them through new eyes each day? Or does the habitual labeling of the thinking mind get in the way?

Can you imagine being able to see everything (including yourself) with this same sense of freshness, wonder, and open-mindedness? The trees you see every day? The streets you see every day? Your family and the people you see regularly? And most importantly, yourself? This is the root of what is referred to in Zen as "beginner's mind."

Appendix 4

Bringing Relational Mindfulness and Cultural Humility to Group Interactions

As we address the larger work that this day and age require, it is especially important to know how to practice Relational Mindfulness in group situations—from personal conflicts to group meetings of people with differing views.

We have all attended meetings in which people with great purpose do not seem to see and/or listen clearly. We have all experienced situations in which the power of presence could change the whole course of a meeting or a conflict between participants. A commitment to presence is a basic requirement for any successful group interaction.

Relational Mindfulness offers a way to work skillfully with emotions and the shadows behind them and to choose to stay focused, open, and present to interconnection. It invites us to take responsibility for our own shadows and interact within the field of "We" rather than from the orientation of "I" or "me." It helps people to connect from both a more genuine place and to embrace the spirit of teamwork and equality.

We must start from the place of "We" if we are going to show up skillfully and be conscious participants in a group. In order to come from "We," we need to commit to staying present. We can stay present by practicing the following:

- Pausing often enough to attend to our own needs
- Taking responsibility for our "triggers" rather than just reacting to them
- Not taking other people and the things they say personally, but practicing kind neutrality
- When it is time to speak up, doing so with the intention of being of service to the whole rather than speaking from ego
- Modeling the openness, trust, vulnerability, and compassion of mindful inquiry, rather than positioning ourselves as an expert or someone who has the only right answer
- Allowing our awareness to move back and forth between the internal landscape (self-awareness) and awareness of other individuals and the group field, so that we can hold the question, "What is best for all here?"
- Being willing to lead, when the moment calls for it, and being willing to be led
- Modeling acceptance and transparency

Then we are able to:

- Stay present
- Look/see others clearly without the veil of judgment
- Avoid communications mishaps and meet conflict with authenticity
- Contribute to more understanding and efficiency within a group context
- Seek to understand others rather than fight for "being right"
- See the shared nature of human suffering and allow this interconnection to bring us together rather than separate us

- Be of service to the whole
- Participate in co-creativity

What is not particularly helpful in working with groups is:

- Making assumptions
- Taking people's opinions and actions personally
- Projecting rather than seeing/listening
- Having a personal agenda
- Trying to fix/change people with differing ideas or opinions
- Using an intellectual approach to negatively analyze others' ideas or opinions
- Not listening, moving on too quickly
- Holding fast to a position that might require flexibility

Glossary

Authentic Power – The ability to give and receive love. Authentic power is accessed through remaining open, receptive, permeable, and vulnerable with others rather than interacting through a mask or the lens of ego. While ego, feeling separate and under threat, seeks to have "power over," authentic power is an expression of "power with."

Authentic Self – True nature, essence, or who we really are beneath our conditioning. Authentic self is unburdened by the ego and expresses qualities of peace, well-being, acceptance, ease, and wholeness. Each of us has an innately unique expression of authentic self. It is synonymous with True nature or no-self, in Buddhism, because it is who we really are when we allow ourselves to embody the spaciousness of presence.

Awareness Practice – The practice of bringing consciousness to our life experience, moment by moment; being more aware of our thoughts, emotions, bodies, and habit patterns. Meditation and mindfulness are both forms of awareness practice.

Center – The embodiment of present moment awareness in which we are not distracted by our conditioned thoughts but are paying attention in the moment. At center we feel clear, grounded, and able to make conscious rather than unconscious choices. We have a degree of freedom from of the conditioned mind and its stories and distortions because we can see more clearly. We are able to see ourselves and others from compassion.

Compassionate Awareness – The field of ever-present and accepting awareness that contains all of our life experience and all of life's ups and downs.

Conditional Love – The dualistic assumption that some aspects of our self are lovable and some are not, that parts of humanity are acceptable and parts are not, that we deserve reward when we are "good" and punishment when we are "bad."

Conditioning/Conditioned Mind – The habitual thoughts and patterns that fill our minds and thus direct our life experience, if we are not practicing awareness. Conditioning is all of the messaging and beliefs we have taken in from society, family, religion, media, past experience, and negative imprinting.

Consciousness – Consciousness comes from the Latin root meaning "to know" and is synonymous with awareness or wakefulness.

Deep Listening – The practice of giving our full focused and relaxed attention to listening. We can deeply listen to another person, to the sounds in our environment, or to our own inner being.

Dharma – Dharma refers to the wisdom teachings of the Buddha, or in a larger sense, the teachings of truth. Its root, *dham*, means "to support" or "uphold," and the teachings support people in seeing clearly and accessing consciousness.

Disidentification – The act of stepping back from identification with the suffering parts of our self in order to return to center, the field of present moment awareness from which we can see ourself with compassion. For example, we can either identify with and be caught in our anxiety, anger, or attachment to "being right" or we can step back, acknowledge and witness that aspect of us, and be with the anxiety, anger, or attachment. When we disidentify and return to center, we see the part of our self that is suffering clearly and we access the compassion required to meet that life experience. Rather than shutting down around an emotion/trigger, disidentification requires us to remain open. Disidentification is a means for taking responsibility for ourselves, our lives, and our actions.

Dukkha – Suffering or "subtle incessant dissatisfaction." The roots in Buddhism of the word *ukkha* are found in Pali, Sanskrit, and Tibetan, and the term is also referred to in Hinduism.

Ecological Design – An approach to designing systems (for instance, homes, gardens, buildings, or cities) that work with rather than against nature, mimicking the principles of sustainability as modeled by the natural world to guide graceful, efficient, and sustainable design.

Ecosystem – A community comprised of living biotic organisms in conjunction with the abiotic aspects of their environment (such as water, air, and soil), interacting as a system.

Engaged Meditation/Engaged Mindfulness – The framework for integrating meditation and mindfulness into all aspects of life, including work, community, family, and political engagement. Engaged practice is a path for taking greater responsibility for one's participation in the world and one's choices in response to global awareness. It is the path of mindfulness as an expression of activism.

Eros – In Greek mythology, Eros was the Greek god of love. Eros can be thought of as intimate and sexual love, but in the broader sense, eros means "life force." Eros points to vitality, sensuality, and vibrant aliveness, as well as our connection with the natural world.

Erotic Intelligence – Our innate capacity to be guided by eros and authenticity in the realm of sexual intimacy, free of the distraction of the conditioned mind. While the mind of separation ties sexuality to the duality of good/bad, repression/explosion, approval/judgment, and goal orientation, mindfulness offers tools to deepen our embodiment of erotic intelligence.

Essence – The unique presence or signature that we each carry, which comes from our core or inner being, rather than from the ego or personality. Our essence is the unique beauty and wholeness that is who we are seen through the eyes of compassion. It is the unique way that consciousness illuminates us.

Giving Back to the Soil – Within the framework of organic farming, this refers to replenishing the soil or humus after nutrients such as nitrogen have been leached by crops. This practice feeds long-term sustainability of the earth. Within the framework of personal sustainability, this phrase refers to radical self-care. To give back to the soil—in the context of the personal sustainability—means to continually replenish and regenerate ourselves so that we do not become depleted.

Illusion of Separation – In the mechanistic paradigm that has pervaded human thinking for much of the past two centuries, the operating belief system has taught that humans are separate from the planet and reign over nature. The mechanistic era has also taught that we exist in competition, separation, and domination/subordination with one another. If we look more closely, we see that this way of perceiving also causes fracture or disconnect within our self.

Interconnection – The intricate web of life's interdependence that includes all beings and all forms of life on this planet. Relational Mindfulness emphasizes that interconnection is our natural state and separation is a delusion.

Kind Neutrality – A quality we can cultivate through meditation that allows us to welcome our life experience with spaciousness, acceptance, and nonjudgment. The more we learn, through practice, to see clearly and to not take life personally, the more we are able to meet all of our experiences with kind neutrality rather than judgment or reactivity.

Koan – Buddhist teaching offered as a paradoxical-seeming story.

Middle Way – In Buddhist philosophy, the Middle Way refers to the point beyond duality and beyond extremes. Instead of making choices through ideas about morality, practice invites us to turn to our authentic self and find the place of absolute sufficiency and balance for ourselves.

Mind of Separation/Separate Self – The mind of separation is synonymous with the conditioned mind; however, this phrase focuses on how the conditioned mind ultimately causes disconnection rather than oneness within our self, with our experience of life, with other people and life forms, and with the planet.

Mindful Eating – The art of paying attention more subtly to our sacred relationship with food and approaching the process of eating as a meditation in itself. This can mean pausing at mealtime to be aware of our experience of hunger and our motivation for eating, acknowledging gratitude for our food and its source before eating, and paying subtle attention to each of our senses, feelings, mind, and body while we eat.

Mindful Inquiry – The practice of bringing curiosity, nonjudgment, and honesty to our internal process in the moment. Rather than try to analyze, fix, or understand, we turn toward our experience of suffering with a spirit of exploration and patience. Inquiry helps us to see clearly what is happening internally, which allows for disidentification, insight, and compassion to arise.

Mindful Sexuality – The art of bringing awareness to the realm of sexuality. Rather than operating through unconsciousness or autopilot, we pay attention more subtly to our physical, mental, emotional, and spiritual experience of sex. Sexuality can be another means to expand our embodiment of Relational Mindfulness.

Mindfulness – The practice of meeting life, moment by moment, with openness, gentle curiosity, kindness, and a willingness to be with what is. This helps us disengage from habitual, conditioned, unsatisfying, and unskillful habits and behaviors. Mindfulness helps us to see clearly, as old habitual ways arise, that we have the opportunity to make another choice.

Passionate Responsibility – The more we practice, the more we realize that we hold the power of conscious choice in every moment. We make a connection between our personal actions and our ability to impact our world at large. This inspires a sense of empowered and joyful responsibility for how we engage in the world. Rather than feeling powerless or believing the popular story that taking responsibility is boring, we become passionate about taking responsibility for our actions.

Relational Mindfulness – The practice of using all of our interactions—with self, one another, and the planet—to wake up from the mind of separation and remember the interconnected consciousness that is who we really are.

Shadow – Shadows can be defined as those attributes and qualities that are inconsistent with the self-concept we are trying to maintain, but that we are often not aware of

Showing Up – To meet life wholeheartedly and with presence; to resist the temptation to escape, distract, or numb out. For example, whether we are at work, being intimate, or in conversation or conflict with a loved one, we can genuinely pay attention and engage fully, or engage in a distracted or halfhearted way.

Spaciousness Within, The – Spaciousness is an innate quality of present moment awareness. When we are not focused on the busyness of the conditioned mind or our surface thoughts, we gain more access to a peace, calm, and spaciousness within.

Stillness – In sitting meditation, the instruction is to sit without moving, in stillness, in order to allow body, mind, and feelings to settle. On a broader level, stillness refers to the energetic state of calm and expansive settledness that we find through present moment awareness.

Sustainability – This is an approach to life that views environmental, human, and economic well-being as one and the same. Sustainability honors life, and the interconnection in the web of life, as far into the future as one can imagine. A system is only sustainable if it is designed to take care of all components of that system—now and into the future.

Sustainable Agriculture – While conventional farming focuses on producing "the most, the fastest, the cheapest," sustainable agriculture carries a commitment to working with nature to assure long-term sustainability rather than short-term profit.

Wholeness – The felt experience of being complete and not lacking within ourselves.

Zendo – A meditation hall or space for meditation, in the Zen tradition.

Index

fatigue, accepting, 89–90
fear. *See also* mind of separation;
relationships; vulnerability
FEAR (False Evidence Appearing Real) response to expanding awareness, 296–97
Fear of Missing Out (FOMO),
269
feedback
ignoring/fearing, 20–21, 204
opening to, 31, 82–83, 86, 109,
149, 252, 259, 286
feelings, acknowledging and
expressing. *See* relationships;
transparency; vulnerability
Fox, Matthew, 224
frailty, accepting, 23
Francis (Pope), 293
freedom, true. *See also* authentic
self; beginner's mind; transparency
and letting go of ego needs,
55–56, 163–64, 178
and questioning conditioning,
28–30, 242, 297
and releasing the lens of other,
186–87
and sufficiency/sustainability,
232–33
and transparency with others,
122, 135–37
Fukuoka, Masanobu (*The One-
Straw Revolution*), 204–5
Fukushima nuclear disaster, 277–
78
future self, conversation with,
306–7

G
gardening, organic, parallels with
Zen practice, 199–204

global uncertainty. *See also* environmental responsibility;
nature; sufficiency
cultivating resiliency in the face
of, 286–87
and despair, 279, 281
dichotomous responses to, 277–
79
and grieving, 281–84
and taking compassionate
action, 279–81, 285–86, 288–
89
gratitude, 208, 253–54
Greenswald, Gerry, 34
grief, grieving, 48–49, 281–84
group practice, 7, 323–24

H
habits. *See also* practice
approaches
beneficial, and "we" consciousness, 108–10
ego-based, examining and letting go of, 8, 43, 54, 101–4
healing, personal and global. *See
also* environmental responsibility; nature; self-awareness;
wholeness
collective, 183–84, 192–93, 197
grief as, 49
and mindful sexuality, 168,
171–73, 175–76
organic approaches, 3–4, 203–
4, 224
of others and the "We" mentality, 105, 107–8, 118
and self-healing, 57–58, 104
helpfulness, conditioned, 152–
53, 155, 157–61, 250. *See also*
authentic service; compassionate action

U

Uji ("being-time") practice, 77–78
uncertainty. *See* global uncertainty; mind of separation/separate self
unconditional love
    and finding the authentic self, 55
    and loving fearlessly, 146–48
urban lifestyle. *See* city life/urban lifestyle

V

vulnerability, resisting, 13–18. *See also* transparency

W

"We" consciousness. *See also* identity; others, the other; wholeness
    and compassionate awareness, 105–6, 194, 197, 280, 288, 308
    experience of, at Zen monastery, 28
    practices that support, 98, 103, 108–10, 142, 323–33
    and value of deep listening, 117
white privilege
    characteristics of, 182–83
    and marginalization of the other, 182, 189–90
    owning, taking responsibility for, 184–85, 195
    using to benefit others, 191–92
wholeness. *See also* authentic self; awareness, mindfulness; interconnection/nonseparation; sufficiency

affirming through meditation, 69
    as inherent and constant, 38, 55–57, 299–300
    learning to accept and experience, 29, 52, 57, 135, 206
    opening to, 184
    sources of guidance about, 38
    and the spaciousness within, 33, 78–79, 208–10, 234
women, objectification of, 168
working meditation, 304–5

Z

Zen monastery
    discipline and simplicity of life, 28
    experience of interconnection, 27–28
    and learning about sufficiency, 227–28
    and questioning, 242
    tasks and the "not enough time" story, 79–80
    working meditation, 304–5
Zen teachings/traditions. *See also* meditation; practice approaches; Relational Mindfulness, basic principles and tools
    and accessible approaches to mindfulness, 7–8
    and focusing on process, 204–5
    importance of schedules, 84–87, 304
    the priority of spiritual growth, 28
    and the wisdom of not knowing, 281

About the Author

DEBORAH EDEN TULL, founder of Mindful Living Revolution, is a Zen meditation and mindfulness teacher, public speaker, writer, and activist. She spent seven years as a Buddhist monk at a silent Zen monastery and teaches the integration of compassionate awareness into every aspect of our lives. She offers retreats, workshops, and consultations nationally, and offers a podcast. Eden's teaching style is grounded in compassionate awareness, experiential learning, mindful inquiry, and an unwavering commitment to personal transformation. She assists people in releasing the myth of separation and reclaiming the authority of the heart. A teacher for UCLA's Mindfulness Center, she also facilitates The Work That Reconnects, which was created by Buddhist activist and eco-philosopher Joanna Macy. Eden lives in an eco-village in Western North Carolina with her partner, and spends as much time as possible in places and contexts that celebrate true nature—from the garden to the wilderness to nurturing relationships. Through her love of service, Eden feels a sincere commitment to a relationship with you, the reader, and to all who wish to embody the teachings of Relational Mindfulness.

For more information please visit deborahedentull.com and mindfullivingrevolution.com.

What to Read Next
from Wisdom Publications

INTERCONNECTED
Embracing Life in Our Global Society
The Karmapa, Ogyen Trinley Dorje

"We are now so interdependent that it is in our own interest to take the whole of humanity into account. Hope lies with the generation who belong to the twenty-first century. If they can learn from the past and shape a different future, later this century the world could be a happier, more peaceful, and more environmentally stable place. I am very happy to see in this book the Karmapa Rinpoche taking a lead and advising practical ways to reach this goal."—His Holiness the Dalai Lama

WAKING UP TOGETHER
Intimate Partnership on the Spiritual Path
Ellen and Charles Birx

"A tribute to splendid marriage, [from] wise and spirited guides."—Raphael Cushnir, author of *Setting Your Heart on Fire*

AWAKENING TOGETHER
The Spiritual Practice of Inclusivity and Community
Larry Yang
Foreword by Jan Willis
Foreword by Sylvia Boorstein

"I don't see how *Awakening Together: The Spiritual Practice of Inclusivity and Community* could be better. It is so wise, thoughtful, and dedicated to our healthful growth, ease, and enlightenment through the Dharma, that I know I will be reading it for years to come. Larry Yang seems to have thought of everything we will need as we venture bravely forward—through racism, prejudice, ignorance, and poor home training—into the free spiritual beings we were meant to be. Together."—Alice Walker, author of *The Color Purple*

About Wisdom Publications

Wisdom Publications is the leading publisher of classic and contemporary Buddhist books and practical works on mindfulness. To learn more about us or to explore our other books, please visit our website at wisdomexperience .org or contact us at the address below.

Wisdom Publications
199 Elm Street
Somerville, MA 02144 USA

We are a 501(c)(3) organization, and donations in support of our mission are tax deductible.

Wisdom Publications is affiliated with the Foundation for the Preservation of the Mahayana Tradition (FPMT).